The Oracle and the Curse

The Oracle
and the Curse

A POETICS OF JUSTICE FROM THE

REVOLUTION TO THE CIVIL WAR

Caleb Smith

Harvard University Press

Cambridge, Massachusetts · London, England

2013

Copyright © 2013 by the President and Fellows of Harvard College
Printed in the United States of America

Library of Congress Cataloging-in-Publication Data

Smith, Caleb, 1977–
The Oracle and the Curse : A Poetics of Justice from the Revolution
to the Civil War / Caleb Smith.
p. cm.
Includes bibliographical references and index.
ISBN 978-0-674-07308-1 (alk. paper)
1. American literature—History and criticism.   2. Law and literature—
United States—History.   3. Social justice in literature.   I. Title.
PS169.L37S63 2013
810.9'355—dc23   2012041347

For S.A.S.

Contents

Preface   ix

Introduction: The Poetics of Justice   1

1. Oracles of Law   37

2. Oracles of God   64

3. Blasphemy "At the Court of Hell"   96

4. Evil Speaking, "A Bridle for the Unbridled Tongue"   128

5. The Curse of Slavery   151

6. Words of Fire   176

Epilogue: The Curse at Sea   207

Notes   217
Acknowledgments   255
Index   257

Preface

Long before today's secular justice system confronted the resurgence of so many violent fundamentalisms, the developing legal order of the post-revolutionary United States reckoned with the incendiary speech acts of dissenters, militants, and self-styled martyrs who invoked a "higher law." *The Oracle and the Curse* reconstructs the law's public sphere, from the age of revolution through the slavery crisis, as the scene of this unresolved conflict. An impersonal rule of law and a religiously animated resistance: these two enemies sometimes appear to come from different worlds or different times. I argue that they belong to a single, modern formation that emerged when the ceremonies of justice were refashioned for circulation in popular literature and the developing mass media. My archive includes some familiar essays, novels, and poems, as well as many other texts—legal treatises, execution sermons, criminal confessions, convicts' autobiographies, trial reports, and slave narratives—which invited their readers into rituals of judgment and punishment. My aim is to introduce a historical poetics, or an account of the varieties of nonrational persuasion that these documents were thought to exercise on their first publics.

Early American legal institutions prided themselves on reason and a freedom from religious dogma, but they depended nonetheless on elaborate ceremonies. Criminal trials, especially, were occasions for the legitimation of state power. Addressing publics which had come to be imagined as sovereign peoples, the courts secured their authority by invoking natural order and popular customs. Judges suppressed their own voices so that a transcendent justice could speak through them; they played the living oracles of law. In time, though, some offenders learned to use oracular performance in other ways, vindicating themselves in the name of a higher justice and weakening popular support for legal institutions. The oracle was answered by the curse.

In its broad contours, the history of these two speech acts is not difficult to see. Over the course of a century, the foundations of legal authority in the United States were secularized. During the earliest decades under consideration here, the clergymen and judges who presided over ceremonies of justice still sometimes posed as the ministers of a sacred order. By the middle of the nineteenth century, the courts had recast themselves as the enforcers of a rational code, written and published by the people's representatives; they no longer claimed to be following the commandments of the Almighty. In the meantime, the moral sanction that had been abandoned by the courts was taken up by dissenters who used it to call for legal reform, for principled acts of civil disobedience, or, in the extreme case of a Nat Turner or a John Brown, for militant resistance. Often dismissed as the vestiges of an earlier, unenlightened age, the antebellum period's martyr figures were really the unruly children of a coldly rationalized modernity. As the oracles gave up their claim to a righteous, vengeful justice, the curse began to make itself heard.

The invocation of impersonal justice by a judge or an offender was a speech act, but it was not easily consigned to a preliterate past. One of my premises is that the distinction between orality and literacy, as paradigms of culture, is of little use in analyzing the law's public sphere. In the early United States, even intimate talk (a confession, a promise) was often scripted according to the conventions of writing. More significantly for a poetics of justice, the printed word itself came to be endowed with the dangerous power to mystify the people or to summon an insurrectionary movement. Exploring the period's own ways of understanding the publication, circulation, and reception of popular legal literature, I recover luminous fantasies of sovereign peoples enchanted into submission, of dissenting factions called to arms, by texts which carried the scene of judgment far beyond the courthouse and into an indefinite future. Along the way, I join other revisionist critics in suggesting that the history of the public sphere, that imaginary space where the legitimacy of state institutions is judged by the sovereign people, has been too narrowly focused on representative legislation and deliberative reason. To make sense of the public culture of justice, even in a secular modernity, requires thinking about the rituals of law and the self-justifying prophesies of martyrs, the oracle and the curse.

I began my research with an interest in the summoning power of these self-abnegating modes of address, their capacity to constitute moral communities by calling people to a side in a struggle over justice. Oracular address, it seemed to me, was a style of dominion more enchanting than ideology. The curse was a style of protest more dangerous than critique or sentimentality. The conflict between the oracle and the curse was more furious than any debate about sovereignty. As I worked on the book, though, I saw that many of the most vivid depictions of justice's performative invocations had come from authors who took an interest in regulating their power. One example was already apparent in the rationalization of the law's theoretical foundations. In refusing to call down the wrath of God, judges displayed their own reasonableness. They distinguished themselves from the priestcraft and lawcraft of a despotic, superstitious past. They were perhaps not so much forsaking the summoning power of oracular address, though, as reinventing it under the signs of reason and popular sovereignty; they preserved the ceremonial function of the legal ritual by seeming to purge it of its much-disputed theological content. Another, less predictable example involved the suppression of fanaticism within the rising social movements and reform crusades of the early nineteenth century. Even those who appealed to a moral law, hoping to expand the boundaries of the public sphere and to save the country from such "crimes" as slavery, were careful to police themselves against an incendiary, militant enthusiasm. They wanted to redeem the national community, they said, not to rend it into factions.

Much of my work, then, developed into a study of the curiously productive suppression and chastening of certain menacing styles of public address. In some cases, these procedures took on the character of legal rituals in their own right. My middle chapters explore the popular literature that emerged from the prosecution of the word crimes known as blasphemy and evil speaking. Associated with the undisciplined voices of social classes that were normally disenfranchised and dispossessed, these two offenses made the dynamics of factionalizing speech a matter of explicit controversy in the Jacksonian period. These conflicts over justice, that is, were also struggles over access to publication and over the meaning of public address itself. Carried on at a time when the infrastructure of print circulation was dramatically expanding, they were about who had the right to speak before the people, and in what style, and with what effects. As the actors in these legal dramas tried to silence the blasphemer or to speak out against oppression, to bridle the evil speaker's tongue or to give voice to God's will, to smother the incendiary or to move the hearts of their brothers and sisters—as they waged their campaigns for justice, they were also redefining the relations between language and power.

More subtly but also more deeply, the regulation of the curse shaped the development of distinctly literary subcultures. According to one familiar account, literature in the conventional sense, as a semi-autonomous field with its own standards of aesthetic value and moral truth, emerged in the United States by slowly, fitfully extricating itself from the authority of the ministers and lawyers who had once controlled the press. By the mid-nineteenth century, authors like Nathaniel Hawthorne and Herman Melville were publishing fiction preoccupied with the injustices of law, exposing the hypocrisy of judges and the martyrdom of moral innocence. Unlike the public ceremonies of trial and punishment, the introspective literary imagination could explore the ambiguities of consciousness, the subtleties of desire, and the mysteries of the heart.

Staking its claim to autonomy in such terms, however, literature tended to withdraw to the margins of the public sphere, to concern itself above all with matters of conscience. Even Harriet Beecher Stowe, whose novels were expressly designed to bring about legal reforms, linked the persuasive ambitions of her most famous book to the influence of women's voices, speaking in the private space of the kitchen or the fireside. Stowe defined her literary endeavor against the calculating rationality of legal authorities, but she wanted no association with the obscene, public performances of ranters and exhorters. When they invoked a moral standard in opposition to the law's institutions, most of the other canonical authors of the antebellum period also identified literature with a private sphere. And when they represented a martyr's curse, which they often did, they were careful to distance themselves from its incendiary power.

To account for the law's public sphere, then, it was not enough to narrate the decline of the oracle and the rise of the curse. I also had to describe the regulation of incendiary speech acts within the reform movements and to consider the role of literature in that precarious operation.

Still, regulation was not the same as exclusion. It was a performance of self-discipline which gave writers access to special kinds of authority. The poetics of justice was most carefully described, most elaborately imagined, in the literary field. Detaching itself from legal authority, literature also discovered several postures, never identical to each other, which can be understood as modes of estrangement, enabling various modes of dissent. After all, the story does not end with a withdrawal into the sanctuary of conscience. By the time of Turner's insurrection in 1831, and especially after 1850, the crisis of slavery was profoundly straining the law's claim to legitimacy. In reactionary sermons and popular legal texts, obedience was once more demanded in the name of God and country. But the ongoing struggle also generated a fierce protest literature, animated by the principle of higher law and endowed with the incendiary power to ignite a factional war. The undead presence of the martyr's voice was reawakened, and its power idealized, in surprising ways. The oracle and the curse alike were ominously revived.

The Oracle and the Curse

Introduction

The Poetics of Justice

In the fall of 1859, the abolitionist John Brown was captured and tried in Virginia. Badly wounded in the fighting with Robert E. Lee's troops at Harper's Ferry, he lay on a pallet in the courtroom, charged with high crimes—conspiracy, murder, treason. When the jury found him guilty, he took the occasion to address the court and the assembled public. "Now, if it is deemed necessary that I should forfeit my life, for the furtherance of the ends of justice, and mingle my blood further with the blood of my children, and with the blood of millions in this Slave country, whose rights are disregarded by wicked, cruel, and unjust enactments,—I say, let it be done!"[1] Just afterward, the death sentence was pronounced. Brown would hang on December 2.

He spent his last days in the Charles Town Jail, praying over his Bible, receiving visitors, and writing letters to his friends and family. In the letters, as in his widely reprinted "Address to the Virginia Court," he freely confessed that he had broken the laws of the state, but he appealed to the higher code of justice he called the "law of God." "I feel no consciousness of guilt," he wrote, "nor even mortification on account of my imprisonment and irons." It was the wicked law and its enforcers, not the martyred rebels, who would be damned when the day of reckoning arrived. "I, John Brown, am quite certain that the crimes of this guilty

1

land will never be purged away but with blood." Composed in his cell, just before he went to the gallows, this was his verdict and his sentence against the nation.[2]

In broadsides, in newspapers, and in such books as James Redpath's *The Public Life of Captain John Brown* (1860), Brown's prison writings were reprinted and circulated around the Atlantic.[3] They helped to take his case far beyond the courthouse, transforming a legal process into a political event on a national scale. "With the Alleghany mountains for his pulpit, the country for his church, and the whole civilized world for his audience, he was a thousand times more effective as a preacher than as a warrior," Frederick Douglass remembered.[4] The New York minister William Henry Fish, writing for the *Liberator,* was one of the many readers who responded to the power of the condemned man's prophetic words: "What a text John Brown has given us!"[5] In the next century, W. E. B. Du Bois would call Brown's dispatches from Virginia "the mightiest Abolition document that America has ever known." "That John Brown was legally a lawbreaker and a murderer all men knew," Du Bois observed. "But wider and wider circles were beginning . . . to recognize that his lawlessness was in obedience to the highest call of self-sacrifice for the welfare of his fellow men. They began to ask themselves, What is this cause that can inspire such devotion?"[6] Brown's works seemed to have called their audience to the cause of a justice higher than the statutes of the land.

Among Brown's readers was another well-known dissenter from the law, Henry Thoreau. A sworn enemy of slavery, Thoreau had felt, throughout the 1850s, a growing tension between legal obligations and the dictates of the moral conscience. In essays like "A Plea for Captain John Brown," he had explored the idea that violent action might be justified as a way to enforce the laws of nature in a corrupt world.[7] On the Fourth of July, 1860, he was invited to speak at a memorial service in Brown's home village of North Elba, New York. Thoreau declined to make the trip—"for my own part, I commonly attend more to nature than to man"—but he sent some pages from his journal to be read aloud to the congregation. First published in *The Liberator* alongside eulogies by Douglass, Redpath, and others, "The Last Days of John Brown" now belongs to the canon of American protest writing, and of American literature in general. Thoreau hailed Brown as a fallen hero who was bound for heaven. "Now he has not laid aside the sword of the spirit, for he is pure spirit himself, and the sword is pure spirit also." Most of Thoreau's memorial remarks, though, were less concerned with Brown's weapons than with his words, and with what happened to the people who encountered them. Thoreau's essay was a tribute to a martyr who had taken some of his own arguments about civil disobedience to a violent conclusion. It was also a reflection on the power of publicly circulating legal literature, the capacity of the printed word to call readers to a side in a struggle over justice.[8]

Thoreau observed two different circles of readers, two responses to Brown's writings. There was one audience that condemned the old man as a vigilante, a false prophet, and a disturber of the peace: "They read his letters and speeches as if they read them not. They were not aware when they approached a heroic statement,—they did not know when they *burned*. They did not feel that he spoke with authority, and hence they only remembered that the *law* must be executed. They remembered the old formula, but they did not hear the new revelation." These readers took the part of the judge and jury. They joined their voices to that of the Virginia court, condemning "an ordinary felon" who deserved to hang. Considering these responses, Thoreau saw how Brown's controversial trial had given the court an occasion to revive the democratic sanction of the rule of law. As the judge pronounced the death sentence, and as word of this sentence circulated in print, a reading public authorized the court's decision, retroactively, with its blessing. Suppressing his own voice, the judge became the oracle of the sovereign people.

Gathering in opposition to the law's ideal public, in Thoreau's account, was another circle—the men and women who *burned*. To them, Brown had exposed a truth about justice that was ordinarily shrouded by the language of jurisprudence. "They saw that what was called order was confusion, what was called justice, injustice, and that the best was deemed the worst." Moved by Brown's incendiary revelation, they heard the institutions of state indicted according to a higher law. An editorial essay in the *Independent,* a New York paper sympathetic to the antislavery cause, foresaw that "the brief address of Brown to the Virginia court about to sentence him . . . will outlive that sentence, and in the opinion of mankind will make Brown the Judge and the Court the Criminal."[9] If the court's sentence could ratify itself by gaining the assent of one public, the rebel might appeal to a counterpublic for vindication.

Brown's prison writings did not persuade their readers through the rigor or the clarity of their reasoning. They performed a summoning. Thoreau wondered if "a new sect of *Brownites*" might be gathering "in our midst." The condemned man's address, he suggested, would lead these righteous people to feel that the slaveholding legal order had no foundation in their will. It would align the spirit of a new moral community with another, more just law that awaited a revolutionary founding. The doomed embodiment of the higher law would be remembered as a martyr. Its darkly prophetic invocation in language would be apprehended, by Thoreau and others, as a peculiar kind of performative speech-in-print that stirred up a dissenting faction against the laws of states. Oracular as a court's sentence, yet spoken from the other side of legal authority, this is the kind of utterance that I call the *curse*.

How was it that the addresses of a judge and of a condemned man, transmitted across the continent by the press, could seem to call together two irreconcilable moral communities? *The Oracle and the Curse* sets out to compose a critical genealogy of the conflict between human law and higher law, and of the juridical public sphere where it was waged, from the Revolutionary period to the Civil War. This is a book about scenes of judgment in American literature, very broadly defined, and especially about the popular genres that emerged at the boundary between legal institutions and the public at large, inviting common readers into ceremonies of justice. I gesture toward the broad scope and rich diversity of this body of work, some of which has been forgotten by literary historians, but I rest my claims on close, contextualized readings of a few especially self-conscious texts. Attending to the conceptions of public address and popular reception that were worked out in and around these documents, I set out to develop a historical poetics of justice—that is, to describe the styles of nonrational persuasion they performed and to analyze how they came to be understood as capable of summoning the assent or dissent of lawgiving publics, even of that elusive, chimerical audience known as "the people."[10]

The judges and offenders who spoke in these texts, I argue, appeared to suppress the private self so that the commandments of some transcendent, impersonal power could speak through them. They sentenced their addressees to terrible, but just, fates. And they invited an audience to recognize their performances as expressions of its own collective spirit, indeed as the very medium of its community. Both the oracle and the curse, that is, were thought to convoke a collective subject which could grant them a retroactive legitimacy. I show how the martyr's curse emerged as the prophetic retort to the judge's oracular condemnation, but in the end I find that the perceived force of these two speech acts depended on common fantasies about persuasion and performative self-authorization through the circulation of printed texts.

Taking John Brown's martyrdom as its centerpiece, this introduction begins to tell the three stories that will be developed in the rest of the book. First is the story of the oracle, in which legal authorities position themselves as the mouthpieces of a law whose origins are elsewhere. It begins with the common law judges of the Revolutionary era, men who mystified their own power by invoking the commandments of God and the ancient customs of the people. It ends with the legal rationalists of the antebellum decades, the secular oracles of the rule of law. Second is the story of the curse, the invocation of higher law by unapologetic offenders, righteous dissidents, and defiant martyrs. It tells how the law of God, gradually abandoned by the secularizing courts, was picked up and wielded as an instrument of reform and rebellion in a diversifying mass press. Finally, there is the story of how the curse came to be imagined, from a distance, by writers like Thoreau. More and more estranged from the authority of legal institutions, literary authors saw how the laws of God might summon a faction, igniting a conflict over the foundations of justice. They were troubled by the violence of the curse, but they were also intrigued by its power, and from their encounter with the law's public sphere were conceived distinctive new ideas about the politics and pleasures of literature itself.

The Oracular Public Sphere

"He is no longer working in secret," Thoreau said on the occasion of Brown's capture and trial. "He works in public." As Thoreau knew well, the condemned man could not create a revolutionary movement merely by mimicking the rhetoric of the death sentence. The force of his words depended on the material and cultural contexts where they were received by reading publics. An editorial in New York's *Weekly Anglo-African,* run by the black abolitionist Thomas Hamilton, described the infrastructure of this transmission. On the day of Brown's execution, the paper reported, "the lightning wires of the press summoned a larger number of witnesses than ever before looked upon the dying of one man."[11] In an antebellum society where imagined communities were formed and sustained, in large part, through the circulation of documents, Brown and his supporters used the press to carry his message to a wide, diverse audience. Behind Thoreau's depictions of the oracle and the curse was an understanding of how a mass medium could appear to create an arena for the disputation of justice. Thoreau conceived of Brown's various readers, wherever and whenever they might have encountered his words in print, as a collective body assembled in a space of common presence.

What Thoreau was imagining was a kind of *public sphere,* a virtual forum where legal institutions encountered the people at large. The concept has been used in several ways, but it received its most influential treatment in the philosopher Jürgen Habermas's field-defining study, *The Structural Transformation of the Public Sphere.* Tracing the sources of the public sphere to the rise of the printing press in the sixteenth and seventeenth centuries, Habermas describes how modern states began using print to publicize their decrees, as "the press was systematically made to serve the interests of the state administration." When certain readers were identified as the intended audience of official speech, "the addressees of the authorities' announcements genuinely became 'the public' in the proper sense."[12] Commonly identified with the population of a region or the citizenry of a nation, a public is something other than a living community. "Public speech," as Michael Warner explains, "lies under the necessity of addressing its public as already existing real persons," but "publics do not exist apart from the discourse that addresses them," and such discourse, whether explicitly or not, is always involved in a "subjunctive-creative project" of conjuring the audience whose existence it pretends to take for granted.[13] A public is a peculiarly modern fiction, born out of print-mediated circuits of performative address and reception, and "the" public came into being, in its modern form, as an assembly of strangers called together by the voice of power.

Over the course of the eighteenth century, this new entity began to negotiate its own position in relation to the state. The public would not simply obey the published commands of government officials. It would conceive of itself as a sovereign body, a *people,* whose consent gave the rulers their legitimacy. "A political consciousness developed in the public sphere of civil society which," Habermas writes, "ultimately came to assert itself (i.e., public opinion) as the only legitimate source of [the] law."[14] In a growing number of newspapers, journals, and pamphlets, private citizens submitted official policies to a putatively impersonal critical reason, often calling for reform in the name of the common good. The public sphere took shape as the virtual space where this kind of public address was thought to do its persuasive work. There was a changing communications infrastructure, and there were various statements made about law and policy; the public sphere was an image that mediated between the two. In this sense, the public sphere has no stable location in the geographic or social world. It is an idealized picture of the space of textual circulation, a dream-world where various acts of publication and reception are harmoniously synchronized, and it is called into being anew with each act of public address. Toward this imaginary sphere, authors cast their arguments about the utility and legitimacy of law.

Thus the emergence of the public sphere was linked to the rise of a new lawgiving institution, the representative assembly, whose legitimacy depended on its claim to speak for the people. John Adams, for instance, used metaphors drawn from the arts to describe the lawmakers' relation to the people at large: "The end to be aimed at, in the formation of a representative assembly, seems to be the sense of the people, the public voice. The perfection of the portrait consists in its likeness." Other claims to legitimacy, such as the divine right of kings and the customary authority of Common Law courts, appeared to be on the wane because they lacked a foundation in the people's sovereignty. "The voice of the people is the voice of God," Adams wrote, "which the voice of the prince is not."[15] One of Habermas's critical moves, in relation to such ideology, was to defamiliarize the commonplace idea of the people. He exposed the technological and ideological changes that produced the public sphere as an imaginary gathering place for a sovereign community and, along the way, gave legislatures their strong claim to the popular voice.[16]

Just as the virtual entity known as the public is distinct from the heterogeneous population, and just as the public sphere is distinct from any material space, public opinion is not just any sentiment. It is a specific, regulated kind of discourse. "The classical bourgeois public sphere of the seventeenth and eighteenth centuries," Craig Calhoun observes, "was constituted around rational critical argument, in which the merits of arguments and not the identities of arguers were crucial."[17] Entering the public sphere, authors invoked the impersonal standards of reason and the common good. In other words, they acquired a special kind of authority by performing their own self-discipline, disavowing private interests and overmastering unreasonable passions. Argumentation in this "deliberative" public sphere appeared to depend on the making of publicly verifiable claims—it emphasized the substance of the proposition, not the moving power of the performance. As the most recognizable form of law became the printed statute, the idiom of public opinion was the reasonable, if polemical, language of the newspaper editorial or the political pamphlet.

While Habermas described the public sphere as an imagined arena of negotiation between state authorities and the people, then, his characterization remains distant from Thoreau's vision of ceremonial legitimation and prophetic resistance. The history of the public sphere, as written by Habermas and his followers, is mainly a secular history of the relation between legislation and the public use of deliberative reason. It has little to say about how the law's foundations might be contested in the sensational popular literature that circulates around controversial trials, and only very recently has it begun to reconsider the enduring power of religious discourses in a secular age. Since the era of its emergence in the seventeenth century, Calhoun acknowledges, "religion has been a source of anxiety for the liberal public sphere."[18]

For these reasons, among others, scholars of American cultural history have sometimes charged Habermas with idealizing a scene of debate which excluded the unlettered and the undisciplined. Outside the borders of Habermas's deliberative public sphere, John L. Brooke suggests, there has always been a darker, wilder territory of "persuasion," characterized by "nondeliberative discourse."[19] The men and women of the eighteenth and nineteenth centuries practiced many kinds of public address which departed from the rationalist norms of Habermas's deliberative public sphere. That much is clear to anyone who looks into the period, with its fantastic carnival of riots, rabble-rousing, revivals, jeremiads, exhortations, sentimental appeals, and literary experiments—in all of which, somehow, the will of the people could appear to be at stake. In the chapters that follow, I turn away from the scenes of legislation and learned debate, toward the courthouse and the gallows, the blasphemer's prison cell and the lonely haunts of outcast enthusiasts.[20] I adopt a broad definition of public address, expansive enough to include all attempts at persuasion in language whose subjects discipline themselves, according to normative conventions, in order to elicit a public's legitimating recognition. The rational-critical idiom described by the Habermasians is one example, but so, in time, would be the martyrs' self-annihilating invocations of a divine justice.

What seems worth preserving from Habermas's account, though, is his original emphasis, perhaps diminished in the later work, on the performative summoning of publics which can be imagined, in retrospect, as lawgiving communities. In its most nuanced versions, public sphere theory shows how insecure is the boundary between rational-critical discourse and the types of nonrational persuasion against which it routinely defines itself. By nonrational persuasion, I mean modes of address and affirmation which involve not the critical evaluation of propositions but the affective and aesthetic response to justice's performative invocation. I mean the love that binds subjects to power, the beauty that enchants, and (in the case of the curse) the fiery righteousness that animates dissent. Often, a promise of belonging is implicit in these styles of conviction, and I attend, especially, to the feeling of taking a side in a collective conflict, joining a community which knows its identity in opposition to its enemies.

Just as speech act philosophy comes around to recognizing an illocutionary function at work even in the most straightforward assertion of a proposition, a poetics of justice will discover the ceremonial, summoning force of juridical performances, even when they cloak themselves in the language of reason. The fantasy that discourse can conjure a legitimating public is not entertained only in regimes of spectacularly ritualized statecraft. It lives on in self-consciously modern styles of verbal governance, too. Such styles, I argue, continue to cherish a ritual, performative design even as they disavow the excesses of theocratic mystification. Legal authorities deliberated. They made arguments. They composed opinions. And all the while they were known to be involved in mystification. Their call to submission exceeded rational persuasion. It was rich with terror and pleasure, the menace of violence and the blessing of domestic peace.

Legal historians of the early United States almost always emphasize the rise of constitutionalism and representative lawmaking, the codification of the law, the disestablishment of the churches, and other shifts away from theocratic and aristocratic customs, towards the statute-centered rationalism of the mid-nineteenth century. Even Perry Miller's magisterial literary study of the American legal "mind" describes a movement from postrevolutionary confusion into the learned, professional legal culture of the antebellum period. The legal reasoning of the high courts, according to Miller, became a bulwark against the rising evangelicals, who valued the sentiments of the Christian heart over the calculations of the head, and against the literary Romantics, with their contempt for traditional institutions. The authority of such eminent judges as James Kent and Joseph Story "guaranteed that the mind of the Republic would never be swept wholly into the enthusiasms of revivalism or Transcendentalism."[21] Law, so the story goes, withdraws from the worlds of religion and politics. The courts recreate themselves as dispassionate bodies whose business is to interpret and enforce law, not to speak it into being.

In the long feud between the disciples of Thomas Jefferson and the Federalists allies of the Marshall Court, it was finally the representative assemblies which came to be seen as unstable entities, liable to be possessed by momentary passions, and the courts assumed the mantle of rationality. As Miller argues, "the Jeffersonians . . . by their veneration for 'reason,' had . . . played into the hands of James Kent."[22] The trouble with this account, though, is that it regards the conflict over the grounds of law's authority as a kind of debate, where the most convincing argument wins the field. The national mind is finally persuaded by the august rationality of the jurists, and there the story ends.[23] By way of a poetics of justice, attending less to arguments about the nature of authority and more to the ceremonial exercise of power, another narrative can be unfolded. The story of the legal oracle, between the Revolution and the Civil War, is one in which judges display their own reasonableness so that they can appear to give voice to the spirit of the sovereign people. The oracular ceremonies of justice are not forgotten; they are reinvented for a secular age.

By the time of the Revolution, the transformation was already underway. In his *Dissertation on the Canon and Feudal Law* (1765), John Adams contrasted the enlightened legal system of the New World to the despotic superstitions of ancient regimes. The modern champions of "popular power," he wrote, "saw clearly, that of all the nonsense and delusion which had ever passed through the mind of man, none had ever been more extravagant than . . . those fantastical ideas, derived from the canon law, which had thrown such a glare of mystery, sanctity, reverence, and right reverend eminence and holiness, around the idea of a priest, as no mortal could deserve."[24] According to Adams's liberal narrative, modern societies had emancipated themselves from this theocratic authority through a discipline of self-education and critique. The people had learned the secrets of natural law and political science, and they had used the press to hold their governments accountable to the standards of reason. They could now make their voices heard in print, and lawmakers would be able to claim legitimacy only when their statutes were in harmony with the *vox populi*.

In the view of his more radical contemporaries, even the ceremonial utterances of judges in courtrooms appeared to be vestiges of the superstitious, unlettered age that Adams identified with the reign of priests and lords. Just as Adams produced his *Dissertation,* in 1765, the English jurist William Blackstone brought out the first volume of his monumental *Commentaries on the Laws of England*. Reflecting on the sources of judicial authority, Blackstone argued that the body of concepts and precedents known as the Common Law belonged to a single customary system, founded in the laws of nature and passed down through the generations. Judges, Blackstone wrote, were not the authors of this law. They were its "living oracles."[25] The utilitarian philosopher and reformer Jeremy Bentham—Blackstone's former student at Oxford—responded to the

Commentaries with a fierce critique of the judge's bewitching rhetoric. The "enchanting harmony" of Blackstone's treatise, Bentham claimed, had seduced the public into being "governed by the ear."[26]

Bentham argued that Blackstone's text, with its invocation of an ancient, occult national spirit, had mystified the foundations of legal authority. In twentieth-century critical theory, this kind of persuasion would be given several names. Louis Althusser would develop the idea of *interpellation,* describing how state institutions establish a hold on their subjects that goes deeper than the conscious processes of rational deliberation or consent.[27] Diagnosing *misrecognition,* Pierre Bourdieu would argue that "the language of authority never governs without the collaboration of those it governs."[28] In a poststructuralist analysis of law-giving speech acts, Jacques Derrida would describe "a performative . . . violence that in itself is neither just nor unjust and that no earlier and pre-viously founding law, no preexisting foundation, could . . . invalidate."[29] Bentham and his followers took their terms—mystification, enchantment, masquerade—from the lexicon of feudal domination. They depicted their conflict with the courts as a struggle against obsolescent superstitions. The reformers were, in their way, the agents of the progressively rational-izing, secularizing modernity described by Habermas and others, nota-bly Max Weber. At the same time, though, they were testifying, as if in spite of themselves, to the new power that the oracles acquired when they entered the public sphere of print. Blackstone's text was no relic from an unlettered past. Its summoning power depended on its wide circula-tion, and Bentham knew it. He was describing the re-enchantment of the world, the re-enslavement of the public by the judge's siren song.

While the quarrel between Blackstone and Bentham played out in England, the American courts were confronting the urgent problem of rebuilding the foundations of their own legitimacy after the Revolution. "The establishment of republican governments with the people as the ultimate source of authority," as Richard E. Ellis observes, "raised the radically new question of the extent to which the judiciary should be dependent upon and responsive to popular influence."[30] The legitimacy of the legislatures, and of statute law, was secured with the ratification of the state and federal constitutions, but the question of the common law lingered, unresolved. In an 1822 polemic, Henry Dwight Sedgwick used the image of a rotting corpse to describe the persistence of English customs in American courts: "Nothing shews the superstitious veneration of men for *established forms,* more than the practice of the English common law, for the forms have been carefully preserved, long after the spirit and design which they were originally intended to subserve has passed away. The life has departed, and the soul has gone; but the body is embalmed, and kept to future ages in a useless state, between preservation and decay."[31] Assaulting the power of the courts in the name of reason and the *vox populi,* Jeffersonian Republicans like William Sampson and Jacksonian Democrats like Robert Rantoul brought Bentham's call for codification to the new world.

American judges reacted by following Blackstone's lead, producing an elegant treatise literature that sought to justify the common law with the assent of the people. In the most philosophically and rhetorically ambitious of these documents, jurists like Jesse Root of Connecticut identified the common law with the divinely authored laws of nature. "The sublimity of its principles," in Root's sermonic phrases, "the purity, excellency and perpetuity of its precepts, are most clearly made known and delineated in the book of divine revelations; heaven and earth may pass away and all the systems and works of man sink into oblivion, but not a jot or title of this law shall ever fail."[32] Root was a prominent Federalist, but he was also a former minister in the established church. He saw a beautiful continuity between the laws of scripture and the precedents of the courts. The oracles of law, in this orthodox Congregationalist's reworking of Blackstone, were really the oracles of God.

While this metaphor shaped the theory of legal authority laid out in the legal treatises of New England conservatives, it also informed the ceremonies of criminal justice and the popular crime literature of the era. The clergy, gradually yielding power to the ascendant lawyers, would concede that the authors of the law were the people and their representatives, not the Almighty. They would draw an ever sharper line of demarcation between the commandments of the creator and the rules enforced by civil governments. But as they considered the common people who gathered around the scaffold on execution day, they would also insist that such a public was best controlled through the invocation of a higher sanction.

On one hand, the imposition of terror: to deter the wicked from crime, it was necessary to menace them with the fear of retribution. "It would be well, could we, in inculcating morality, prevail with all by representing the reasonableness, excellence and advantages of virtue," one New England minister preached on execution day. "But we are compelled to persuade men by the terror of future judgment, and future wrath."[33] On the other hand, the cultivation of faith: to quell riot and suppress dissent, it was best to supplement the justice of the laws with a spiritual blessing. "Where the divine law is written in the heart," another minister promised, "it will and must produce a regular and cheerful subjection to human laws framed for the good of society."[34] Both of these preachers at the gallows indicated the nonrational, affective aspects— the terror and the cheer—which would characterize a people subdued by oracular justice.

It was not only the ministers who spoke this way. Judges, too, cast themselves as the oracles of God. These lines, for example, were reportedly spoken from the bench, addressed to a migrant peddler called Isaac Coombs, upon his conviction for the murder of his wife in Salem, Massachusetts, in 1786: "If Cain of old, who first slew his brother, was cursed by God from the earth, condemned to be a fugitive and a vagabond, with perpetual horror of conscience and terror, lest every man, that found him, should slay him; so that he was forced to cry out, even in this world, that his punishment was too much to bear; what vengeance must await you, in the world that is opening before you. . . , *unless* repentance, and your peace with Heaven, prevent the fatal doom!"[35] Transcribed and published for general circulation, such performances reflected the enduring alliance between religious and legal institutions, nowhere stronger than in New England. In that benighted region, as Jefferson said with contempt, "priestcraft and lawcraft are still able to throw dust into the eyes of the people."[36]

"Lawcraft," even in its old-fashioned, spectacular forms, proved difficult to chase from the shores of the republic. As late as the Jacksonian period, when the power of the judiciary and the cultural authority of the legal profession had been more firmly established, a reactionary literature for popular audiences could still revive its ceremonies. In 1831, for instance, after Nat Turner's rebellion traumatized the slaveholding

order in Virginia, the pamphlet that purported to transcribe his confession also gave voice to the restless spirits of the dead, invoked by
the chief judge in Turner's case, Jeremiah Cobb: "the blood of all cries
aloud, and calls upon you, as the author of their misfortune."[37] Perhaps
legal institutions no longer needed to summon the people to submission,
but a cheap pamphlet could still invite a traumatized community into a
mass-mediated ritual of oracular justice. In the decades after Turner's
rebellion, too, when the struggle over slavery threatened to break apart
the nation, ministers and others unearthed the moth-eaten notion that
obedience to law was enjoined by the Almighty, and the fiery condemnation of abolitionists and insurrectionists was performed in that supposed
citadel of reason, the federal Congress.[38]

American courts rebuilt the foundations of their own legitimacy, then,
not only by winning a debate against rationalist reformers, but also by
appearing to give voice to a transcendent justice. Even New York's Chancellor Kent, the most respected legal thinker of the antebellum period
and no friend of fanaticism, aligned the common law with Christian
principles as he pronounced judgment in a blasphemy trial: "The people
of this State, in common with the people of this country, profess the general doctrines of Christianity, as the rule of their faith and practice."[39]
The opinion of the court in *People v. Ruggles* was widely reprinted in
evangelical periodicals, and today it has been granted a strange afterlife
as a favorite text in the right-wing mythology of the nation's Christian
"origins."[40] This misreading would have been repugnant to Kent, who
looked on revivalism and atheism with equal suspicion, and academic
historians have little trouble exposing its fallacies. Kent's argument virtually reduced religion to an instrument of social control, a bind that held
the poor in consoling subjection. In this way it took a deeply secular, if
not a cynical, view of faith. But it is a more difficult challenge to understand how the opinion of the court, with its oracular mode of address,
makes itself available to such mystifying receptions.

In Herman Melville's *Pierre,* a novel preoccupied with the encroachment of the law into the most intimate quarters of private life, the hero
asks the object of his desire for a strange blessing. "I call thee now,
Isabel, from the depth of a foregone act, to ratify it, backward, by thy
consent." Oracular justice has the same design. The execution sermons

preached on the occasions of felons' deaths, the sentences pronounced in controversial cases, the opinions delivered by appeals courts—these events, enacted in language, sought to produce a people through its performative invocation. They were juridical speech acts comparable to the political ones that Jason Frank calls "constituent moments."[41] The print-mediated ceremonies of justice continually recreated the sovereign public in whose name they spoke. Far-flung strangers were invited to imagine themselves as a people when their common faith was invoked, retrospectively, as the original power that found its expression in the voice of the court. As the intimacy of Pierre's invitation suggests, too, there are aesthetic, affective, and erotic dynamics involved in this mode of domination. Oracular summoning is partly seduction; it has a history, but it also has a poetics.

Over time, of course, the churches were disestablished, and the courts sought to transcend the passionate conflicts that divided religious factions. In the canonical treatises of the late eighteenth and early nineteenth centuries, American legal professionals would distance their practice from both Blackstone's aristocratic assumptions and the New England judges' theocratic ones. They harmonized the imported customs of common law with the postrevolutionary state and federal constitutions, and they were more likely to gesture toward liberal theories of the social contract than to cite scripture. Their project, they said, was to demystify the law, to make plain the origins of its power and the methods of its practice. The reason of law looked down, with lofty detachment, on the passions of personal interests, situated politics, and religious antagonism. It was the judiciary's development of a self-enclosed, procedural rationality that provoked Louis Hartz to observe that "law has flourished on the corpse of philosophy in America."[42]

And yet, as Hartz's gothic metaphor suggests, the lifeless husk of legal rationalism's enemy lingers, incompletely buried, and its evacuated form continues to nourish the living. The struggle between lawcraft and deliberative reason has commonly been regarded as a political conflict between Federalists and Republicans (later, between Whigs and Democrats), between the courts and the legislatures, between religious authorities and the common people. But the critique of lawcraft was undertaken most rigorously within the legal profession itself. It was an internal process of abjection, purification, and rebirth—an act of verbal self-discipline which endowed its subjects with a new kind of power.

Some attorneys "involve themselves in a *thick Mist* of Terms of Art," said the jurist James Wilson in his 1791 lectures on American law, but "the Knowledge of those rational Principles on which the Law is founded ought, especially in a free Government, to be diffused over the whole Community."[43] In passages like this one, legal rationalism's public address clarifies itself by suppressing a ghostly, irrational other. It defines the enlightened discipline of law—its principles but also the voice in which it speaks and the "community" to which it addresses itself—against the superstitious despotisms of the old world. In the process, the performance of self-abnegation is reinvented as a way of enforcing reason against the passions, the constitution and the statute book against the fanatical mob. The oracles of law are refashioned as the ministers of reason.[44]

Part of Wilson's task was to construct a foundation for legitimacy that would be valid across the nation—to distinguish America's republican legal system from England's imperial one in a way which preserved some continuity but which, more pressingly, linked together a variety of colonial ones. Part of the story of the oracle, too, is the gradual and halting movement toward the supremacy of federal law. The coherent organization of American law could hardly be taken for granted in the wake of the Revolution, and many of the nineteenth century's struggles for justice were also struggles for position within a hierarchy of legal authority. Indeed, some of the interest of a poetics of justice lies in the prospect of decentering the nation as the dominant horizon of political and cultural history. Recent scholarship on American history and culture has been concerned to redraw the map, situating the nation within broader patterns of transnational exchanges and oceanic flows. For a poetics of justice, the issue is less one of cartography than one of *jurisdiction,* the multiple, overlapping scales on which legal speech authorizes the exercise of power through the performative constitution of lawgiving publics.[45]

Between the Revolution and the Civil War, law's publics were of several kinds, imagined in relation to many territories. There was not only the nation, with its revolutionary heritage and its precarious cohesion.

There were also the residents of local and regional districts; the citizens of the several states, who authorized the law in civil and criminal matters; and the transatlantic network of peoples held together by the shared tradition of the common law. Within each of these communities, too, there were some who enjoyed the privileges of enfranchisement, and there were more—women and children, convicts and wards, the dispossessed and the enslaved—who were subjected to legal authority without being fully recognized as legal subjects. Every act of lawcraft oriented itself toward one public while suppressing or antagonizing others. The oracles demanded obedience, but they also promised sovereignty and supremacy to the people who answered their call.

At the conclusion of John Brown's trial, after the jury had returned its verdict and the defense counsel's motion for arrest of judgment had been denied, after the defendant had delivered the address that would be reprinted across the continent and around the Atlantic, Judge Richard Parker prepared to pronounce the death sentence. It was a modest, restrained performance. The court did not invoke the vengeance of God or the blood of the innocent. It made no effort to justify the system of slavery, which had the full support of the statute book and was not under consideration in a criminal case. It soberly reminded the defendant that he had received a fair trial, had been assisted by a competent attorney, and had voluntarily confessed to serious crimes. "For each of these offenses," Parker said, performing his own disappearance, "the law provides the penalty of death, and now it only remains for me, as the minister of the law, to pronounce judgment upon you." Brown would hang by the neck until he was dead. The sentence concluded with the conventional blessing, "May God have mercy on your soul."[46]

Parker insisted, however, that the execution should not be performed behind the walls of the Charles Town Jail. It should be a public ceremony, "carried out in open day and before all men." The judge reminded the convict and the assembled public that the law imposed the death sentence "in mercy to our own people—to protect them against similar invasions upon their rights—in mercy and by way of warning to the infatuated men of other States who, like you, may attempt to free our negroes by forcing weapons into their hands." Here the Virginia court, whose jurisdiction ended at the Potomac, quietly acknowledged that the ritual of punishment had become a political event, and that it was conducting its proceedings before a national audience divided over the burning question of slavery. The court identified its task as the preservation of law and order, the protection of the people's security.[47] It mentioned religion only in the guise of fanaticism, the antagonist of domestic tranquility. But the same legal authority recognized its obligation to exercise a ceremonial persuasion—against a few, to suppress crime through terror; for the rest, to repair the breach in the community that had been inflicted by an act of treason. Here was the endpoint of the rationalizing transformation of oracular jurisprudence, between the Revolution and the Civil War.

From the Oracle to the Curse

The justification of the Common Law by appeal to higher law, according to Robert Cover, "was Blackstone's blessing and curse."[48] If the judges' self-representation as the oracles of a transcendent law had enabled the people to recognize courts' decisions as emanations of their own collective spirit, other speakers would adopt the same role to summon moral communities in opposition to legal institutions. In the secularizing nineteenth century, the law of God, gradually dissociated from the laws of states, was turned against them. "Many of my brethren . . . will rise up and call me cursed," the antislavery militant David Walker wrote in his 1829 *Appeal*. "But against all accusations, I appeal to Heaven for my motive in writing."[49]

The first accounts of American offenders' public speech had been produced by religious authorities in the form of the confession, a genre designed to warn sinners and to model penitence. In the beginning, popular crime literature bound the privilege of self-expression to the performance of submission. "I James Morgan," as one convict confessed in 1686, "being Condemned to die, must needs own to the glory of God, that he is Righteous, and that I have by my Sins provoked him to destroy me before my time."[50] In such performances, the felon was constituted as a speaking subject, but only to justify his conversion into an object of punishment. The confession, according to Michel Foucault's devastating critique, is a "ritual of discourse . . . that unfolds within a power relationship, for one does not confess without the presence (or virtual presence)

of. . . the authority who requires the confession, prescribes and appreciates it, and intervenes in order to judge, punish, forgive, console, and
reconcile."[51] To become a speaking subject, under such conditions, is to
enter the bind of subjection. In popular crime literature, moreover, this
drama does not play out in the hidden space of the confessional booth
or the prison cell. It is staged for a reading public as part of a ceremony
of legitimation. The pressures of coercion and compulsion shape the
offender's testimony as a blessing on the institution that condemns him.

In the early modern period, Shakespeare's Caliban spoke of this linguistic bind with a ferocious eloquence: "You taught me language," he
says to his masters, "and my profit on't / Is, I know how to curse."[52] By the
nineteenth century, though, a diversifying mass press had begun to produce new genres of popular legal literature—criminal autobiographies,
prison poetry, propagandistic trial reports, romances of martyrdom, and
so on—which depicted offenders addressing the public in unorthodox
ways. Many openly sought to justify themselves and to protest the institutions which condemned them. Often, these documents took their titles
from the vocabulary of the law. They went by such names as the "plea,"
the "appeal," and the "address." To emphasize a peculiar kind of verbal
performance that could seem to expose, and perhaps to create, a fatal
corruption in the foundations of the common order, I gather them under
the term *curse*.

Why call it that? Cursing is an ancient practice whose early history
might be traced from the curse tablets of the classical age down to Shakespeare's "abhorred slave." According to some modern accounts, too, the
curse is a form of practical magic or everyday obscenity, and such noise
has little to do with questions of justice. I use the term in another sense,
one which was developed in the eighteenth and nineteenth centuries and
which allows me to analyze a certain structure of vatic address and collective reception that belonged to the period's repertoire of contestation.
The curse's politics might be radical or reactionary, and it could divide
communities along unexpected lines. Pronounced in various ways, with
various effects, however, it was a speech act of a distinctive kind. Its
speakers performed the abnegation of the self in submission to a higher
power. In many cases, they addressed their words to an embodiment of
legal authority like a judge or a prosecutor ("God will give him blood to

drink!"), but they expected to be heard by a wider audience that could be imagined as a moral community. They called on this audience to recognize their invocation of a transcendent justice, to mobilize for reform or resistance.

Cultural historians have mainly studied such performances according to a problematic of inclusion and exclusion. "The public sphere in its classical liberal/bourgeois guise," as Geoff Eley writes, "was constituted from a field of conflict, contested meanings, and exclusion."[53] According to such accounts, the arena of educated, reasonable opinion guarded its boundaries against speakers who appeared unwilling or unable to deliberate under the norms of a bourgeois rationality. However antagonistic they might take themselves to be, disputes conducted within the deliberative public sphere actually serve to reinforce an unspoken consensus among the governing powers—an "order of the visible and the sayable," in Jacques Rancière's phrase.[54] The public sphere is regulated by social norms which, before disagreements can even be articulated, establish that certain subjects can speak sensibly and consigns others to a fate of unintelligibility or silence.

A task of revisionary scholarship has therefore been to seek out these other voices. Animated by an ethics of recognition, such work expands the bounds of the public to include subjects who had no access to the elite culture of deliberation. In the popular literature of crime and punishment, this kind of criticism discovers an especially rich archive. Daniel Cohen argues, for instance, that early American crime genres routinely violated a general "rule of exclusion" from the arena of print. By the late seventeenth century, felons drawn from the ranks of the common people were being called to tell their stories in published confessions and convict narratives. Here, the categories of "race, class, gender, age, and deviant conduct" were no bar to public address. The privilege of self-expression, even self-creation, was extended to men and women whose voices might never have found their way into print under other circumstances.[55]

It is tempting to view popular legal literature as a precious archive, preserving the elusive voices of the excluded and the dispossessed—not least because, from such a perspective, critical scholarship can see itself as a contribution to the reparation of past injustices. Yet the story of the curse that I tell here is not, finally, one of self-assertion against forces

of exclusion. One reason is to be found in the structure of this mode of
address. The curse depends for its summoning power on the speaker's
renunciation of personal subjectivity. Especially in the context of a criminal trial, where the prosecution's task is to demonstrate the defendant's
mental and spiritual responsibility for a transgression, the condemned
seek ways out of the bind of subjection. In pronouncing the curse, the
offender or the dissenter becomes the mouthpiece of an impersonal justice whose origins are elsewhere. Although it was often misrecognized as
an arrogant, presumptuous demand for recognition, the curse was a style
of self-abnegation, not self-expression.

Another reason is in the variety of strategies by which the menace
of the curse was managed and contained. Identifying the freedom of
expression as a crucial principle for progressive causes, the main line
of liberal cultural historians has emphasized the official and unofficial
censorship that sought to exclude radical reformers like David Walker
from the public sphere.[56] But the suppression of the offender's curse was
not only enforced by the state or its apologists; rather, the regulation of
this potentially incendiary mode of address was undertaken within the
reform movements themselves. The internal purification of legal institutions, especially the disavowal of a theocratic lawcraft, had enabled
authorities to reinvent oracular justice for a secular age. In the same way,
the self-discipline of the reformers, the restraint of an incendiary enthusiasm, would generate distinctly modern styles of persuasion and poesis.
Exclusion is negation, silence; regulation is coercion, but it is also production. The story of the curse, then, is neither the story of its exclusion nor that of its gradual maturation into self-expression. It is the story
of the simultaneous, ongoing emergence and regulation of the martyr's
righteous address.

The antagonism between legal rationalism and moral protest would
reach its crisis in the antebellum struggle over slavery, but it shaped
many other, earlier conflicts over language and power. In the eighteenth
and nineteenth centuries, Calhoun notes, "much thinking about the
public sphere was devoted . . . to disciplining participants so that . . .
faith would not become 'enthusiasm'—the determination to act immediately on inspiration and without the mediation of reflection or reason."[57] In colonial New England, the disorder called enthusiasm had

been persecuted in the figure of James Davenport, the itinerant evangelical who attacked the authority of the orthodox ministry. In the early national period, it was used to explain the terrible crimes committed by such murderers as William Beadle, who claimed that he was acting as an instrument of God, and James Yates, the deist whose confession became a source text for Charles Brockden Brown's *Wieland.* Abraham Lincoln was drawing from this long tradition when, in the wake of the Harper's Ferry raid, he denounced John Brown as an "enthusiast [who] broods over the oppression of a people till he fancies himself commissioned by Heaven to liberate them."[58]

The question of exclusion was raised most explicitly, however, in the popular legal literature that emerged from two sets of trials in the 1830s. The first were the blasphemy cases, decided by such masters of legal rationalism as James Kent and Lemuel Shaw. In *People v. Ruggles,* Kent had reaffirmed the Christian character of the common law in the new republic. A decade later, as Massachusetts reluctantly moved toward disestablishment, the freethinker Abner Kneeland was arrested for scoffing at religion in the pages of his popular newspaper, the *Investigator.* Locked up in the Common Jail of Suffolk County, Kneeland composed a trial report for mass circulation: "I have never courted the crown of martyrdom," he declared—"nor have I shrunk from it, nor shall I, when it comes."[59] Appealing to a spirit of justice higher than the statutes of the land, Kneeland called the common people to tear down the vestiges of the old theocracy. The prosecution was, in part, an effort by New England's Whig elites to retain their ideological dominance in the age of the mass press, which enabled the unrefined, Jacksonian multitude to address the public in print. Even today, Kneeland is mainly remembered as one of the last victims of an obsolescent alliance between church and state. In his own time, though, he was regarded by his most important defenders as a nuisance and a crank. It mortified them that such a figure "should, by a sentence of the law, be exalted into a martyr, or become identified with the sacred cause of freedom."[60] On these grounds, they petitioned the state for his pardon. The Transcendentalist reformers wanted no affiliation with this fanatic or his unruly mob.

In the same years, as the evangelicals sought to cultivate a Second Great Awakening, they attacked enthusiasm as the source of "evil speaking." Through the formal excommunication of unordained preachers like Sally Thompson and the informal persecution of exhorters like Elleanor Knight, they rid themselves of unrefined public speakers who offended polite society. In published narratives of their "trials," both Knight and Thompson argued that male authorities had unfairly silenced their voices. "Perhaps some that may read these pages, will consider me an enthusiast," Knight wrote; "I felt that it was not my duty to give way to injustice any longer."[61] They understood their cases as instances of exclusion, and they sought to demonstrate that they could adopt the disciplined rationalism of the deliberative public sphere.

But the evil speaking trials were episodes of internal regulation rather than exclusion. As the Methodist preacher Israel Chamberlayne wrote in an 1849 discourse, the punishment of evil speaking meant to provide "a bridle for the unbridled tongue"—not to silence speech but to rein in its inhuman excesses.[62] Bridling the enthusiasts, the evangelicals positioned themselves as the custodians of a reasonable and refined Christianity, a true religion that would move the people towards a moral regeneration without dividing them into factions. The Congregationalists and the Methodists shied away from the spectacle of women's public speech; in the process, they developed the powerful mode of nonrational persuasion known as *influence*, a corrective to masculine reason that was associated with the moral sensibility of women. Influence was a style of public persuasion that had the gentle, intimate feeling of a plea whispered in private. The monuments of this domesticated version of enthusiasm were the sentimental antislavery texts, works like Lydia Maria Child's *Appeal* and Harriet Beecher Stowe's *Uncle Tom's Cabin,* which sought to redeem the nation from its peculiar sin.

As these reformers saw it, the slave codes had made a peculiar contribution to legal rationalism. Here, especially, the struggle between reason and religion came to stand for a conflict between two sources of law. Slavery, as Deak Nabers shows, was unlike "all other social institutions recognized in the law" in that it was understood to have been explicitly created by statutes: "Not only . . . was slavery sanctioned by the laws; its existence required such a sanction."[63] This insight did nothing to diminish the binding force of the slave codes. Instead, it seemed to make them irresistible. As the North Carolina Supreme

Court justice Thomas Ruffin declared in the notorious opinion he delivered in *State v. Mann* (1829), "The struggle . . . in the Judge's own breast between the feelings of the man, and the duty of the magistrate is a severe one. . . . It is useless however, to complain of things inherent in our political state. And it is criminal in a Court to avoid any responsibility which the laws impose." Such was the duty of self-annihilation imposed on an oracle of law.

Even Northerners like Lemuel Shaw and Joseph Story, who considered themselves antislavery men, decided that their oaths required them to remand fugitives, punish civil disobedience, and respect the authority of the statute book. As they justified these decisions, Cover observes, they "tended to extreme protestations of powerlessness or helplessness, [and] to excessive reliance on mechanistic formalism."[64] Shaw, for instance, was reported to say that, in his courtroom, the laws of Congress "were to be obeyed, however disagreeable to our natural sympathies or views of duty."[65] Thus the judges who decided controversial cases involving enslaved persons helped to bring about the triumph of positive law over natural law and custom. If they had succeeded in grasping the mantle of reason from the likes of Sampson and Rantoul, they had also conceded that the command of the legislator, as inscribed in the statute book, was supreme.

Indicted for his efforts in support of fugitives, the radical minister Theodore Parker described the triumph of federal compromises over the discretionary power of Northern courts this way: "the moral sense became extinct, and the legal letter took the place of the spirit of Justice which gives life to the People."[66] In the wake of the Revolution, the courts had been accused of a corrupt intimacy with priestcraft, a habit of mystifying their own power with invocations of a divine blessing. Now, on the eve of the Civil War, they heard the opposite claim, that they had abandoned God and become the servants of worldly power. In this context, popular legal documents like Parker's trial report oriented themselves toward an arena of mass public opinion that was imagined as a higher authority than the courts, both more democratic and more capable of honoring the moral law. As Jeannine DeLombard observes, "abolitionists redirected the legal tactics of earlier reformers into the mass medium of print, converting antebellum print culture itself into an alternative tribunal."[67] Their campaign meant to drive a wedge between the judiciary and the collective conscience of the people. The sanction of moral authority, and with it the assent of a significant popular faction, was now being turned against the institutions of law.

Confined to a Missouri penitentiary in the 1840s for his attempt to spirit enslaved people across the river to the North, the young divinity student and poet George Thompson saw a greater victory in martyrdom than in any formal, legal vindication: "I shall be acquitted at the great and supreme tribunal of the universe. Then my dear Savior will act as judge, and the world will see and acknowledge the justness of my cause. Then those who are now my enemies, and rejoice and clap their hands at my condemnation, will be covered with shame."[68] Denied justice by the state, Thompson expected exoneration in heaven and vengeance in the court of public opinion. His prophesy that "the world will see" shows how the martyr's fantasy internalizes and sublimates the forms of public address, reception, and reform that were enabled by print. Thompson foresees the transmission of his testimony into an indefinite future, where it will find its true addressee, and where the present hierarchy will be overturned. Here, too, it becomes clear that the story of the curse is the counterpart and complement to the story of the oracle. As the higher law was left behind by the secularizing courts, it was picked up in mass politics, especially by the rising evangelical movements, as a way to inspire reform and to justify disobedience.

While the martyr's voice was widely revered for its persuasive force, however, it was also feared for its incendiary potential. Introduced to bring about the moral and legal redemption of the community, it threatened to divide the public into irreconcilable factions, even to kindle insurrection. Awaiting trial and punishment, the Nat Turner of the *Confessions* asked his accusers, "Was not Christ crucified?"[69] The violence of Turner's uprising was quickly associated with religious delusion. Many in the proslavery press blamed the fiery rhetoric of radical abolitionists like David Walker and William Lloyd Garrison. Part of the reaction was the imposition of formal and informal censorship—the prosecution of blasphemous and incendiary speech, "gag rules" against the discussion of controversial problems, laws prohibiting the circulation of offensive texts. Another part was the internal regulation of abolition's public sphere, the disciplining of the movement to distinguish its own appeals to higher law from a fanatical militancy.

At just the time when the development of large-scale distribution networks had enabled something like a national audience to be addressed in print, the conflict over slavery made the relation between the formal laws of states and the higher law of God a burning question.[70] Preaching to a congregation in Brooklyn, New York, in December of 1850, the Presbyterian minister Samuel T. Spear suggested that the "great politico-moral question" of the higher law had cleaved the nation into two irreconcilable circles, "each repudiating and violently denouncing the other." There was no longer a single public mind; there was the antagonism between "the law-abiding conscience" and "the higher law conscience." One revered the oracles of law, and the other answered the call of the curse. The law-abiding conscience, Spear wrote, "affirms the sanctity and authority of law, and by consequence, the obligation of obedience." Its counterpart, the higher law conscience, is animated by the old revolutionary faith that "resistance to tyrants is obedience to God." "Every professed martyr virtually appeals to posterity and to God, to review his case, and settle the question whether he was a martyr or a fool." The martyrs suffer their punishment today, but they expect to find vindication over the course of a longer history, in the eyes of heaven and of the people.[71]

In Spear's vision of an irreconcilably factionalized community, the precarious relation between legal rationalism and moral reform was collapsing. Each of these polite discourses had devolved into its suppressed, incendiary other. The struggle over slavery seemed to be dividing a national mind into two minds, a reasonable polity into "two fanaticisms."[72] The effect was what the political philosopher Nancy Fraser calls a "heteroglossia of justice discourse." Under the conditions of "normal" justice, Fraser explains, "contestants share some underlying presuppositions about what an intelligible justice claim should look like," and "their contests assume a relatively regular, recognizable shape." Under the more radically oppositional conditions of "abnormal justice," by contrast, we lose "the ordering force of shared presuppositions," and "the grammar of justice itself" becomes a matter of contestation.[73] The two sides do not simply disagree about particular cases of harm or retribution; they seem to lack a common language for the negotiation of their claims. Two incommensurable standards of justice are invoked, and no legal institution is able to resolve their dispute. The intrusion of the higher law opens the ceremonies of justice to the antagonisms of politics. The oracle and the curse return in their undisciplined forms.

Into this flammable situation, Brown, the meteor of the war, came crashing down in 1859. Brown's trial not only deepened the national divide over slavery. It also reopened an old fissure within the antislavery movement itself. For some, Brown's martyrdom signaled that the time for reform had lapsed; the higher law justified open acts of civil disobedience, even of rebellion against the state. As the radical abolitionist George B. Cheever saw it, Brown's militancy was "the curse of God against political atheism"—the very spirit of the divine law, avenging itself on a corrupt nation.[74] Most of the leading evangelical reformers, however, still recoiled from the violence and the apparent folly of Brown's doomed endeavor. Garrison continued to hold fast to his peace principles. Child, in a widely reprinted letter, expressed her sympathy for Brown's suffering but condemned his effort to stir up an armed insurrection in the South. Even as the prisoner was led to the gallows, the reformers were making their last efforts to suppress the incendiary power of enthusiasm, to preserve the peculiar styles of persuasion that had promised to contain the fire of the curse.

Martyr Literature

Midway through "The Last Days of John Brown," Thoreau paused to recall that another eminent American had quietly passed away within a week of the martyr's ascension. "The death of Irving, which at any other time would have attracted universal attention, having occurred while these things were transpiring, went almost unobserved. I shall have to read of it in the biography of authors." Thoreau had just been praising a condemned man whose words were so forceful that they had cleaved the national community. Now he took a moment to point out how small, in light of this epoch-making event, a literary life appeared. Even Washington Irving, the most celebrated American fiction writer of the early nineteenth century, a man sometimes credited with founding a national tradition in *belles lettres*, looked like a petty trifler next to the mighty Brown. The announcement of his death was not even news. It would circulate in a genre of polite literary history, of interest mainly to pedants and amateurs. Indeed, Thoreau may have been writing a renunciation, a death notice for the insubstantial tales on which Irving had built his career. Thoreau's alliance with Brown's cause seems to have called him away from any literary endeavor which could make so little difference in the world where justice was at stake. To reckon with the curse was also to question the value of literature itself.

The relation of literature to law, in Thoreau's time, was one of deep familiarity and deepening contempt. Around the Revolution, the legal profession had become a dominant force in the culture of letters. Taking the mantle from the ministers, the lawyers set the standards of taste, defining the role of *belles lettres* as a supplement to state authority. It was not until the 1830s, perhaps, that their grip on the literary field had itself begun to slacken. This, as Habermas says, was the age of the public sphere's "disintegration": the division of an apparently coherent culture of letters into so many smaller cultures, the segregation of a presumably unified reading public into myriad publics.[75] Part of this larger transformation was the estrangement of literature from law, the formation of a semi-autonomous literary field where professional writers like Irving did their work.

In the Jacksonian and antebellum periods, literary authors established their autonomy by defining themselves against the social and ideological world of the lawyers.[76] Sometimes they did so through parody or satire, sometimes through the kind of nuanced dissent that has come to be known as critique. In any case, the rise of a literature that could critique legal institutions, as Brook Thomas notes, became possible only after "the breakup of a configuration of law and letters" that had remained in place through the 1820s.[77] By the antebellum period, Wai Chee Dimock argues, law and literature had become "different operative theaters," featuring "different styles of knowledge," and literature began to make its "eloquent dissent . . . from that canon of rational adequation so blandly maintained in philosophy and law."[78] The law's conception of justice could now be brought before the bar of the literary, with its alternative standards of judgment.

According to the prevailing narrative in Law and Literature scholarship, the work began with Charles Brockden Brown, a lapsed law student who fled from Philadelphia to New York to become a philosophical novelist in the English gothic style. Brown openly criticized the obscure jargon of the common law, and in books like *Wieland* he warned his readers against the self-effacing verbal wizardry of deceivers and demagogues. In the 1830s, the endeavor was renewed by such canonical American Romantics as Nathaniel Hawthorne, who exposed the self-interested hypocrisy of legal and religious authorities. It was finished with the so-called American Renaissance of the 1850s. In the years leading up to the Civil War, Melville wrote his gothic fictions of martyrdom, attending to the ambiguities of motive that seemed to fall into the blind spots of a criminal justice system concerned with verifiable facts and a secure social order. Thoreau's essays on civil disobedience set the individual conscience above the authority of the state. And Stowe's monument of sentimental protest, *Uncle Tom's Cabin,* became the definitive literary treatment of the evangelical reformers' doctrine of higher law. The literary field had taken a position of detachment and disenchantment. From this estranged distance, it delivered its critique of law.

For some commentators, the story of American literature's quest for autonomy is a heroic one of Romantic resistance to the banality and sensationalism of mass culture.[79] Others have argued that the ideal of an autonomous literature was a dream of escape from history itself, a withdrawal into a private zone of aesthetic pleasures or domestic attachments. In these critical histories of literary privatization, Hawthorne, for example, is taken to task for his refusal to engage with the great national crisis of his era, the struggle over slavery.[80] Stowe, meanwhile, is charged with misrecognizing the same crisis as a matter of conscience, not of politics. With the rise of sentimentalists like Stowe in the mid-nineteenth century, Lauren Berlant writes, "the political as a place of acts oriented toward publicness becomes replaced by a world of private thoughts, leanings, and gestures."[81] If antebellum literature developed an eloquent dissent from law, it also imagined the forum for its address to the reader as a secluded space at the margins of the public sphere. The secret unity of antebellum literature, the common ground between the rebel Romantics and the popular sentimentalists, perhaps, is to be found in their cooperative production of a private sphere, withdrawn from the public worlds of economics, politics, and law.[82]

In fact, most of the authors of the Law and Literature canon did define their interest in the autonomy and purity of conscience against the public concerns of legal authority. If, as Law and Literature critics maintain, Brown protested the tyranny of the legal profession in the early republic, it was not by identifying with the fanaticism of the murderer Theodore Wieland. It was, instead, by diagnosing the intrusion of law's logics and rituals into intimate relations, even into the structure of consciousness itself—the moral constitution, as Brown called it—and by seeking to preserve the integrity of private life against this subtle enemy. In a similar way, Hawthorne's tales of martyrdom suppressed the temptation to curse and dreamed, instead, of a private space of freedom and chastity: *The House of the Seven Gables* opens with the vengeful imprecation of a condemned man, but the most urgent task for its heroine is to keep Judge Pyncheon, the embodiment of legal hypocrisy, from crossing the threshold into the domestic interior. As for Stowe, she drew from *The Confessions of Nat Turner* to produce the character of Dred, the exhorter whose thundering voice stirs up an insurrection in the Great Dismal Swamp, but she was best loved for the figures of Uncle Tom and Little Eva, innocents who evangelize much more quietly, in private.

Thus it appears that American writers played a part in their own banishment from the public sphere. Contributing to the regulation of enthusiasm, they helped to contain the menace of dissent by sublimating fanaticism into such relatively unthreatening ideals as self-reliance and moral influence. "Literature was a space where enthusiasm gained a relative toleration," as Jon Mee argues in a study of these aspects of British Romanticism, but this "was only because literariness itself came to be seen as part of the process of regulation."[83] The authors of martyr literature tended to limit themselves to a concern for the integrity of conscience, often dramatized in stories of seduction and sexual violation. Indeed, when the curse was spoken in literature, it seemed almost always to be accompanied by another voice, an innocent victim of seduction—Brown's Clara, Hawthorne's Alice Doane—who wished mainly to be cleared of blame and left alone.

If the disentangling of literature from law enabled literary critiques of legal institutions, then, it also threatened to contain and neutralize the public force of critique; the sanctum of conscience could also be a quarantine. The main task of Law and Literature scholarship has been to show how novels and poems took positions in the legal debates of their times.[84] Often, the approach involves recontextualizing the literary work so that it can be recognized as an allegory of injustice. But the critical scholarship on privacy has illuminated what is obscured by any simply allegorical reading, by any strictly literary critique. We have not fully grasped the politics of a text (whether we call it ideology or protest, complicit or subversive) until we understand its orientation toward the public sphere where conflicts over justice are played out. What ideas about address and reception govern its orientation toward its audience? What is its public, and how does it imagine that its reception can make a difference in the world? How, for instance, can the critique of unjust laws be expected to lead to their reformation or their abolition? The power to critique legal institutions through allegories of martyrdom is dearly bought if its price is exile to the margins of power.

Thoreau had a feeling for this predicament. Like many of his contemporaries, he reflected with great seriousness on literature's estrangement from sovereignty and history. Thus, on the occasion of John Brown's funeral, he seemed to bury *belles lettres* and to endow the abolitionist militant, by contrast, with eternal significance: "Literary gentlemen, editors and critics, think that they know how to write, because they have studied grammar and rhetoric, but they are egregiously mistaken. The *art* of composition is as simple as the discharge of a bullet from a rifle, and its master-pieces imply an infinitely greater force behind them." A commitment to public action could seem to require a turn away from any merely literary pursuit.

Yet it would be oversimple to read these statements as total rejections of the powers that literature had acquired through its extrication from the legal field. They were made by an author whose access to publicity depended on the reputation he had built through the writing of memoir and poetry, and they were, in their way, strong assertions of autonomy. Through the strategic disavowal of literary trifling, Thoreau laid claim to a special kind of public authority. Indeed, when critics today indict the authors of the antebellum period for declining to address the people in an effort to transform their world, they inherit an ideal of imaginative literature's public power that was itself developed by some of the same writers as a compensatory fantasy.

Between the Revolution and the Civil War, the disciplinary regulation of the curse involved the suppression of enthusiasm, the persecution of blasphemy, the bridling of evil speech, and the censure of militancy. It also involved the creation of new styles of nonrational public address which, in refusing to curse, could represent themselves as legitimate modes of verbal protest. Nowhere were these modes of peaceable resistance more carefully or more elaborately constructed than in the period's imaginative literature. Again and again, American fiction and poetry dramatized scenes of injustice, of innocence wrongly persecuted and righteousness put to death by corrupt authorities. In revisiting the Law and Literature canon, I give special attention to these fictions of inequity, this martyr literature. The authors of the antebellum period were of course not the first or the last to discover, in stories of martyrdom, a compelling narrative pattern. But this period produced a martyr literature of a particular kind. As its own self-critique suggests, its authors may have been drawn to the martyr for reasons that had less to do with their political commitments on such issues as blasphemy or slavery than with the precarious, marginal condition of literature itself.

Martyr literature, I argue, analyzed the dynamics of public address, developing a poetics of justice. And in relation to the oracle and the curse it defined its own distinctive position, its own forms of seduction and persuasion. Its authors were mourning the loss of a kind of persuasive power that could only be exercised on, and conferred by, a public that imagined itself as a sovereign people. In the story of the martyr, of innocence or righteousness condemned, they discovered a speaker whose words, performed before the people, could seem to authorize the remaking of the world. The martyr became a figure of compensation, even of redemption; the wish for an audience which was not the legitimating public of the existing law, but which could authorize a new law, found its expression in the literary idealization of the curse.

In the end, martyr literature's worst nightmares involved the corruption of the self—the seduction of the autonomous will, the loss of moral purity, or the complicity of conscience in injustice—and it did tend to define the space of freedom as a private realm, protected from the reach of law. But it also gave elaborate attention to the curses which it declined to pronounce. Martyr literature was marked by "the nostalgia for community that," according to John Guillory, "pervades . . . mass culture, in the midst of its carnival of cultural diversity, its infinite dispersal and fragmentation of knowledge."[85] The "nostalgia," however, was not limited to a feeling of personal alienation or resentment. Keeping a gothic presence alive even as they buried it in sentiment, the authors of martyr literature grieved their own estrangement from the public culture of justice. If the curse was repressed, it was also routinely reanimated; it was a monstrous other carried along and nurtured, in a way, within the heart of a sentimental culture.

Throughout *The Oracle and the Curse,* then, my readings of martyr literature attempt to move beyond the critical impasse that arises from the identification of autonomy with privacy. The story of early American literature's poetics of justice does not neatly conform to a pattern of self-enclosure, the cordoning off of a field outside the legal public sphere. In my view, the public sphere itself has no durable structure except as a set of discursive and generic conventions. It is spoken into being anew with every act of public address. In the same way, the projection of an autonomous literary field is a process repeated countless times, in myriad ways. Rather than rehearsing a single narrative of autonomization, therefore, I attend to multiple sites and modes of estrangement, each of which had a distinct politics. The trick is to understand how a given novel or poem marks its own position with respect to the institutionalized struggles of law's public sphere. The really beguiling thing about martyr literature is not the forfeiture of power. It is the performance of strategic disavowal and self-discipline through which literature authorizes its protests against the law.

The literature that identified itself with conscience, whether in Stowe's sentimental mode or in Thoreau's Romantic one, addressed its reader as a private person. To stage such a relation, though, it had to distort the circumstances of its transmission and reception in fantastic ways. These texts asked a mass public of strangers to picture itself as so many discrete and inward-looking souls, and they masked their own broadcast into the networks of general circulation as a strictly domesticated appeal—a quiet entreaty, even a whisper. If Law and Literature criticism has overlooked this aspect of allegorical critique, the scholarship on privacy has perhaps taken the distortion for the reality, emphasizing the sacrifice of power it involved. For a poetics of justice, the problem will be to understand how the performance of domestication or alienation could endow the literary work with a peculiar authority. Both Stowe and Thoreau repaired to the private sphere by way of the perception that the deliberative public sphere had been thoroughly corrupted by a ruthless capitalism in league with the slave system. But even the (highly public) demarcation of a private sphere may not have pointed toward a space of withdrawal. What was called privacy or solitude was, in my view, really the sheltered place for the gathering of a counterpublic: a community of strangers that knew its unity in opposition to the lawgiving people.

By the 1830s, it had already become possible to imagine the summoning and animation of large-scale counterpublics through the channels of the mass media and the itinerant circuits of evangelical exhortation. (These were the menaces imperfectly contained through the suppression of blasphemy and evil speaking.) In poetry and fiction, this prospect was first acknowledged in the act of its disavowal. Thus the speaker of Elizabeth Barrett Browning's "Runaway Slave at Pilgrim's Point," for example, renounced the temptation to pronounce an insurrectionary curse against a guilty land. But in order to dramatize the speaker's choice in this way, the same poem had to accept the premise that a single act of verbal dissent really might summon a slave rebellion on a national scale. It had to reimagine the evangelical public sphere of moral suasion and literary entreaty as an infrastructure that could be weaponized, its private appeal revealed as public dissent. The leap from circumspect imagination to explicit activation, from Browning's Garrisonian disavowal of incendiary speech to Thoreau's embrace of Brown's vatic protest, was significant, but in either case the fantasmatic object of appraisal was the same.

After 1850, and especially in the wake of Brown's raid, there were radicals in the antislavery campaign who gave up on the prospect of reform, and who openly embraced the idea of a prophetic public address that might redeem the nation by stirring up a revolution. Perhaps, as John

Brown said, the crimes of this guilty land would never be purged away but with blood, and perhaps literature might hasten the reckoning. The final chapter of *The Oracle and the Curse* turns to the rhetoric and reception of Harriet Jacobs's *Incidents in the Life of a Slave Girl*, a text which, contrary to its reputation as a sentimental appeal, seemed, to some, to bind the fate of autonomy and chastity to Brown's violent endeavor. As one militant wrote, Jacobs's "words of fire" would provoke readers to "tear down the cursed system which makes such records possible."[86] To a few, at least, Jacobs's testimony resonated with the black militant Martin Delany's vision, in *Blake,* of a general insurrection coordinated by a single prophetic messenger. To be sure, the possibility of a militant counterpublic was created outside the literary field, through ongoing acts of resistance and agitation and the intensifying radicalism of abolition's public sphere. But these transformations also exploited the fantasy of the curse that martyr literature had been developing for decades, precisely by seeming to renounce or regulate its power. The very genres of writing that had been cultivated by the reformers, in the interest of a moral reawakening, now appeared capable of summoning readers who *burned*—circles wishing not to cleanse their consciences but to remake their common world.

CHAPTER 1

Oracles of Law

"Custom, so immemorial, that it looks like nature."
— Nathaniel Hawthorne, *The House of the Seven Gables*

Τhe oracle, the curse, and the estrangement of literature from law—no book knits these three stories together more tightly than Nathaniel Hawthorne's 1851 romance, *The House of the Seven Gables*.[1] Hawthorne begins his chronicle of the Pyncheon house at the primal scene of colonial injustice, the Salem witch panic of 1692. The corrupt, theocratic magistrates who are putting an accused wizard to death stand "in the inner circle roundabout the gallows, loudest to applaud the work of blood" (7). The condemned Matthew Maule, walking "the martyr's path," climbs the scaffold and curses his most eager persecutor, an eminent judge, with the prophecy that "God will give him blood to drink!" (7).[2] And Hawthorne's preface, drawing its subtle distinction between the genres of the novel and the romance, is one of the best-known literary manifestoes of the antebellum period, laying out the "laws" which govern the writer's art (3). As many readers have observed, *The House of the Seven Gables* is deeply engaged with legal history, especially with the transformation of property law between the colonial period and the age of industrial capitalism.[3] The romance positions the affairs of antebellum Essex County, Massachusetts, within regional, national, and transnational legal contexts, insisting that the present has inherited the legacies of a premodern past. But it is also a tale of crimes and punishments in the antebellum present, taking up the relations between rituals of justice and the consent of the sovereign people. The book's visions of domestic happiness and literary autonomy emerge from its reflection on the tyrannizing power wielded, in private and in public, by an oracle of law.

There will be more to say about the cursing of the condemned in Hawthorne, and about the author's cautious positioning of his own literary protest, but first there is the story of the oracle. The villain of the melodramatic plot is Judge Jaffrey Pyncheon, a descendant of Puritan witch-hunters and an ambitious public figure who covers his self-interest in the robes of impersonal reason and legal duty. As the romance approaches its conclusion, the heartbroken Hepzibah Pyncheon confronts the judge about his role in the wrongful conviction and imprisonment of her brother, Clifford. When he was still a young man—"wild, dissipated, addicted to low pleasures"—Judge Pyncheon committed dark crimes against property and family, then framed the innocent Clifford (219). Later, as the convict lives out his days in poverty and seclusion, Hepzibah worries that "he shall be persecuted to death, now, by the same man who long ago attempted it" (160). The judge is indignant. He played his role in the trial, he says, but it was the law, not Jaffrey Pyncheon, that condemned poor Clifford. "Is it possible that you do not perceive how unjust, how unkind, how unchristian, is this constant, this long-continued bitterness against me, for a part which I was constrained by duty and conscience, by the force of law, and at my own peril, to act?" (161).

In Judge Pyncheon, Hawthorne produces the figure of a corrupt, self-interested authority that disavows its own discretionary power. Along these lines, Brook Thomas reads *The House of the Seven Gables* as an "allegory of national politics" which "questions the impersonal claim to authority" made by government officials.[4] Describing a private gathering of a dozen Massachusetts elites, Hawthorne's narrator considers how men of influence like Judge Pynheon mystify the sovereign people: "They are practiced politicians, ever man of them, and . . . steal from the people, without its knowledge, the power of choosing its own rulers. The popular voice, at the next gubernatorial election, though loud as thunder, will be really but an echo of what these gentlemen shall speak, under their breath" (193). According to the ideology of the state, the governors represent and obey the people's will, but in a corrupt world the sequence is reversed, and the crafty elites produce popular opinion as an echo of their own commands.

Thus Hawthorne introduces the problem of mystification, a style of domination that depends on the enchantment of the governed. In an essay on speech acts and power, Pierre Bourdieu sets out to expose how this coercive magic works. Bourdieu begins with a straightforward claim: "Authority comes to language from outside." Contrary to the theories of some linguistic formalists, Bourdieu argues, the illocutionary force brought to bear by performative utterances has little to do with their grammatical form. It has everything to do with the distribution of power. In any given social order, a few are entitled to pronounce judgments in the courthouse or to perform sacred rites at the altar. The rest are expected to obey. The magic attributed to words and phrases, Bourdieu writes, "is nothing other than the *delegated power* of the spokesperson." As he develops this critique, however, the question of delegation turns out to be more complicated than it first appeared, and in the end it leads the philosopher down a circular path. Power, it seems, has to secure the "complicity" of the governed, which "is the basis of all authority"; it seeks to produce and reproduce the conditions of its own legitimacy. It does so, in part, by persuading its subjects to sanction its commands. The moment in which the governed acknowledge the legitimacy of official speech, according to Bourdieu, is always a moment of *misrecognition* because they do not realize that they have cooperated in their own subjection.[5]

Hawthorne's romance gives a subtle turn to this critique of ritualized domination. Judge Pyncheon is not interested in masking the consensual origins of his authority. On the contrary, his self-abnegating performances enchant the people into surrendering precisely by insisting that he speaks in their voice. *The House of the Seven Gables* is a Jacksonian Democrat's critique of Whig sophistry, but it is also an investigation into the peculiar vulnerability of a legal order founded on the people's will. A fashionable, modern man with "the genuine character of an inquisitor," Judge Pyncheon is "doing over again, in another shape, what [his] ancestor before [him] did" (155, 168). And if the romance insists on the continuity between the colonial past and the Whig-dominated present, it calls attention, as well, to the new "shape" assumed by authority in the postrevolutionary age. In the judge, Hawthorne develops the portrait of a subtle tyranny which preserves the character of an older, theocratic one but legitimates itself in a new way, in relation to the "popular voice." *The House of the Seven Gables* is a story not only about the undying presence of oracular mystification, but also about its refashioning.

With Hawthorne's gothic romance of a house accursed in mind, this chapter explores the poetics of justice, the conceptions of juridical address and public reception, that emerged in the transatlantic, intertextual conversation about the grounds of legal authority in the era of the Atlantic revolutions. My focus will be on the common law treatise, the genre in which jurists made their case for the legitimacy of customary law by positioning themselves as the custodians of the people's will—as the oracles first of the community's faith, then of its reason. In these documents, more explicitly than anywhere else, legal professionals defined the sources of their authority and the proper modes for its ceremonial exercise. Some of the minor legal writers who produced the treatises have been all but forgotten by literary critics since Perry Miller examined their work in the 1960s. It is a curious case of amnesia or neglect, since literary scholarship has become, in the meantime, so much more explicitly concerned with questions of justice and law. But these treatises reveal aspects of the law that not many critics have gone looking for—the precariousness of legal authority, the delicate intellectual and political procedures by which it protected itself against the revolutionary threat. In these overwrought, occasionally desperate instances of public address, legal professionals, no less than other verbal artists, wrote from beyond the boundaries of a secure legitimacy, seeking the people's blessing.

Historians often describe the legal debates of the early republic as battles between antagonistic camps: the courts defend the interests of the propertied classes against the leveling demands of debtors and the disenfranchised; the judiciary protects the Federalists against the Republicans, the Whigs against the Democrats. But these were also conflicts over the nature of law's public sphere. They defined the modes of persuasion through which legal authority might properly secure the assent, or respond to the dissent, of the sovereign people. Out of a long, unresolved struggle between an old-fashioned, theocratic lawcraft and a critical reason associated with public opinion, the distinctive verbal style of modern legal formalism would be conceived. The oracles would shed the costumes of the theocratic past and reappear in a new shape, as the guardians of reason and the rule of law.

Lex non Scripta

The foundations were laid in William Blackstone's *Commentaries on the Laws of England* (1765–1769).[6] Blackstone's subject was the Common Law, a body of customs that he sometimes called the *lex non scripta,* or unwritten law, to distinguish it from the written statutes of Parliament (I: 63). The Common Law, as Blackstone imagined it, was the most venerable standard of civil justice in the British empire. It was in harmony with the divinely authored laws of nature. It was as ancient as English civilization, and it expressed the unique character of the English people, with their profound devotion to liberty. It had been preserved through centuries of invasion and rebellion, and its long history had been documented, though imperfectly, in a tradition of court records and legal treatises, including Blackstone's own. The Common Law was natural law, embodied in the customs of the nation's people, and the judges were its living oracles.

The first Professor of English Law to be appointed at an English university, Blackstone was endeavoring to create a new discipline—or, as he put it, to nurture through its "infancy" a "most useful and most rational branch of learning" (I: 3). In his long Introduction to the *Commentaries,* he made the case that his subject belonged among the noble disciplines, alongside natural science and moral philosophy. He placed the civil laws within the broader framework of a divinely ordered universe, grounding their legitimacy in the all-governing commandments of God: "This law of nature, being co-eval with mankind and dictated by God himself, is of course superiour in obligation to any other. It is binding all over the globe, in all countries, and at all times: no human laws are of any validity, if contrary to this; and such of them as are valid derive all their force, and all their authority, mediately or immediately, from this original" (I: 41). Even as he was preparing to teach the history and procedures of the civil law, Blackstone was eliciting his readers' assent to a shared creed. By his sermonic cadences no less than by his rehearsal of familiar ideals, his audience was invited to recognize the common, transcendent standard that was the basis for every worldly dispensation of justice.[7]

Blackstone has been called "the high priest of the English legal system," and his account of natural law was marked by his piety and his conservatism.[8] Since the fall of Adam, he said, "[man's] reason is corrupt, and his understanding full of ignorance and error" (I: 41). Dictated by God but only partially revealed in scripture, the law of nature was finally mysterious, beyond mortal understanding; the surest guides to its principles were the traditions of religious institutions. The maxims of the Common Law, too, were "of higher antiquity than memory or history can reach" (I: 67). They had been composed, gradually and organically, as the laws of nature and the spirit of the nation inscribed themselves in the customs of the people. Thus Blackstone took his stand against the liberal theorists of natural right, who traced the origins of the legal order—and the right of revolution—to a mythical social contract.

For a study of his poetics, though, Blackstone's resistance to the radical implications of natural law theory may be less significant than his curious insistence on national forgetting. It was precisely the disappearance of the Common Law, its unwritten and potentially unknowable character, that gave the judges their claim to authority: "How are these customs or maxims to be known, and by whom is their validity to be determined? The answer is, by the judges in the several courts of justice. They are the depositary of the laws; the living oracles, who must decide in all cases of doubt, and who are bound by an oath to decide according to the law of the land" (I: 69). Blackstone was expounding the doctrine known to lawyers as *stare decisis,* the obligation of the courts to follow precedent. Every judge, he recalled, was required "to determine, not according to his own private judgment, but according to the known laws and customs of the land; not delegated to pronounce a new law, but to maintain and expound the old one" (I: 69). This was a familiar proposition. Blackstone's innovation was in his peculiar conception of the oracle's function in a present which has lost touch with its distant origins.

There is a subtle, half-repressed acknowledgment of political and social modernity in Blackstone's depiction of oracular jurisprudence. Ancient customs and maxims are unknown. The validity of justice claims is in doubt. In these troubled circumstances, Blackstone claimed, the Common Law courts served their indispensable function, preserving national traditions from the oblivion of history and the confusion of modernity. The judge was not delegated to speak in his private voice. He gave expression to the ancient ways of a nation that had forgotten its past, its true self. With the trope of the oracle, Blackstone mystified the origins of juridical authority by suggesting that the judge's public address called the people of the present to obey the laws which, in spirit, they had always known.

Blackstone's vision of English history involved its own kinds of retrospective mythmaking. The principal sources for his treatise had been produced in the early modern period, when jurists began to draw up general codes of customary law for a centralizing state. By the seventeenth century, the king's courts had overwritten a variety of regional practices, and only then, as J. G. A. Pocock argues, did it become plausible for the jurists to suggest that "the common law was the only law their land had ever known."[9] In this way, legal literature had contributed to the rise of national imaginaries. According to Guyora Binder and Robert Weisberg, "the modern idea of a sovereign people or nation emerged out of the early modern idea that any group obedient to a common customary regime was a distinct people."[10] The new genre of the common law treatise, in other words, helped to persuade the subjects of the emerging nation-states that they belonged to a people whose spirit reached back to an era before recorded history.

Blackstone used the term "municipal law" to refer to the laws of England, "for, tho' strictly that expression denotes the particular customs of one single *municipium* or free town, yet it may with sufficient propriety be applied to any one state or nation, which is governed by the same laws and customs" (I: 44). In such passages, he took his place in the tradition of "juridical nationalism"; repressing the history of local and regional differences, conquests, and revolutions, he invited his readers to imagine the kingdom as a coherent normative community, held together by the same beliefs and traditions.[11] In this sense, the lawgiving national people invoked in the *Commentaries* was not a historical entity at all. This public was a retrospective illusion—a function of legal authority, summoned into being by the performative power of the judge's oracular address.

Blackstone's invocations of natural law and national traditions, as David Lieberman observes, "reflected the special demands created by his audience and the specific type of legal literature he designed for it."[12] The peculiar challenge Blackstone confronted was to defend the Common Law in a period when the center of sovereignty seemed to be drifting from the crown and the courts to Parliament.[13] He had to justify the legitimacy of obscure, unwritten customs to a public that had taken its modern form in relation to the ideal of written legislation, accountable to the will of the people.[14] Responding to the rising prestige of the statute books, Blackstone was careful to acknowledge the "absolute despotic power" of Parliament, which "hath sovereign and uncontrollable authority in making . . . laws" (1: 56).[15] Among his unspoken ambitions, however, was to bring about a world in which the courts would never come into open conflict with the legislature. He would seek to fortify the legitimacy of the judiciary through innovations in education and, more broadly, in the public sphere of print.

Here, for Blackstone, was the crucial importance of the discipline of legal study and of his own work as the teacher of a rising generation of elites. As Lieberman shows, Blackstone endeavored "to disclose the legal structure upon which responsible lawmaking might in future occur."[16] "How unbecoming it must appear," Blackstone remarked, "in a member of the Legislature to vote for a new law, who is utterly ignorant of the old! what kind of interpretation can he be enabled to give, who is a stranger to the text upon which he comments!" (I: 9). Although he used the metaphor of the "text," Blackstone insisted, throughout, that this quasi-sacred document existed nowhere in space or time. More like the English language itself than any particular piece of writing, it was legible only in its partial, local manifestations.[17] What Blackstone sought to teach, in the end, was not just the collection of customs and precedents that he recorded in his four volumes but, more fundamentally, the discursive system that held them together, the very grammar of the law. If he succeeded, then the power of the courts would never have to display itself in contradiction to the legislature. Statutes contrary to the reason of the Common Law—that is, against the norms expounded in the *Commentaries*—would simply become unspeakable.

Prospective legislators, however, were not the only audience for these lessons. The *Commentaries* became "the most popular treatise in common law history," appearing in twenty-three editions and sixty printings in its first century.[18] From the beginning, its reception was informed by a sharp awareness of its transatlantic popularity—as readers encountered this monument of legal literature, they knew that they were in the presence of the learned classes of the Anglophone world. St. George Tucker, the son of Bermuda planters who became a prominent Virginia judge and professor of law at the College of William and Mary, expressed the received wisdom when, in his own elaborately annotated edition of Blackstone's text, published in 1803, he called the *Commentaries* "a work . . . which has undergone so many editions in England, Ireland, and America, as to have found its way into the libraries of almost every gentleman whether of the [legal] profession or otherwise."[19] Blackstone had inherited the ideologies and doctrines of earlier generations of jurists, but his book endowed them with a new power by transmitting them to far-flung, nonspecialist reading publics. With the figure of the oracle, he had suggested a mode of address through which judges might summon the assent of the people; with the publication and distribution of the *Commentaries,* he had enacted this mode in the public sphere of print, where legitimacy was to be won and lost in rituals of reading.

Or, as Jeremy Bentham put it, mixing admiration with resentment, Blackstone's "works have had beyond comparison a more extensive circulation, have obtained a greater share of esteem, of applause, and consequently of influence . . . than any other writer who on that subject [the law] has ever yet appeared."[20] No one felt Blackstone's power more intensely than Bentham, and the quarrel between them has long been recognized as a significant episode in the history of English legal thought. Blackstone, according to Donald Kelley, carried on the "conservative and conservationist attitude" of the customary judiciary; the utilitarian Bentham, by contrast, was "an extreme example of an anti-jurist who wanted to discard all old legal tradition."[21] Where Blackstone defended the unwritten Common Law of the courts, Bentham called for a *Pannomium,* a single master code of statutes, to be published by Parliament. But this debate over the constitutional distribution of legal authority was also, crucially, a conflict over the proper idiom of law's public address.[22] While so many others were admiring Blackstone's gift for rational synthesis, Bentham argued in *A Fragment on Government* that the *Commentaries* was a work of verbal wizardry whose "enchanting harmony" appealed "powerfully to the imagination and the ear" (22–23). Championing a public sphere where legislation encountered a rationalist public opinion, Bentham composed a vivid portrait of its menacing counterpart, a public culture of justice where the oracles of law summoned the people to obedience.

Bentham's critique of Blackstone's legal theory emerged especially from a reckoning with the judge's language. "Had there been sense" in the arguments of the *Commentaries,* he wrote, "I should have attached myself to the sense: finding nothing but words; to the words I was to attach myself, or to nothing" (111). The *Fragment* is a marvelously subversive display of close reading—a rambling, vicious deconstruction of Blackstone's treatise that develops by quoting long passages, then pointing out their contradictions, vagaries, and reversals. In order to follow his critique, Bentham advised, "it will be proper the reader should have [Blackstone's text] under his eye" (36). As the antidote to the enchantment which possessed men to be governed by the ear, Bentham prescribed the silent, skeptical mode of reading enabled by print.

Schooled in Enlightenment philosophies of language, Bentham was familiar with the distinction between what were known as sentences of "assertion" and sentences of "volition"; anticipating the speech-act theory of the twentieth century, his contemporaries had described the difference between analytic propositions, or constatives, and the ritualized utterances that would come to be known as performatives.[23] Bentham's critique of Blackstone made the most of this distinction. "Throughout the whole of [the *Commentaries*]," he wrote, "what distresses me is, not the meeting with any positions, such as, thinking them false, I find a difficulty in proving so: but the meeting with any propositions, true, or false, . . . that I can find a meaning for. If I can find nothing positive to accede to, no more can I to contradict" (50). It was no use weighing the validity of the judge's arguments; he had not really made any coherent arguments at all. Through the magic of the performative, he had attempted to speak the Common Law into being. Blackstone's persuasive power, in Bentham's view, was entirely in his "oracular" style (110).

Much like Pierre Bourdieu, Bentham aligned the linguistic distinction between performatives and propositions with the constitutional distinction between the legislator and the private citizen. As the origin of law's authority, Bentham imagined neither the ratification of a social contract nor the emergence of a Common Law from the customs of the people. He saw only a structure of command and submission: "the establishment of names of office: the appearance of a certain man, or set of men, with a certain name, serving to mark them out as objects of obedience" (45). The "constitution," if there were such a thing, was only the organization of society into the few who could pronounce law and the rest who must obey.[24] Law, as Bentham understood it, was an authorized command, a special kind of performative that transformed the world in which it was spoken. The authority to speak in this way, he insisted, was strictly reserved for the legislator, granted through the constitutional and political distribution of power.

The legitimate counterpart of the lawmaker's sovereign performatives, in Bentham's scheme of things, was the critical opinion of the private citizen, as expressed in the deliberative public sphere. In a free society, the "person at large" could expect to have "the reasons publicly assigned and canvassed of every act of power that is exerted over him" (97). Reading the statutes of Parliament, the public could submit those reasons to critique and call for the revision of the law, in the press. This was Bentham's "motto" for the "good citizen": "*To obey punctually; to censure freely*" (10). The liberal cause of improvement would be served as the commands of law were reformed by the legislator, in response to the propositions of critical reason in the public sphere.

"A book of expository jurisprudence, is either *authoritative* or *inauthoritative*. It is styled authoritative, when it is composed by him who, by representing the state of the law to be so and so, causeth it to be so; that is, of the legislator himself; unauthoritative, when it is the work of any other person at large" (424). Even as he laid out the distinction between the legislator's command and the subject's opinion, however, Bentham perceived that it was a delicate one. The problem that dogged him, after all, was the pervasive "influence" of Blackstone's work. As an argument about the origins of legal authority, the *Commentaries* was absurd, a piece of "obscure and crooked reasoning" (4). But through its performative invocation, Bentham suggested, the "shadow" called Common Law had taken on a different kind of power. The *Commentaries* "teach men . . . to yield the same abject and indiscriminating homage to the Laws here, which is paid to the despot elsewhere" (12). The "timid and admiring" public, dazzled by Blackstone's language, had been all too willing to submit to the "shackles of authority" (111–112).[25] An enchanted people had surrendered its sovereignty to the judge.

Analyzing how it had happened, Bentham came to recognize that performative speech could be authorized not only prospectively, by constitutions, but also retrospectively, by reading publics. "The ultimate efficient cause of all power of imperation over persons," he admitted, "is a disposition on the part of those persons to obey: the efficient cause then of the power of the sovereign is neither more nor less than the disposition to obedience on the part of the people."[26] The power to pronounce law was not permanently fixed through the delegation of titles. It was grasped and yielded in ongoing linguistic negotiations between legal authorities and the people. It could be ratified backward, by consent. Bentham wanted to expose the invocations of the Common Law as "the mere opinions of men self-constituted into Legislators."[27] "What is called the Unwritten Law," he argued, "is made not by the people but by Judges: the substance of it by Judges solely."[28] But Bentham also saw how Blackstone had bewitched readers into believing that arbitrary commands uttered by judges were not, in fact, commands, but oracular revelations of the national spirit—in other words, that the subjects who obeyed the law were also its original authors.

According to the prevailing account in legal historiography, Blackstone represents the conservative judiciary, an institution that spoke an arcane language known only by a few specialists, and whose authority was granted from above, not founded on the will of the people. His adversary, Bentham, represents a legal rationalism which inaugurates a new age of codification. Certainly Bentham described himself as an advocate of the forms of deliberation and publicity associated with print, against Blackstone's enchanting harmony—his endeavor was to "teach [the reader] to distinguish between showy language and sound sense" (112). But he also came to understand Blackstone's work as an innovation in the law's public address. Blackstone had not simply repeated the old arguments of the Common Law tradition. He had developed a new genre of legal literature in which the ceremonial invocation of natural order and national heritage could be communicated to a wide public and ratified in rituals of reading. Bentham had set out to expose Blackstone as a relic from a superstitious, unenlightened past, but he ended up accomplishing something like the opposite: he perceived the dangerous new power of oracular address in the modern age of print and popular sovereignty.

"Written upon the Table of Our Hearts"

Bentham published his polemic against Blackstone in 1776, just as a group of colonists on the other side of the Atlantic was composing its own document of performative self-authorization: "When in the course of human events it becomes necessary for one people to dissolve the political bands which have connected them with another, and to assume among the powers of the earth, the separate and equal station to which the Laws of Nature and of Nature's God entitle them, a decent respect to the opinions of mankind requires that they should declare the causes which impel them to the separation." The Declaration of Independence invoked no customary institution. It meant to speak a new sovereignty into being.

Bentham respected the ideals of the revolutionaries. In a long note composed for the 1789 edition of his *Introduction to the Principles of Morals and Legislation,* he referred to the United States as "that newly created nation, one of the most enlightened, if not the most enlightened, on the face of the globe." But he was disturbed by the irrational language of the Declaration. The document's "loose and inadequate terms" seemed to reflect no understanding of "the science of legislation": "Who can help lamenting, that so rational a cause should be rested upon reasons, so much fitter to beget objections, than to remove them?" (434–435 n.1). Bentham perceived a curious affinity between the enlightened republicans and the reactionary Blackstone. Each had sought the grounds of sovereignty outside the halls of Parliament, and each had introduced the bewildering noise of performative speech into the public sphere. The Americans saw themselves as the vanguard of political rationalism, submitting facts to a candid world, but Bentham accused them of founding their new order in a mystical language. In his ongoing critique of law-craft, he perceived the dynamics of performative self-authorization in the Declaration that would be taken up by late modern analysts of its language, from Hannah Arendt to Jacques Derrida.[29]

In fact, there was an affinity between the revolutionary cause and the Common Law. Across the British empire, nowhere more so than in the American colonies, Blackstone's treatise had become essential to the ideology and practice of law. "Americans," Lawrence Friedman notes, "were [Blackstone's] most avid customers."[30] The Philadelphia printer Robert Bell produced a pirated edition of the *Commentaries* as early as 1771, explaining that a local printing would "produce mental improvement, and commercial expansion."[31] In all, Bell's 840 subscribers ordered 1,557 copies of Blackstone's four-volume work, "an astounding response" by the standards of colonial publishing.[32] Others in the colonies paid to have more expensive editions imported from English publishers. According to Morton J. Horwitz, "none of the persistent hostility to English legislation that prevailed throughout the colonial period seems to have influenced [the colonists'] commitment to common law doctrines."[33] Like the natural law of Locke and Montesquieu, the Common Law represented an alternative code of rights and responsibilities that could be invoked against the oppressions imposed by the crown and Parliament.[34]

After the Revolution, however, the customs of English jurisprudence became a matter of controversy. The legal culture of the early Republic, as Maxwell Bloomfield argues, was characterized by the "unresolved tensions between the millennial spirit and the common law." While the assemblies worked to build a new kind of representative government on the foundations of popular sovereignty, the courts held fast to English customs, and "lawyers seemed a counterrevolutionary force, blocking the emergence of a truly free republic."[35] Thus the attorneys of the early republic found themselves involved in what Horwitz calls "a distinctly postrevolutionary phenomenon: an attempt to reconstruct the legitimacy not only of statutes, but of common law rules, on a consensual foundation."[36]

In the factional struggles of the early republican decades, the protest that had begun with Bentham's polemic against Blackstone would take on a distinctly American accent.[37] Thomas Paine bitterly announced in

1805 that the United States had "not yet arrived at the dignity of independence." A great war had been waged; the colonies had broken their
political bonds with England; new lawgiving institutions had been established—but the "chicanery of law and lawyers" was a chronic affliction.
The legal system continued to "hobble along by the stilts and crutches
of English and antiquated precedents," like some wounded but undead
creature, in thrall to the Common Law.[38] The courthouses seemed to be
haunted by the phantoms of the old world.

The call for reform did not come only from deists and radical democrats. Peter Van Schaak of New York, a moderate who had spent the war
years in exile in England, returned to protest the "cobweb niceties and
refinements" of English concepts as lingering signs of decadence and
disability: "I would as soon suppose the flannels and crutches of a gouty
debauchee to be necessary for a robust American, or the appendages of
an old dowager's toilette ornamental to the bloom of nineteen, as that the
complex subtleties of [English] practice would be proper for the sim-
plicity of our courts."[39] Along the same lines, Jesse Root, a Federalist
stalwart who became Chief Justice of the Superior Court of Connecticut,
wrote in 1798 that English laws "were inapplicable to an infant country or state, where the government was in the peoples." "Let us, Americans," Root went on, "duly appreciate our own government, laws and
manners, and be what we profess—an independent nation."[40] The U.S.
courts could not claim, as Blackstone had, the unbroken continuity of
legal institutions. They would suggest, instead, that their common law
expressed the shared norms of American communities, which, in turn,
conformed to the universal laws of God.

From the Revolution through the early nineteenth century, Root and
other legal professionals produced a popular literature that invited reading publics to recognize the common law as an expression of their own
sovereign will. The American courts would work to distinguish their
customary traditions from the Common Law of England, with its aristocratic conventions and arcane ceremonies; they would claim to be
enforcing a simpler, clearer, and more liberal law than the one Blackstone had so elaborately defended. Yet the American judges had inherited more from Blackstone than a system of procedures and precedents.
They had learned his distinctive mode of legitimating legal authority in

the public sphere. According to the legal historian James Q. Whitman, the lawyers of the revolutionary generation tended to "confuse custom and reason"—to blur the boundary between the national traditions of common law and the rational principles of natural law itself.[41] For a poetics of justice, the problem might be framed not in terms of legal writers' conceptual errors, but of their effort to rebuild the foundations of authority. The invocation of natural law was a way of summoning the assent of reading publics, cultivating popular support for the institutions of law. The distinctive function of the legal literature of the early republic was to harmonize the power of the courts with the principle of popular sovereignty by way of the mediating invocation of natural law.

Nathaniel Chipman, a Revolutionary War veteran who would become Chief Justice of the Vermont Supreme Court, argued in his *Sketches of the Principles of Government* (1793) that the civil state in America, properly cultivated, would manifest a divinely authored state of nature, where all were free yet bound by their mutual obligations. Unlike English laws, which were often so artificial and arbitrary that they required complex mechanisms of enforcement, the common law in America would be "founded in natural principles" and recognized by all citizens as a sacred code of rights and duties.[42] Here, Chipman approached Perry Miller's "American paradox": "the more we perfect our legal system, the more natural we shall become."[43] The common law has a paradoxical grandeur. On one hand, it is nothing less than the highest law of the universe, demanding an absolute obedience. On the other hand, it is so perfect, so free of arbitrary or unjust schemes, that it hardly needs to be enforced at all.

The authentic common law, Jesse Root wrote in *The Origin of Government and Laws in Connecticut* (1798) "is the perfection of reason, arising from the nature of God, of man, and of things, and from their relations, dependencies, and connections: It is universal and extends to all men . . . and embraces all cases and questions that can possibly arise."[44] According to his 1824 obituary, Root had "experienced the renewing influence of the Holy Spirit" when he was four years old. He was educated at Nassau Hall and then at Andover, where he studied for the ministry under the Reverend Samuel Lockwood. After a few years, he decided to pursue a career in law, but "he carried his religion from the desk to the bar."[45] Even as he sat on the judge's bench, he thought and spoke like a Congregationalist minister: "Common law is the perfection of reason, arising from the nature of God, of man, and of things." Root went on, at length:

> It is in itself perfect, clear and certain; it is immutable, and cannot be changed or altered, without altering the nature and relation of things; it is superior to all other laws and regulations, by it they are corrected and controlled. All positive laws are to be construed by it, and wherein they are opposed to it, they are void. It is immemorial, no memory runneth to the contrary of it; it is co-existent with the nature of man, and commensurate with his being. It is most energetic and coercive, for every one who violates its maxims and precepts are sure of feeling the weight of its sanctions.
>
> Nor may we say, who will ascend into heaven to bring it down, or descend into the depths to bring it up, or traverse the Atlantic to import it? It is near us, it is within us, written upon the table of our hearts, in lively and indelible characters; by it we are constantly admonished and reproved, and by it we shall finally be judged. It is visible in the volume of nature, in all the works and ways of God. Its sound is gone forth into all the earth, and there is no people or nation so barbarous, where its language is not understood.
>
> The dignity of its original, the sublimity of its principles, the purity, excellency and perpetuity of its precepts, are most clearly made known and delineated in the book of divine revelations; heaven and earth may pass away and all the systems and works of man sink into oblivion, but not a jot or title of this law shall ever fail.[46]

The language of the common law was perhaps never more lovely or more persuasive than in this memorable passage from Root's *Origins,* which revises key themes from Blackstone in the style of a New England sermon. Root absorbs and transforms Blackstone's representation of the law of nature, fusing it with the traditions of the courts. As he invokes this mystical standard of justice, his language takes on the cadence of a hymn, even slipping into the archaic idioms of scripture—"its sound is gone forth into all the earth."

Such representations of the common law won their authority, in part, by denying their own dependence on language and print. Bound books like Blackstone's *Commentaries* had to be copied and imported from across the Atlantic, but Root's ideal code was so indelibly inscribed in nature and in the hearts of the people that it needed no artificial documentation. The true common law was "original," "written upon the table of our hearts," and "delineated in the book of divine revelations." It was a universal code, etched in every soul and legible in the works of God. Its "language" resolved the discordant dialects of diverse "people" and "nations"; it was "understood" by all. In an enchanting rhetoric that called his readers to assent, the judge appealed to a standard of justice older and truer than any text. He asked his readers to obey not his own opinions or the maxims of any treatise but a higher law which, in their hearts, they already knew and revered.

The common law in America, as Root envisions it, "is clothed with an energy, derived from a source, and rendered efficacious by a power, unknown in foreign governments, *(viz.)* the attachment of the citizens who rejoice in being ruled and governed by its laws, by the blessings it confers." It encodes only those rights and duties "which are reasonable and beneficial, and which have the sanction of universal consent and adoption amongst the citizens." Expressing the nature of the citizens and their common good, therefore, these "customs and regulations . . . have the force of laws under the authority of the people."[47] According to the ideology of the judiciary, the enforcement of the law was not oppression but the cultivation of a higher liberty. The free citizens of the United States would "rejoice in being ruled"—they would sanction their own submission to the power of the courts. And the scene of their rejoicing would be a scene of reading, the people's imagined assembly in the public culture of the law.

To the followers of Bentham and Jefferson, naturally, Root's Christian jurisprudence looked like the relic of a dead age. They continued to attack the common law in the name of representative lawmaking and a rationalist public sphere. Thus Robert Rantoul, known to modern legal historians as "a Jacksonian Benthamite," argued in a July Fourth oration of 1836 that "all American law must be statute law," so that it would express the will of the people through their representatives, and

that "the whole body of the law must be codified" into a single great statute book, so that it could be clearly understood and reasonably debated
in the public sphere.[48] Rantoul grotesquely satirized a maxim from the
Commentaries in which the Blackstone, like his American followers, had
aligned the common law with the principles of reason: "The Common
Law is the perfection of Human Reason—just as alcohol is the perfection of sugar. The subtle spirit of the Common Law, is Reason double
distilled, till what was wholesome and nutritive, becomes rank poison."[49]
By the arts of intellectual and rhetorical alchemy, the common law judges
had contrived to work their mischief on the American body politic. The
Revolution, Rantoul told the crowd on Independence Day, would not be
complete until this poison had been leeched from the nation.

"The common law," the New York attorney Henry Dwight Sedgwick
wrote in *The English Practice* (1822), "is not compatible with the spirit
or character of the age." Echoing Paine, Sedgwick called on his fellow
attorneys to abandon the "useless mysteries" they had inherited from
English customs, "and make legal science more consonant to common
sense and sound reason."[50] A review of Sedgwick's book in the *Literary
and Scientific Repository* welcomed this attack on the lingering authority
of imported customs. It was time to expose "the disposition, too manifest, which the members of the learned professions have exhibited to
make themselves oracles, rather by involving their sciences in maze and
mystery, than by plain and obvious intellectual strength and vigor." The
"solid reason" of Sedgwick's "propositions" would disenchant the public, a victory for critical reason against the oracles of law.[51]

No attack on the common law provoked a livelier controversy in the
world beyond the courthouse than the one delivered by William Sampson.[52] Sampson was an Irish patriot who had studied law at Lincoln's Inn
before he was banished by the English and made his way to the United
States. He had published vivid accounts of the persecution and imprisonment he endured under the despotic regimes of the old world, and in
the early nineteenth century he took part in a number of famous trials,
including the 1809 prosecution of New York's Amos Broad for cruelty
to his slaves. In a trial report prepared for general circulation, Sampson
celebrated the enlightened jurisprudence of a nation that defended the
security even of its most vulnerable subjects: "The justice of this land is

public justice," he said. "I wish this trial, with the just sentence which shall follow it, may be mounted on the wings of the air, and spread where the winds can blow, or ships can sail; because wherever it goes, it will be an example to the guilty, and a trophy to humanity. It will be a magnificent testimonial of a nation's justice."[53] This was a glorious vision of circulation and reception—the law's public sphere as a heaven on earth.

In his *Anniversary Discourse* (1824), though, Sampson turned on the American courts. He took up the line of critique that had begun with Bentham, calling for legal reforms responsive to the critical reason of the public sphere—demystification, rationalization, codification. The law, Sampson wrote, "is supposed to be the public reason, uttered by the public voice." "The well-being of society requires that a subject of such vital importance, should be brought to the test of reason in the open light of day." But the persistence of the common law in the American courts had tarnished this enlightened ideal; the administration of justice had not yet been "stripped of the parasitical growths that darken and disfigure it" (122, 123). Sampson continued: "[The American people], long after they had set the great example of self-government upon principles of perfect equality, had reduced the practice of religion to its purest principles, executed mighty works, and acquired renown in arts and arms, had still one pagan idol to which they daily offered up much smoky incense. They called it by the mystical and cabalistic name of Common Law" (123). The history of the early republic, as Sampson recollected it, was an unhappy parable in which enlightenment failed to dispel the enchantment of lawcraft.

But Sampson, like Bentham, knew that the common law was not only a relic of barbaric times. It acquired its legitimacy through a circuit of publication and reception; "the efficacy of the law," as Sampson acknowledged, "depends upon the confidence it creates" (122). He gave special attention to the men he called "panygerists," the authors of legal treatises in defense of the common law, from Blackstone forward. "If this Common Law is but oral tradition," he asked, "how comes it to fall about our ears in overwhelming showers of printing?" (123, 126). Legal literature, Sampson argued, had bewitched the American public into accepting the commands of a judiciary whose power had no basis in reason or popular sovereignty. Just beneath the surface of his rationalist polemic against antiquated precedents was the wary recognition that the common law had undergone its own transformation in the public sphere. This print-mediated arena was not only a forum for the exercise of critical reason. It could also be turned into a theater of ceremonial legitimation. The rituals of the courts were denounced as so much benighted idolatry, but the critique of the common law also described its rebirth in the postrevolutionary culture of letters.

Sampson's attack provoked the legal establishment once again to defend the foundations of its authority. A long, hostile review in *The Atlantic Magazine* announced that Sampson "has been fighting with a phantom conjured up by his own ardent imagination."[54] It was not the lawyers but their rabble-rousing antagonists, the author suggested, who practiced the arts of mystification. The Jeffersonians and Jacksonians liked to imagine the common law as a superstitious idol, but in the long struggle over the grounds of legal authority the judges would develop their own critique of lawcraft, making a claim to the mantle of reason and the consent of the people. As they looked back on the history of their profession in America, nineteenth-century lawyers would remember Jesse Root with an appreciation for his effort to organize the decisions of Connecticut courts into a useful set of precedents, but they would also confess to being embarrassed by his "florid" way of writing, "a quaintly discursive and elaborate style, in which form of expression receives quite as much attention as accuracy of reasoning."[55] Legal authority no longer wished to associate itself with an established church or with the preaching style of a New England minister. It wished to speak in the voice of cultivated reason.

The reformation of law's public address had been undertaken, for example, by James Wilson, a Scottish attorney who served as a U.S. Supreme Court Justice and a professor of law at the College of Philadelphia. Delivering his 1791 *Introductory Lecture* on American law, Wilson began with some praise for the acknowledged masterpiece of legal literature, Blackstone's *Commentaries*. "[Blackstone's] Manner is clear and methodical; his Sentiments . . . are judicious and solid; his Language is elegant and pure." But Wilson, not unlike Bentham, worried that Blackstone's elegant language may have been too persuasive. "He deserves to be much admired; but he ought not to be implicitly followed."[56]

Wilson was especially concerned with the problem of revolution. For Blackstone, a true revolution would have broken the continuity between the laws of the present and the customs of the ancient realm, severing the power of the courts from its legitimating source. Wilson did not accept such a conclusion, at least not in the American context: "*we* have *acted* upon *Revolution* PRINCIPLES, without offering them up as *Sacrifices* at the *Shrine* of *Revolution Precedents*."[57] Against Blackstone, Wilson argued that the precedents of common law might endure a political revolution. To hold their validity, however, these customs would have to be aligned with the sovereign power of the new nation, the people themselves.[58] The "*vital* Principle" of American law, Wilson wrote, "is this, *that the supreme sovereignty or power* of the society resides in the citizens at large."[59] Blackstone had anchored the Common Law in the ancient customs of the nation. Unable to appeal to such a tradition, Wilson found a new sanction for legal authority in the will of the people.

The written law, including the statutes and the constitutions of the newly independent states, had been composed by the people's elected representatives. But the enduring customs of the common law would have to be connected to the *vox populi* in some other way. Wilson described the common law in America as a force "springing warm and spontaneous from the Manners of the people."[60] Leaving behind the ways of the old world, he explained, the colonists had composed their own distinctive set of customs. Because they had enjoyed a near perfect freedom and equality, distant from the corrupting influence of the aristocracy, their manners had given living form to a common law virtually identical with the laws of nature. Wilson was a severe critic of tyranny and of lawcraft. He devoted substantial passages to the principle of religious toleration, and he insisted that the power of the judiciary had to be rationalized. "Law and liberty cannot rationally become the objects of our *love,* unless they first become the objects of our *knowledge*."[61] The purpose of legal education, and of treatise literature, was to disclose to the public the reasonable foundations of the law's authority, the principles of natural order to which they had already given their love and their consent.

In 1826, when James Kent published his monumental *Commentaries on American Law,* the rationalization of the common law was more or less complete. Kent would not invoke the sanction of scripture. He would provide, instead, a history of popular habit, natural justice, and cultivated reason. "A great proportion of the rules and maxims which constitute the immense code of the common law, grew into use by gradual adoption, and received, from time to time, the sanction of the courts of justice, without any legislative act or interference. It was the application of the dictates of natural justice, and of cultivated reason, to particular cases."[62] The will of the people, as inscribed in the constitution and the statute book; "cultivated reason," applied by a disinterested judiciary—these were the twin pillars of Kent's legal formalism. They were built not only in the debate against Jeffersonians like Sampson and Jacksonians like Rantoul, but also in the conservative judiciary's efforts to purge itself of superstition.

A generation later, in 1858, the Chief Justice of the U.S. Supreme Court would look back to the Revolutionary moment and describe, in miniature, the foundations of American jurisprudence. "The American Revolution was not the offspring of fanaticism, nor was it produced by the wild theories of political dreamers. It was not designed to subvert the established order of society and social relations, nor to sweep away traditional usages and established opinions. On the contrary, it was undertaken to maintain ancient and established rights which had been invaded by the British Government. The colonists claimed the rights of Englishmen. . . . They did nothing more."[63] These lines from Roger B. Taney's "Supplement" to the notorious opinion of the court in *Dred Scott v. Sanford* (1857) stitched together a transatlantic network of moral communities, bound by the customs of English law. As the court denied Scott's claim to freedom, as it refused even to acknowledge his right to file such a claim, it aligned the common law with a measured and conservative reason, against the "fanaticism" of some "political dreamers" in the past—and, in the present, against a moral crusade that invoked a higher law. The business of the court was not, in Taney's view, to abrogate longstanding traditions. It was to carry on the work of the ancient oracles.

Oracles at the Gallows

Taney's invocation of the revolution's conservative spirit shows how the ideal of a dispassionate and transcendent justice could be wielded in a deeply contested and highly publicized trial, where the very boundaries of the sovereign community were being redrawn. Even as the judiciary disciplined itself to address the public in a more reasonable style, however, it seemed to bear the old oracularism of lawcraft within itself. The specter of a divine justice was a latent presence that could be revived in the ceremonies that were performed in the courthouses, at the scaffold, and in the popular legal literature that transmitted these spectacles of justice to the broader, more dangerous public known as the common people. Chapter 2 will outline a historical poetics of the popular crime literature of the early republic. For now, one example may suggest how the theory of oracular address, as developed in early American law treatises, shaped the practice of ceremonial condemnation.

Here, the story circles back again to Hawthorne's territory. In May of 1786, Isaac Coombs, a migrant peddler of handmade tools, was arrested for murdering his wife, Sage, in Salem, Massachusetts. His trial was held in Ipswich, but the state-appointed defense attorney, William Pynchon, appealed the conviction on the grounds that members of the jury had discussed the case with the patrons of a local tavern before delivering their verdict. Months later, the appeal was heard by the state supreme court, and the conviction was upheld. Coombs was put to death on December 23.[64]

In the meantime, the press had taken an interest in the case, and various accounts of the defendant's life and crimes appeared in newspapers up and down the Atlantic coast. According to one, Coombs had been born in Southampton, Long Island, and his given name was John Peters.[65] According to the sensationalized "Sketch of the Life and Confession of Isaac Coombs," he was born in Martha's Vineyard and had wasted most of his years in idleness, drink, and crime.[66] Coombs was said to have taken part in a human sacrifice among the Mohawks near Montreal. He was reported to have experienced a mystical vision in his jail cell, where the spirit of his murdered wife, accompanied by devils and imps, came to torment him.[67] Each of these accounts, in its way, emphasized the condemned man's status as an outsider to the social order of New England—his race, his poverty and vagabondage, his intemperance and indifference to Christian teaching.

An execution sermon was preached by the Reverend Joshua Spalding, then published in pamphlet form. The minister pledged himself to "great plainness of speech." He asked the public to view the ceremony with solemnity, renewing their own humility before a divine judge. He exhorted the wretched sinner to repent. Unlike some of the other writers on Coombs's case, Spalding did not describe the felon on the gallows as an exotic or inhuman creature. He addressed him as a child of God who was about to stand for eternal judgment: "You have a soul of infinite value."[68] But Spalding also recognized that Coombs "[had] not appeared to be a true penitent"; as the historian Alan Rogers notes, Spalding's complaints about the condemned man's public behavior "suggest[ed] the clergy's loss of mastery over the execution ceremony."[69] It was now the magistrate, not the minister, who would deliver the definitive address to the felon and to the public.

The death sentence was a rigidly conventionalized utterance, imported to North America as part of English criminal procedure. The penalty for most crimes was established by statute, and, as Blackstone observed, "the court must pronounce that judgment, which the law hath annexed to the crime"; in delivering the sentence, judges denied their own discretionary power and identified themselves as the living oracles of a law whose authority arose, ultimately, from the consent of the governed.[70] Virtually the same phrases were uttered at the conclusion of all capital cases where the defendant had been convicted and exhausted the available appeals. The court ordered the condemned felon to return to prison, and there to await the appointed date of execution. It specified the method, usually hanging by the neck until death. Ordinarily, it concluded with a brief, formulaic prayer. Thus the court in Coombs's case advised him that it was "obliged to pronounce the solemn judgment of the law": "You shall go from hence to prison, from whence you came, and from thence to the place of execution, and there be hanged by the neck, till you are dead! And the Lord have mercy on your soul!"

In certain notorious cases, the utterance of the death sentence was transformed from a legal procedure into a religious and political ceremony; it became a genre of lawcraft, embellished with long, exhortatory addresses to the condemned and to the public. The text in Coombs's case was probably written and read aloud by the state supreme court's chief justice, William Cushing. The published version appeared under the title "Sentence of Death," without any signature. According to the conventions of the genre, the sentence communicated the decision of the court, and of the law itself, rather than the opinion of any human author. In practice, too, the judges who appeared to condemn convicts in published sentences and trial reports were produced through the work of many hands. The "Sentence of Death" was not an official court document. It was designed not only for legal professionals but also, perhaps especially, for the general public. First printed in the *Salem Mercury*, the court's address to Coombs may have followed Cushing's own draft, or it may have been transcribed by some other attorney or layperson, then edited at the offices of the newspaper. Within a few weeks, it had been reprinted in papers throughout Massachusetts, Connecticut, New York, and Pennsylvania.[71]

The "Sentence of Death" reminded the defendant that he had received a fair trial, in accordance with the customs of a free country, and had been found guilty by an "impartial jury." It recounted the "horrid" details of the murder, performed with a "sharp stone." And it insisted on the deep connection between the statutes of the commonwealth and the immutable dictates of divine law:

> The great law of your Creator, and the laws of society, which will not suffer a murderer to live, require, that whoso sheddeth man's blood, by man shall his blood be shed; that your life go as an atonement for the innocent blood of your wife, and that you be suddenly cut off from the society of men, as unfit and too dangerous to be trusted in it: even the bloody stones rise up in judgment against you; the earth lifteth up its voice, and her blood from the ground crieth aloud for justice and satisfaction against her cruel, murderous husband; and you must soon appear, for another and infinitely more solemn trial, before the tremendous bar of Almighty God, the Supreme and final Judge of all mankind, to answer for your horrid unnatural crime.[72]

Full of righteous fire, the speaker of the death sentence condemned the murderer as an offender against the laws of God and man, an "unnatural" creature whose victim cries out, from beyond the grave, for his atoning blood. The court advised Coombs to spend his final days in penitence.

He could expect no mercy from the magistrates, but he might find it at the bar of the creator.

The court's elaborate address to the condemned, performed for a wide reading public, invokes the universal code of justice that was so reverently imagined by Blackstone and Root: "Ignorance you cannot plead; for that sacred law which Almighty God, in mercy and wisdom, hath written in strong characters in the hearts of the most ignorant of mortals, must have clearly dictated to you, the wickedness and enormity of such a conduct." The clear function of this performance was to sanction the exercise of state violence with reference to higher law and the faith of the sovereign people. If the crime literature that emerged from Coombs's trial demonstrated the faltering authority of the clergy and the rise of a secular basis for law's authority, then, it also testified to the ongoing collaboration between priestcraft and lawcraft. In a sensational and controversial case like this one, where the act of legal judgment was known to be a political event, the judge sought a legitimating sanction for his authority by appearing before the common people as the oracle of a transcendent law.

CHAPTER 2

Oracles of God

"**I**f most of the law and lawyers were concerned with the civil dealings which propertied men had with one another," Douglas Hay writes in a classic essay on eighteenth-century English legal history, "most men, the unpropertied labouring poor, met the law as criminal sanction: the threat or the reality of whipping, transportation and hanging."[1] The ongoing debate over the moral and political foundations of law was carried out in a treatise literature designed for polite circles of educated readers. Blackstone's lectures were delivered at Oxford, and the four bound volumes of the *Commentaries* found their way into the libraries of gentlemen around the Atlantic. The subscribers to Jesse Root's *Origins* were almost all New England attorneys. Scholars like St. George Tucker and James Wilson were doing their best to establish law as a discipline of higher education. While the theoretical grounds of legal authority were being contested in learned treatises, though, the sites for the exercise of that authority were the courthouses and the public square. The crucial meeting place between the law's agents and the common people was the scaffold. The date of their encounter was execution day.

This chapter turns from the treatises of legal professionals to a range of other, more popular and more sensational genres that depicted the ceremonies of justice. We are accustomed to think of the gallows as a theater where sovereignty showed itself in its awful grandeur, overmastering the offender's body and terrorizing the public into submission—a "formidable spectacle," as Hay calls it; an "elaborate ritual of the irrational."[2] But if punishment was an occasion for the dramatic display of state power, it was also the topic of a vast and various popular literature. From the colonial period forward, religious crime genres, including execution sermons and criminal confessions, made hanging day in North America, especially in New England, a ceremony that affirmed the moral authority of the ministry and the congregation's common faith. By the time of the Revolution, the secular press was generating trial reports, convict narratives, execution ballads, and other ephemeral works that addressed the changing relationship between punishment and the moral life of the community.

At one level, these documents showed church and state officials speaking before the common people, investing the ceremony of justice with meaning and power. At another level, the ministers and judges were also writing for each other, reflecting on the peculiar kinds of public address that might secure the assent of multitude. To turn from common law treatises to popular crime genres like the execution sermon and the gallows confession, therefore, is also to turn away from the self-abnegating subject of oracular address, toward the public which that address was thought to summon and to regulate. What will become clear, through a close study of a few especially reflexive texts, is that the public known as the common people was itself something of a construct, an imaginary audience to which the rituals of law addressed themselves. In the end, a poetics of justice might come around to a reversal of Hay's elegant formulation. It was not only the case that "most men" confronted the law as the threat of violence. It was also that, in the genres of lawcraft associated with the ceremonies of punishment, authorities came to know the common people as the public whose submission was crucial to their legitimacy.

The popular crime genres of the late eighteenth and early nineteenth centuries have mainly been studied as artifacts of cultural history. David Brion Davis undertook his path-breaking book on murder and culture with the premise that such texts "would reveal certain beliefs and values which, in turn, would elucidate more general problems in American civilization."[3] This premise enabled cultural historians to recover and interpret documents which would have been forgotten by literary critics. In time, it also opened the way to a critique of the ideologies and power dynamics that structured evolving discourses on crime and punishment, from the spectacle of the scaffold to the silent, regimented discipline of the penitentiary.[4] With its emphasis on the social values expressed in crime literature, though, cultural history did little to investigate how the society in question understood the persuasion exercised on reading publics by the oracular voice of power—that is, about the juridical public sphere where legal rituals, including rituals of punishment, were imagined to secure the assent of the people.[5]

Rather than attempting to reconstruct the ideologies that find expression in popular crime genres, then, this chapter asks how such genres seemed to constitute their publics as normative communities. Early American crime literature did less to voice the universal beliefs of the people, perhaps, than to mediate fantasies of belonging—to elicit the submission of a heterogeneous multitude by enabling it to imagine itself, retrospectively, as a lawgiving community. Where scholars of crime and culture have tended to view the common people as a social entity, a poetics of justice will concern itself with a fictive, sometimes spectral body, conceived and governed in acts of performative invocation. Where historians have narrated the secularization of crime genres and the rationalization of power, a poetics of justice will be just as concerned with the afterlives of enchantment.

This methodological difference—from cultural history to the poetics of justice, from theories of legitimacy to verbal acts of self-authorization—will provide, in turn, an alternative perspective on early American rhetorics of dissent. According to the prevailing account, the subversive capacities of crime genres emerged as effects of their secularization. When the ministry lost its monopoly over the press, the submissive confession gave way to self-expression and vindication, and the sacrificial condemnation of the offender was opened up to the prospect of a sentimental identification. But did an expanded print marketplace really unsettle orthodox authority in these ways? After all, it was often the ministers of justice themselves who insisted on the autobiographical integrity of the accused and who cordoned off a space of compassion for the condemned. They did so, in part, to insist that Christian mercy was a private sentiment, outside the forum of public justice. In fact, what seemed most to threaten the ceremony of punishment was not the human self-expression of the accused. It was the offender's self-authorizing invocation of a divine command, a factionalizing and incendiary higher law. Thus the rise of sensational and sentimental genres, often described as menaces to institutional authority, could serve instead to quarantine the energies of protest. And thus a diversifying crime literature would begin to negotiate with the law's public sphere from a position of estrangement.

The Spectacle and the Sermon

By the turn of the eighteenth century, a richly inclusive, polyvocal public culture of justice had taken shape around sites of punishment in England. The historian V. A. C. Gatrell writes that "people's cries and movements at the scaffold's foot, their feelings about death, the ballads they listened to, and the images they consumed, spoke for something more complex than assent, and often for its opposite."[6] London hanging days featured speeches by judges, sermons by clergymen, the cries of hawkers, and, from time to time, the rumble of a riot. Sometimes felons, in their final moments, offered humble words of penitence. Sometimes they went down ranting at the magistrate and the hangman.

The marketplace of print, no less than the scene of the spectacle, was diverse enough to include perspectives ranging from the piously somber to the subversive and the profane. The English press generated execution ballads, trial reports, and sensational narratives. The "canting dictionaries" of the underworld documented a whole vernacular language of criminal life, where the awful rite of the execution was recomposed as a dark comedy. "To be hanged," Peter Linebaugh recalls, "was to be jammed, frummagemmed, collared, noozed, scragged, twisted, nubbed, backed, stretched, trined, cheated, crapped, tucked up or turned off." The scaffold at Tyburn was designed to be the site of a solemn ritual. It had become a grotesquely ornamented Maypole, the "deadly nevergreen," for a carnival of the multitude.[7]

Across the Atlantic, meanwhile, in the penal ceremonies of seventeenth-century New England, there seems to have been no such noise. Among the Puritans, the legal historian Edgar J. McManus argues, "the whole point of lawmaking was to promote public morality by translating God's moral precepts into criminal statutes and regulations"; the criminal justice system "dealt in fear, pain, and death, but it also stood for the moral ideals and social values" of a community.[8] Nathaniel Hawthorne, in *The Scarlet Letter,* would recollect the crowd that gathered around Boston's seventeenth-century pillory as "a people amongst whom religion and law were almost identical," a society for whom "the spectacle of guilt and shame" was to be regarded with "awe" and a "solemnity of demeanor."[9] No ballad lamented the disgrace of Hester Prynne. No broadside recorded the dying curse of Matthew Maule. No riot shook the hanging tree.

To some degree, Hawthorne's image of a unified, reverent public assembly must be an illusion produced by the peculiarly limited archive of popular crime literature that was produced in New England before the eighteenth century. The people of the region, according to Daniel Cohen, "could not purchase an account of the crime itself, or a report of the trial, or a ballad on the execution, or a play reenancting the tragedy, for such popular English genres were not available in the sharply constricted marketplace of late seventeenth-century Boston."[10] There may well have been some gallows humor in early New England, but it never made its way into print. The ceremonies of conviction and correction were recorded and transmitted only in the ordained ministry's execution sermons.

The evolution of this genre, over the course of the eighteenth century, provides an illuminating case study in the transformation of ceremonial justice under the pressures of popular sovereignty. A double movement will come into view. First, the bond between church and state is weakened, and punishment is justified in terms of the social contract and the security of property, rather than the moral codes of scripture. Second, and more surprisingly, the divine law takes on a new power, becoming a matter of controversy as the ministers and their antagonists contend for legitimacy in the presence of the common people. From this perspective, the special interest of eighteenth-century New England is not that the region was the original source for a later, national culture. Instead, the history of crime literature in the region plays out, with unusual clarity, patterns that developed in an uneven way—sometimes sooner, sometimes later—in various jurisdictions around the Anglophone Atlantic. It should perhaps go without saying that the execution sermon emerged from, and positioned itself within, a transnational culture of letters, both before and after the American Revolution, and that its publics included people from many continents and social groups. The heterogeneous and unruly character of the execution-day crowd was precisely the menace that had to be addressed.

Discourses on capital punishment were printed in Cambridge and Boston as early as the 1670s, and the tireless Cotton Mather oversaw the production of "more than a dozen volumes of execution sermons over a period of forty years."[11] These documents were designed for timely publication, cheap sales, and wide distribution. Conventionally, they were prepared for the printer by ministers, using the drafts and notes from which they spoke, but it is difficult to know how closely any given pamphlet may have followed the version that was actually preached. The scene into which these texts invited their readers was, at best, an idealized reconstruction of the embodied ceremony.

Like most other sermons, execution discourses used the plain style, and they followed a highly conventionalized pattern, advancing from scriptural text through doctrinal propositions to a set of applications, or instructions to the congregation. Unlike other sermons, they concluded with a direct address to a condemned felon, and they were self-consciously performed for audiences at the margins of piety and power. Their function, according to Scott D. Seay, was ritually to repair "the breach in the integrity of the community."[12] In New England's unusually circumscribed public culture of justice, crime was a transgression against the commandments of God, and the enforcement of the civil law was conducted as a religious ceremony. The heterogeneous public that gathered around the scaffold was exhorted to reconstitute itself as a community of believers.[13]

In the Preface to his 1771 sermon on the hanging of Moses Paul, Samson Occom introduced himself as an "unlikely instrument" chosen to do the work of God. Born near New London, Connecticut, Occom was a Mohegan Indian who had converted to Christianity under the guidance of the radical evangelical James Davenport. Occom had been educated in colonial schools and ordained into the Congregationalist ministry, and he had traveled to England to raise funds for North American missionary projects. The pamphlet version of Occom's sermon, which circulated in several American and British editions, has been identified as one of the earliest printed texts in English by an American Indian author.

Occom's "unlikely" assignment to perform this service may be explained, in part, by the unusual kind of audience that was to be addressed on execution day.[14] "The books that are in the world, are written in a very high and refined language," he noted, "so that the common people understand little of them. But I think they cannot help understanding my talk; it is common, plain, every day talk." Even "little children," "poor Negroes," and "Indians" would not fail to grasp Occom's meaning. Here were the common people, the semi-literate, potentially dangerous figures, imperfectly integrated into the community, to whom the execution sermon ritually addressed itself.

Occom took his text from Romans 6:23—"For the wages of sin is death, but the gift of God is eternal life through Jesus Christ our Lord"— a favorite passage for ministers on execution day. His sermon reinforced the bond between the authority of scripture and the legitimacy of the colony's criminal statutes; it linked the spiritual abjection of the sinner to the civil death of the felon. "Sinners are dead in state, being destitute of the principles and powers of spiritual life . . . and they are dead in law, as a condemned malefactor is said to be a dead man." Occom invited his listeners and readers to participate in the judgment of sin: "And now judge ye, what agreement can there be between them! God is a holy and pure God, and a sinner is an unholy and filthy creature."[15] The authorities who had sentenced the murderer to hang were to be recognized as "oracles of God," the voices of a transcendent justice and of the congregation's common faith.[16]

As Occom's sermon acknowledged, though, the spiritual unity of the crowd could no longer be taken for granted. New England had been transformed by the development of a mercantile economy, the growth of urban centers, the mingling of populations, and the accelerating circulation of people and goods. The region's various colonial legal systems had been brought more and more into line with the English imperial model, where the preservation of property, rather than the policing of morality, was the primary task of the criminal courts. (Although secularists liked to depict the Puritan system as benighted and cruel, given to witch-hunting and other persecutions, the colonial codes that followed scripture had been relatively less severe than the criminal statutes of Parliament, which imposed the death penalty for a far greater number of offenses, especially crimes of poverty.[17]) The evangelical movements of the 1730s and 1740s had cleaved congregations into factions, and the spiritual cohesion of the first Puritan villages, if it had not always been a nostalgic fantasy, was a distant memory.

"Be advised not to make this melancholy Sight a Matter of *vain Curiosity*," preached the Congregationalist minister Charles Chauncy before a hanging in 1754; "let it be your sincere Endeavor to get your Hearts impressed with a deep Sense of Sin."[18] Chauncy was a stalwart of the Old Lights who held his position at Boston's First Church for sixty years, from 1727 forward, a career that spanned the crises of the First Great Awakening and the American Revolution. The audience that assembled around the scaffold, as he imagined it, was not only mixed and unrefined; it was an unruly, undisciplined body. His call to somber observance was an effort to reassert the clergy's control over the spectacle in an era when crowds had grown to ten thousand or more, and when the solemn ritual of punishment was turning "carnivalesque."[19] Chauncy had not only to call the people from sin to piety but also to deal with a new style of irreverence. Vain curiosity was neither sin nor piety; indifferent to these moral categories, it was an appetite for grotesque entertainment.

Thus Chauncy's sermon marked the intrusion, into the scene of ceremonial justice, of an attitude that was most often associated with the reading of profane texts, especially sensational fiction. Even as he spoke, the "ministers were losing their cultural monopoly" over the juridical public sphere.[20] New Englanders were gaining access to a wider variety of crime genres, including execution ballads, trial reports, and convict narratives imported from Europe. The execution sermon had become just one among the several genres of lawcraft, and the common people seemed to have acquired an appetite for the sensational. The new task for this old genre, as Chauncy understood it, was to make a deeper impression on their hearts.

In his 1784 sermon on the execution of John Dixson for burglary, the Reverend Peres Fobes of Massachusetts directed his words to the condemned man, but he was performing for the people, calling for their sanction. "Behold the numerous guard about you, the executioners of justice await your doom, the instruments and appendages of death are in sight, a coffin and a grave for you are open, a prisoner in chains, and you cannot escape; this, ah all this, have you merited at the hands of your injured country, by the laws of which your mortal life is forfeited, and now demanded as the sacrifice; condemned also you are by the law of God, which extends to thoughts and intents of the heart. The wages of sin is death."[21] The hanging was a ritual of sacrifice. The statutes of the land were aligned with the law of God. The minister was the oracle of an inescapable commandment. New England clergymen had been saying more or less the same thing for a century. But Fobes preached the familiar lesson in changed circumstances. He addressed a postrevolutionary assembly that was asserting its own power to judge the legitimacy of punishment.

The pamphlet version of Fobes's sermon reported that, "for the sake of accommodating a very numerous assembly," made up of "all ranks, ages, sexes and complexions," the minister was obliged to speak from "a gallery window" to the people below. Many in the audience were openly hostile to Fobes's message: "A considerable number . . . manifested their doubts and dissatisfaction concerning the lawfulness of the intended execution; others *'raged and were confident'* that it would be a murderous bloody deed, and wished that [the prisoner] might escape." During the "clamour" over Dixson's trial and punishment, Fobes recalled, "the judges and jury, the sheriff and state's-attorney, the prosecutor and the preacher, received in turn, each one *his bitter portion in due season*." State and church alike were rebuked by a riotous public. Here, the crisis was not the common people's idle curiosity. It was their open hostility to power. To secure the scene, the sheriff was obliged to muster a guard of 130 men.[22]

Fobes refashioned the execution sermon for this postrevolutionary situation, and his discourse has been recognized as a transitional text in the history of the genre. In an appended essay, "On Burglary," he justified the death penalty not only in relation to scripture, where he found feeble support, but also in terms of the public good. His reasoning, according to Cohen, showed how the ministry was accommodating itself to the legal culture of the early republic, developing increasingly secular arguments for the exercise of state power.[23] It might even be suggested that the minister found himself in the unusual position of defending a criminal statute against a protest that had the authority of scripture on its side.

Reflecting on the withering power of the clergy, Fobes acknowledged that secular authorities now set the terms for the public conversation about crime and punishment. But Fobes was disgusted by the boldness and hostility of the common people, and he resented the indignity of having to shout from a window. He wished that he could "speak in thunder, and [his] voice be heard from pole to pole," like the voice of God.[24] If, as Cohen argues, Fobes was reduced to serving as a "quasi-official apologist for the legal authorities" who held the real power, his sermon was also animated by the reactionary memory of a lost era when the laws of the land had been fortified by the unshakeable authority of divine justice.[25]

To some extent, perhaps, all execution sermons measured the corruption of the present against the dream of a more devout past. In the tradition of the jeremiad, they lamented the depravity into which the community was falling, and they aimed "to restore a backsliding New England people to their earlier relationship with God."[26] In Fobes's sermon, though, this typological narrative was laid over the specific history of the American Revolution, a reordering of authority which led the minister to reconsider the dynamics of address and reception. Fobes acknowledged that the people themselves had assumed the sovereign responsibility for the creation of the criminal codes. He hoped "that not one among all, will ever again open his mouth, to curse or revile the rulers of his own choice, while in the honest, but painful execution of a law, a righteous law of his own enacting."[27] The crucial task of religious authority, as Fobes saw it, was to reconcile the disaffected common people to laws that were supposed to express their own will.

How, Fobes asked his readers, was the "impetus of zeal" to be silenced? "Could reason do it," he suggested, "the talk were easy and soon finished." In this case, however, reason had failed to subdue the multitude. To restore the disintegrating bond between the law and the people would require another kind of public address. It called for an oracle. "If all the statutes, customs and codes of uninspired law, could obtain faith," Fobes imagined, then "all clamour [would] cease."[28] In cultivating the people's spiritual commitment, transforming the clamor of factions into the uniform submission of a moral community, the exhortations of priestcraft would become a crucial supplement to the propositions of reason. Rage and riot would give way to a ceremony of submission; the curses in the mouths of the people would be converted into a blessing. Here, the subtle modernity of Fobes's reactionary fantasies reveals itself. His dream of a broadcast transmission "from pole to pole" was an image of a single, well-regulated public sphere on a national scale.

Three years later, the task laid out by Fobes was taken up in an execution sermon preached in Berkshire County, Massachusetts, by the Reverend Stephen West.[29] The felons on the scaffold were two obscure men, John Bly and Charles Rose, who had been convicted of burglary, but everyone involved with the case knew that it was not only about a couple of ordinary, petty crimes. It concerned the legitimacy of legal institutions in the wake of the most famous outbreak of organized resistance to state power in postrevolutionary New England. In 1786, under the leadership of Daniel Shays, hundreds of indebted farmers and others sympathetic to their cause had taken up arms, defying civil authority and obstructing the proceedings of the courts. In the context of an ongoing dispute about the distribution of power in the new republic, Lawrence Friedman writes, "it was easy [for the rebels] to attribute class bias to the courts, and attribute this class bias in turn to the antiquated, oppressive, inappropriate common law."[30] The insurrectionists turned the ideal of popular sovereignty against a judiciary which seemed to be the servant of wealthy elites. Shays's Rebellion brought the force of the people to bear against the entrenched interests of the lawyers and their patrons—and, especially, against that unwritten manual of mystification, the common law.

As the uprising was put down, many of the rebels were brought to trial on charges of treason, insurrection, and riot. Eighteen were condemned to die. In almost all of these cases, however, the defendants were pardoned or their sentences were commuted to a lesser penalty. (Some were marched through the streets to the gallows and forced to stand with the noose around their throats until the last-second reprieve was pronounced.) The state's legal and political leaders seem to have recognized the precariousness of their position, the need to negotiate with a restless population. Leonard L. Richards argues that the "authorities were clearly afraid of repercussions," especially when the offender had the support of an influential faction. Bly and Rose, though, were "laborers with few connections."[31] Their offenses, which involved the theft of weapons and ammunition, were obviously extensions of their participation in the uprising. The state, however, charged them with burglary, rather than insurrection. It distinguished the defendants' crimes against property from the Shaysites' acts of political violence. Bly and Rose were familiar with the other cases, and they expected some clemency. It never came, and they were hanged, side by side, on December 6, 1787.

"The gallows literature that emerged from the spectacle," Louis P. Masur observes, "demonstrates that by executing Bly and Rose civil authorities intended to send a message to western Massachusetts, and to those people who might consider rising against the state again."[32] If the government had displayed its mercy in reprieving other offenders, these two would serve as examples of its power to enforce the peace, when necessary, by recourse to the ultimate penalty. A dying speech printed in New England papers and attributed to Bly made the point clear. In a direct address to the fugitive Shays, Bly announced, "Our fate is a loud and solemn lesson to you who have excited the people to rise against the government."[33] Here, as elsewhere, the political force of the penal ritual depended less on the drama of spectacle than on the mediation of print. Shays was not present for the hanging of Bly and Rose, but the circulation of the text invited readers to imagine a scene of somber, almost intimate address.

The work to be done by West, then, was to justify the death penalty in cases of burglary and, along the way, to restore the people's faith in the legitimacy of legal institutions—or, as he put it, to "turn our attention to the nature and importance of civil government, and lead us to prize and revere it as a divine institution." What makes West's sermon such an unusual document in the history of the genre, however, is the strong distinction, the "wide and material difference," that it marks between the divine law and the codes enforced by civil magistrates. West's justification of the hanging left behind the revelations of scripture for the reasoning of social contract theory: "as you have set yourselves against the community," he said to Bly and Rose, "so the community now set themselves against you." Indeed, the minister went so far as to recommend that juries and judges, when they determined verdicts and sentences, should exclude all religious questions from consideration. "Nothing can be more absurd than to suppose that *men* should be judges and avengers in the cause of *God*." The soul of every sinner and of every saint would surely have to be judged by the divine creator. In the meantime, the courts ought to enforce the earthly law for the good of the living community.[34]

Like Fobes, West had to concede that there was little support in scripture for the hanging of a petty thief. The penalty to be imposed against Bly and Rose thus seemed, to some dissenters, to show a contradiction between the laws of God and the criminal codes of the state. In taking two men's lives without a Biblical sanction, the magistrates were exposed to the charge that they were committing murder in the eyes of God. But "God," West told his audience, "has appointed civil rulers to bear his sword, to avenge the wrongs of society, and to execute wrath upon evil doers."[35] In other words, the divine sanction for civil authority had been secured as soon as the rulers took their offices. It was not to be raised and disputed again with each case that came before the courts. Crimes against property and social order, no less than sins against the divinity, were punishable by death, and the enforcers of the civil law were not to be accused of overstepping the bounds of their legitimate power.

Observing the traditions of the genre, West addressed the condemned men, exhorting the "poor, unhappy, wretched creatures" to reconcile themselves to the court's verdict and to prepare for the divine one. "But oh! with what voice of thunder, and in what solemn and piercing accents, will you soon be addressed from the throne of everlasting judgment."[36] Finally, West turned to the common people. The state had been careful to identify Bly and Rose's case as a matter of criminal procedure rather than of war, of law rather than of politics, but West took the opposite view. He reminded his audience that all crime tended toward rebellion, and all rebellion was abhorred by God. Capital punishment displayed the wrath of the state. It restrained through terror those few hardened souls who were beyond the reach of reason and moral suasion.

For most of the people, though, there was a gentler lesson to be learned. "We are now called upon humbly to adore and bless God, that there is a way, of his own appointment, in which the world may rid itself of those who, by their crimes and violence, have made themselves intolerable to society." It had not been left to the common people to decide whether the commands of the sovereign had the sanction of scripture. Instead, the distinction between divine and human authority worked, paradoxically, to establish civil authority as a sacred institution in its own right. "Laws framed for the good of civil society, are indeed binding upon the consciences of men." The apparent rupture between the obligations of conscience and the dictates of law was magically reconciled. The enforcement of the burglary statute called for the blessing of the people, spoken in unison, as the discord of faction was overmastered in the harmonious reconstitution of civil order.[37]

Between the Confession and the Curse

"A true penitent," Peres Fobes said before the hanging of John Dixson, "is always willing and ready to confess his sins."[38] Fobes and other gallows preachers did what they could to impose a coherence of faith and a uniformity of submission on an increasingly diverse, unruly society. The publication of Occom's discourse, in particular, shows how the genre could enlist even a converted "heathen," whose "plain" speech seemed well suited to the common people. In the same period, and with similar justifications, condemned offenders were drawn into the practice of lawcraft, as the New England press began to print accounts of their lives for general circulation.

The confession was a precious piece of evidence in the colonial legal system. Most of the New England colonies, following the guidance of scripture and the customs of English jurisprudence, required the testimony of two witnesses to convict a felon. When the accused gave confessions, however, "the two-witness rule was dispensed with," and they could be put to death based on their own words.[39] Beyond the courthouses, too, printed confessions were useful to civil authorities. Their political function, according to Cohen, was to verify "the justice of courtroom verdicts" and to deter crime by imposing a sense of terror in their readers.[40] Offenders provided brief sketches of their youth, describing how they had strayed from the path of virtue. They recounted their crimes, their feelings of guilt, and their awakenings to belief. They acknowledged that they deserved to die, and they prayed for God's mercy. Thus the "Faithful Narrative of the Wicked Life and Remarkable Conversion of Patience Boston" (1738) addressed its public: "I am . . . free and full in confessing my heinous Transgressions. . . , that I may justify God, and be a Warning to Sinners."[41] Confessions such as Boston's called readers to recognize the authority of the ministry and the shared norms of Christian communities, producing subjects whose words reinforced the legitimacy of the institutions that condemned them.

"It is customary," the felon John Lewis was reported to declare as the noose was placed around his throat in 1762, "for Wretches under my unhappy Circumstances to say something at the Place of Execution, to satisfy the world."[42] As Lewis recognized, the gallows confession was a highly conventionalized genre. It had been imported from Europe along with the scaffold, the cart, and the other props of penal dramaturgy. It had been adapted, during the popular religious revivals of the mid-eighteenth century, to the demands of the evangelical conversion narrative.[43] Authorship was attributed to the condemned, but the text was normally composed by religious and civil professionals, based on interviews and other inquiries. Editors and printers made their changes, too. The voice of the condemned was an effect produced through coercion, collaboration, and ventriloquism. For a poetics of justice, though, the focus will be less on the delicate problem of the offenders' intentions or the authenticity of their self-expression than on the public, ceremonial functions that their stories were thought to enact—and to go on enacting, in many cases, long after they had been put to death.

In the early eighteenth century, the public was expected to recognize the condemned as a member of the community, to hear the gallows confession as a call to renewed piety. "The moral and spiritual parity of ordinary sinners and the convicted murderer was encouraged," Karen Halttunen argues, "through the clergy's careful delineation of how the audience was supposed to feel when confronting an exemplary sinner."[44] The ministers who preached on execution day were modeling, for the common people, the proper style of affective response to the felon's words. By the time of the Revolution, though, no such reception could be taken for granted. "Without doubt," the convicted thief Rachel Wall suggested in her *Life, Last Words, and Dying Confession* (1789), "the ever-curious Public, (but more especially those of a serious turn of mind) will be anxious to know every particular circumstance of the Life and Character of a person in my unhappy situation."[45] Following the old script, the text presented Wall's story as a didactic example and composed her prayer for mercy. But it also acknowledged that its audience might bring various, conflicting desires to the text. There was not a single "Public." There were multiple, overlapping ways of reading. Like the execution sermons preached around the same time by Chauncy and others, this "dying confession" attempted to revive the diminishing force of the penal ceremony, to return the common people from vain curiosity to moral seriousness.

The waning of the ministry's control over the popular literature of crime was thus measured, in part, by the rise of new modes of address and practices of reception. Fobes appended a "Sketch of John Dixson's Life" to his execution sermon. This account, according to the minister, had been "taken from [Dixson's] own mouth, while in prison." But Fobes let his readers know that the brief narrative would not adhere to the conventional model. Despite the best efforts of the ministers who had visited him in his cell, the condemned man "was utterly averse to such confessions as have usually been made in such circumstances." The preacher could not hope to reproduce the usual story of conversion and submission. He could only call on the public to abhor a wretched convict whose "mouth was full of cursing."[46]

What happened to the public culture of justice between the time of Patience Boston's faithful confession and the blasphemies of John Dixson? Cultural historians have charted the gradual secularization of the confession. Just as the ministry yielded power to the legal profession, the conventionalized narratives of the colonial era, with their emphasis on conversion and penitence, were displaced by more and more sensational accounts, preoccupied with the details of motive and method. Moral certainty turned to mystery and horror. Along the way, convicts emerged as distinctly individuated subjects, and in a few extraordinary cases they were able to grasp control of their stories, seeking to exonerate themselves before the public. Thus, in the *Memoirs of the Notorious Stephen Burroughs* (1798), the author admitted that he had been guilty of some transgressions, but he also depicted the officials who persecuted him as corrupt, spiteful men, serving their own questionable interests. Burroughs's remarkable narrative, according to Daniel Williams, "explored the boundaries of selfhood and extended the range of individual sovereignty."[47] The rise of the secular press enabled new, peculiarly individuated performances of subversion and self-vindication.

Dixson was a scoffer who interrupted the solemn rituals of correction with rude obscenities. Burroughs depicted a ministry tainted by corruption and fraud. Even more unsettling, perhaps, were the offenders who used the occasion of the confession to challenge Calvinist orthodoxy, asserting their own privileged relation to the will of God. In the *Narrative of Whiting Sweeting* (1793), for example, a convicted murderer, maintaining his innocence, described the redemption that he had experienced in prison. In a strange, sometimes beautiful patchwork of autobiographical sketches, open letters to his family, and devotional poems, Sweeting urged his readers to reject the teachings of the Old Lights and to seek a personal communion with a forgiving God. "I expect there were some of the clergy," Sweeting acknowledged, "to whom my answers were by no means satisfactory as to the murder, and also some principles I believe, that they deny."[48] Shaped by the rising evangelical sects, especially the Baptists, Sweeting's narrative was widely reprinted throughout New York and New England, becoming a key document in the denominational conflicts of the era. By the late eighteenth century, then, a genre that had once served to reinforce the bond between religious and civil authority seemed capable of exploiting the division between them, appealing to the Christian hearts of the people against the secularizing institutions of law.

In crime literature's new capacity to inspire sympathy for the condemned, several commentators have seen a subversive potential. Cohen writes of a "sentimental insurgency" in the confessional genres of the 1780s, which drew from novelistic conventions to challenge the justice of guilty verdicts.[49] Halttunen shows how authorities in the nineteenth century began to diagnose the "moral complicity" of readers who "actively identified" even with murderers.[50] The relation between secularization and sympathy, however, was not a simple one. This new threat provoked new developments in the ritual function of execution sermons and death sentences, too. The ministers and judges worked to regulate sympathy by drawing a distinction between the private attachments of the heart and the public obligations of obedience. Already, the execution sermon had been adapted to justify violent punishments which had no basis in the holy texts by arguing that the laws of God were too sacred to be administered by human judges or juries. Now, the ministry would take the secularization of the gallows ceremony a step further, marking a boundary between the believer's Christian sentiments and the civic duties of the people in their capacity as a lawgiving community.

Among the most sensational stories of criminal adventure to appear in the postrevolutionary years was the *Sketches of the Life of Joseph Mountain, A Negro* (1790).[51] Presuming to relate Mountain's life and crimes in his own voice, the *Sketches* was prepared by the New Haven lawyer David Daggett, who surely had a hand in shaping its content and form. Still, this was no classic confession, praying for mercy. According to Steven Wilf, it marked a radical departure from longstanding generic conventions. In the *Sketches,* "pride replaced the moralism of traditional execution biographies," and Mountain himself provided "the dominant authorial voice."[52] Composed by an attorney who would one day serve on the Connecticut Supreme Court, attributed to an ex-slave who had lived a fabulous life of criminal adventure, provoking responses by prominent legal and religious leaders, the text is an ideal example of how a secular, sensationalized convict's narrative might function in the law's public sphere.

According to the *Sketches,* Mountain had been born in Philadelphia but soon found his way to sea and then to England, where, in time, he established himself as "a highway-man of the first eminence." He was initiated into a band of criminals who robbed merchants and aristocrats, sharing their plunder in common. He joined riots at the doors of Parliament and helped to burn London's Newgate Prison. His circum-Atlantic travels took him to France, Spain, West Africa, and the Caribbean; he "made two voyages to the coast of Guinea, and brought cargoes

of Negroes to Jamaica." He married a white Englishwoman of property, spent all her money, and sent her back to her father in disgrace.
Finally, having returned to the United States, he was convicted of raping
a thirteen-year-old girl. Mountain told Daggett the story of his life in his
jail cell in the days before he was hanged on the New Haven green.[53]

The *Sketches* mocked polite society and celebrated the brotherhood
of thieves. The criminal society revealed in its pages is a world turned
upside down, where the lowly and despised live like kings. Describing
his return to the company of his fellow outlaws after a spree of robberies,
Mountain begins to speak of himself in the third person, as a legendary figure: "I never shall forget with what joy I was received. The house
rang with the praises of Mountain. An elegant supper was provided, and
he placed at the head of the table. Notwithstanding the darkness of his
complexion, he was complimented as the first of his profession."[54] As
Williams suggests, Mountain recounts his crimes to a counterpublic that
knows its own "system of values" in opposition to the norms of church
and state—an audience which, in spite of his race and his crimes, blesses
his name.[55] At the end of the episode, he walks not to the scaffold but to
the seat of honor.

In the classic sermon-confession pamphlets, the oracles of God and
the penitent convict had shared a common ideal of justice. In the intertextual conversation about Mountain's crimes and punishment, this harmony was lost; the voices of Mountain and the authorities who judged
him were irreconcilably at odds. The popular press, collaborating with
lawyers and ministers, produced the elaborate self-expression of one
who had risen from abjection to acquire power and prestige as a hero
among thieves. But the attribution of authorship in Mountain's narrative
was, at best, a mixed blessing. As he faced the courts and the ministry,
his own words became the most damning evidence against him. His narrative was to be received as the performance of an incorrigible villain, a
challenge that could be answered only by putting him to death.

Mountain's death sentence was pronounced by Chief Justice Eliphat
Dyer of the Connecticut Superiour Court, and a version was soon
reprinted in the *Connecticut Courant,* unsigned, under the title "Address
to the Prisoner." It concluded in the conventional way, ordering that the
defendant be "hanged by the neck, between the heavens and the earth,

till you are dead, dead, dead, and the Lord have mercy on your soul."
Preparing to deliver these solemn lines, the court took several para-
graphs to describe the offender's "daring boldness and impudence." It
reflected on the peculiar dishonor that would be endured by the victim
of his assault. It exhorted him to spend his few remaining days in prayer
and penitence. "The crime of which you are convicted, is of a deep dye,
is very heinous in the sight of God and man, and in most if not all of the
civilized nations, punishable with death." The speech was addressed to
the prisoner, but like other works of lawcraft it sought to elicit the assent
of a broader public, linking "the just laws of this state" to transatlantic
norms and the all-governing commandments of divine law.[56]

Justice Dyer's themes were also those of the New Haven minister
James Dana, who preached the execution sermon to a "numerous assembly, of all orders and characters" on execution day, October 20.[57] Dana's
discourse, however, was not the traditional exhortation to an exemplary
sinner. It spoke to the political concerns of the present, defining the uses
of public punishment in the new republic. The minister reproduced a
long quotation from Blackstone's *Commentaries,* demonstrating the
extreme, irrational severity of the English penal code (6–7). It was one of
the blessings of life in the United States, he argued, that the death penalty
was imposed only in the most serious of cases. Still, Dana would not join
the radicals who had begun to call for the abolition of public hangings.
"Confusion and misery would prevail, were punishment, capital punishment, never executed" (11). Contrary to the utopian speculations of some
bookish philosophers, Dana argued, the unruly multitude was not to be
governed by reason alone. The ceremony of punishment, presided over
by the ministry, was a necessary supplement to reason in persuading the
people to obey the law.

Dana's sermon reflected on its own place in a polyvocal, intertextual
ceremony. It called attention, especially, to the story of Mountain's life,
"taken from [his] own mouth, and this day published" (22). The narrative, in the minister's appraisal, was outrageous and offensive. Some
readers would doubt that it could possibly be true. Dana, however,
decided that Mountain should be recognized as the author, and that the
Sketches should be interpreted as his authentic history. "You can reap
no advantage from deceiving the world in which you are no longer to

live" (23). The text, Dana reminded his audience, was no conversion narrative. The offender gloried in the memory of his crimes, and he showed no signs of penitence. Mountain could not be seen as an exemplary sinner. He was an "abandoned character" whose "bold and subtil" self-expression proved that he was "unworthy to live" among the good people of the community (11, 13, 10). "Nothing short of death can expiate his crimes against his fellow-subjects" (15).

In some ways, Mountain's trial and punishment conformed to a pattern that would become terribly familiar in the nineteenth century, when scientific racism and a vengeful justice would be welded together into an iron fist. The published death sentence talked of Mountain's "worse than brutal lusts, and more than savage barbarity," and the court lingered over the dishonor of his young, white victim. The execution sermon associated the offender's pride with an excessively passionate and lascivious nature, unchastened by reason and unrefined by education or religion. The exotic sensationalism of the *Sketches* was intensified by the identification of the author as "A Negro." In a petition for clemency addressed to the Connecticut General Assembly, Mountain offered to undergo castration and to be sold into slavery, with the profits given as restitution to his victim—awful, mortifying prospects, especially for one who had escaped from bondage as a teenager.[58] Just as reformers were beginning to call for a more enlightened and humane legal code, the specter of a monstrous African American predator was raised before the public to justify the state's imposition of the ultimate penalty.

But Dana's sermon, at least, was not exactly an apology for a racialized reign of terror. It followed, instead, the logic observed in Jeannine DeLombard's study of gallows literature: "however race may have skewed the 'justice' that brought them to the scaffold, the black condemned were welcomed as candidates for heaven on roughly equal terms with their white partners in crime."[59] Dana himself was an antislavery man, sensitive to the abuses endured by African people in an Atlantic world dominated by European colonizers. In September of 1790, just a few weeks before he preached Mountain's execution sermon, he had addressed the Connecticut Society for the Promotion of Freedom, producing an extensive history of the slave trade, from the first Portuguese incursions into West Africa through the large-scale British importation of captives to

American colonies in the eighteenth century. Dana denounced slavery as an outrage against Christian principles of brotherly love and human rights. In lines laced with prophetic menace he justified even the desperate resistance of fugitives and insurrectionists: "Under unlimited power, accustomed to the most inhuman usage, no example of mercy relenting for them being exhibited, no marvel that the language of the insurgents is, *Death or conquest.* Their cries will sooner or later reach the ears of him to whom vengeance belongeth."[60]

Indeed, Dana's familiarity with the rhetoric of the transatlantic antislavery movement may have led him to single out Joseph Mountain as one who was likely to inspire a sentimental protest. At the least, he understood that in the New England of his time the public suffering of an African American body could elicit not only a vengeful satisfaction but also the tender pangs of mercy. Of course there was plenty of racism in this eighteenth-century minister's vision of the lower social orders. Dana imagined the poor and the oppressed as populations degraded by vice, governable only through fear. He assumed that the care of their lives was in the hands of the elites who held civil power, and that their benighted souls were the concern of ministers and missionaries. But the political issue at stake in Mountain's case, for Dana and his interlocutors, was the state's right to exercise violence, even to dispense death, in the service of a secure social order. Dana was trying to persuade the public that there was no contradiction between such a power and the imperatives of a Christian justice. In the end, his sermon used the figure of the black convict to distinguish legitimate punishment from the moral crime of slavery; it insisted that the rationalized violence of the criminal justice system was not to be confused with the brutality of the slave system. Thus Mountain's case became a chance to show how the problem of sympathy could be managed by way of an operative distinction between the private and the public, the sentiments of the heart and the obligations of the law.

"However distressed we may feel for him," Dana preached, "we may not . . . give countenance to others, who are warned by this example to *hear* and *fear*" the dictates of law (21). The sympathy which might be inspired by the image of Mountain on the gallows had to be repressed in favor of the disinterested attitude that Dana called, paradoxically, "public compassion" (14). Introducing the court's address to the prisoner, the editors of the *Courant* noted that the chief justice struggled to perform the role of the oracle. "Such were the sensations of a feeling heart, that the Judge could not pronounce the awful sentence without the most visible emotion." Some spectators, too, were moved by the scene: "nor were those who heard, wanting in testimonials of sympathy, towards the poor unfortunate wretch." The delivery of Mountain's sentence, the decision to hang the wretch between the heavens and the earth, became an occasion for the judge and the good people of the state to display their capacity for human sympathy. Such sympathy, though, was a private matter, to be set aside so that public justice could be done. "It now remains for me," the chief justice observed, "on behalf of this court, to pronounce the sentence of law upon you, the solemn sentence of death!" This was the voice of public compassion, addressing the defendant on behalf the people's justice.

"Hand of Heaven"

Eighteenth-century execution sermons expressed the changing ideology of state power. Gradually, New England's theocratic legal orders, grounded in scripture, were becoming secular ones in which the people were supposed to be sovereign. The sermons also showed the shifting style of the law's public address, as the voice of authority responded to the new freedoms taken by offenders and by the common people they addressed. In this transitional epoch, no single solution seemed to serve in every case. Sometimes ministers like Fobes and West tried to rekindle the sputtering flame of the old execution-day jeremiads, calling the people to a more fervent faith in the righteousness of the law. Sometimes the challenge was to erect a firewall between the incendiary potential of religious commitments and the reasonable obligations of the civil order. The public sphere, it seemed, had to be secured not only against irreverence but also against the claims of an overzealous sympathy and, every so often, the self-exonerating curses of enthusiasts. It was here, at the contested boundary between the public demands of law and the private dictates of conscience, that a slowly emerging literary field would attempt to define the conditions of its autonomy.

"My killing my family . . . is as much directed by the hand of heaven as the making of the whole world was."[61] Born in England, William Beadle sought his fortune in Barbados and eventually settled in Wethersfield, Connecticut. He was a prosperous retailer, familiar with the currents of European thought; he supported the Revolutionary cause, read Shakespeare and Montaigne, and took an interest in deism. With the collapse of the continental currency and the fluctuations of the postrevolutionary economy, though, Beadle was ruined, and his shame seemed to drive him into dark, metaphysical ruminations. "I think [man] a perfect machine, that he can do nothing, but as he is operated on by some superior power."[62] Beadle's wife, in her last days, told him that her dreams were haunted by fearful premonitions. He took these signs for tokens that his crime was ordained by a higher power. When he killed his family and then himself, in 1782, he seems to have imagined that he was acting as the agent of an all-governing, irresistible creator.

Beadle's case would be documented by James Dana, who preached on the occasion of the murders; by the local minister John Marsh, who conducted the funeral service for Beadle's wife; and by the Federalist attorney Stephen Mix Mitchell, the "gentleman in Wethersfield" who pieced together a narrative for the press. Because the offender had taken his own life, there was no murder trial, and no death sentence was pronounced against him. What holds the surviving texts together, nonetheless, is a discourse strongly marked by the conceptual world of the criminal law. In the wake of the violence, a jury of inquest was empanelled to establish the forensic details and to analyze the offender's mental state. The findings would determine whether or not he should be granted a Christian burial in the local cemetery. A published report on the case posed the problem this way: "It is difficult to tell where distraction begins. It is very evident [Beadle] was rational on every other subject." A ballad, printed as part of the same broadside, lamented "a deed so black, and yet his mind was sound."[63] Beadle's body, still dressed in his blood-stained clothes, was tied to a sled, dragged out of town, and dumped into an unmarked grave.[64]

For the ministry, as for the jury of inquest, a key point was to restore the burden of culpability which Beadle's writings seemed to have disavowed. Marsh's sermon depicted the murderer as a blasphemer who had presumed to strive against the authority of scripture. Drawing his terms from the vocabulary of the criminal law, Marsh emphasized that Beadle had acted "with deliberation and in cold blood."[65] Along the same lines, Dana's sermon took the human responsibility for evil as its theme: "The violaters of God's laws, inclined to exculpate themselves, impute their crimes to other causes than the real and obvious one—particularly, they may imagine that God is this cause." Such an imputation, Dana insisted, was to be rejected by all right-thinking Christians. "What violence to reason!" Beadle was a "monster of a man," and the motive for his transgressions was to be found in his "evil heart."[66]

As they conducted their investigations, the authorities discovered that Beadle had left behind several letters and "one laboured treatise in justification of his conduct."[67] In their effort to make sense of Beadle's crimes, they were provoked to consider the uses, and the potential abuses, of these confessional writings. Beadle's words were a major piece of evidence, demonstrating that he was of sound mind, legally accountable for the murders.[68] Moreover, the principles that motivated him had to be exposed so that they could be stigmatized and persecuted in others. The case was an opportunity to associate deism with fanaticism, the destruction of the family, and a violent contempt for law. It was not only the offense of murder but also a certain style of thought, an excess of spiritual pride, that was under investigation.

Yet the very texts that revealed Beadle's character and exposed him to judgment seemed to hold an unpredictable, incendiary power. "Much has been said in favour of publishing his writings by those who have not seen them," Mitchell noted. In the end, though, the documents were suppressed, "lest they might have some effect on weak and melancholy minds." The problem was not that the murderer's "reasonings against revelation were in any degree unanswerable"; the propositions that Beadle advanced as he explained his aberrant creed were easily dismantled by well-trained, sober men. The danger, instead, was that Beadle's text might have some unspeakable "effect" on those who responded more readily to the voice of exhortation than to that of reason. By quoting selectively from his writings and surrounding them with commentary, exposing the twisted reasoning of his mind but permitting him to address the public only through their mediating exposition, the ministers and lawyers who presided over the juridical public sphere sought to manage the incendiary potential of a fanatic's self-justifying words.[69]

The troubling relation between religious delusion and criminal guilt came before the public once again in 1796, when journals including the *Philadelphia Minerva* and the *New-York Weekly Magazine* reprinted "An Account of a Murder Committed by Mr. J——Y—— upon His Family."[70] This nightmarish piece of popular crime literature revisited a trial that had been conducted fifteen years earlier. The unnamed author identified herself as a friend of the murderer's family. "From the natural gentleness of his disposition," she remembered, "his neighbors universally esteemed him, and until the fatal night when he perpetrated the cruel act, none saw cause of blame in him" (361). She ended with a confused and ambivalent gesture towards the old conventions of the didactic crime genres: "But what avail our conjectures, perhaps it is best that some things are concealed from us" (365). Between her brief introduction and her uncertain conclusion was the centerpiece of the "Account," the murderer's own confession.

Like other criminal narratives from the era, this document showed how much the confession had changed since its seventeenth-century origins as an appendix to the Puritan execution sermon. Dwelling on the sensational details of his crimes, the murderer described how he bludgeoned his two sons while they slept; killed his infant boy by thrashing him against a fence; followed a trail of his wife's blood across a snowy field; and forced his young daughter to sing and dance before he "cleft her forehead in twain" with a hatchet (362–363). Even as he confessed to these horrible acts, however, he avowed that he felt no shame. He told the court that a spirit had appeared to him while he read his Bible, commanding that he destroy his idols. He knew that the earthly law would condemn him as a felon, but he held to his faith in the righteousness of his inspiration: "No, let me speak the truth, and declare the good motive for my actions, be the consequences what they may" (364). His hands were stained with blood, he admitted, but his conscience was clean.

Scholars have not identified the author of this "Account" with certainty, but the murderer who spoke in its pages was James Yates of Tomhanick, New York. Yates's crime and confession had been discussed, briefly, in posthumously published writings by the poet Ann Eliza Bleecker. Many of the details of the "Account" may also have been informed by Mitchell's well-known account of the William Beadle case, which had been reprinted in 1795, when the controversy over Thomas Paine's *Age of Reason* made the menace of deism a subject of lively debate. Both documents belonged to the growing body of sensational crime literature and to a wider conversation in the press about the dangerous tendencies of unorthodoxy. What has made them so important to the cultural history of the 1790s, though, is that they served as the source texts for the era's most widely studied work of literary fiction, Charles Brockden Brown's *Wieland, or The Transformation: An American Tale* (1798).[71]

Reworking an ephemeral piece of popular crime literature, adapting its material to the literary conventions that he had learned from European romancers, Brown developed a sensational gothic tale in a style that mingled philosophical and psychological speculations and invited careful forensic reading. In Brown's book—he called it a performance, a tale, or a fiction, rather than a novel—Theodore Wieland is prompted by the voice of an unseen speaker to massacre his family. His sister Clara, the only surviving Wieland, is left to narrate his story in letters to a small circle of friends. For Clara, as for the court, the key question is that of Theodore's moral and legal responsibility, the degree to which his terrible crimes might be attributed to a "sudden madness" (170). Clara blames the mysterious drifter Frank Carwin, a "biloquist" (or ventriloquist) who has used his verbal power to wreak havoc on the family. Theodore, she decides, became the victim of deception and perhaps of his own religious fanaticism, which led him into the maniacal delusion that his murders fulfilled "a divine command" (164).

Wieland is a difficult work, formally complex and full of contradictions, and critics have been divided in their interpretations of its politics. One camp reads the book as a Federalist's conservative "allegory" about the dangers of democracy and enthusiasm in the postrevolutionary nation.[72] The violent collapse of the Wieland family's rural utopia, according to Jane Tompkins, is Brown's "direct refutation of the Republican faith in men's capacity to govern themselves without the supports and constraints of an established social order."[73] For another camp, however, the book is most remarkable for its literary resistance to Federalist ideals.[74] From the nineteenth century forward, the legend of Brown's career held that his ambitions as a Romantic artist prompted him to rebel against conventional authority, especially against the citadel of Federalist values, the legal profession.[75] According to Robert A. Ferguson's influential account, Brown's Carwin is "the first clear image of the romantic artist in American literature" and *Wieland* indulges Brown's fantasy "of destroying a world that threatened his own artistic impulse."[76] Where one group sees the book as an apology for traditional authority, another understands it as an act of aesthetic protest against the institutions of law.

Some of these contradictions can be resolved, though, and the politics of Brown's fiction can be clarified, if *Wieland* is reconsidered in terms of the internal conflicts that shaped legal authorities' own endeavors to regulate the late eighteenth century's public sphere. Brown's performance does not simply oppose literature to law. It stakes its claim to a private sphere of conscience which, even according to the Federalists' most sophisticated clerical apologists, was properly beyond the reach of law. It does so by carefully disavowing any affiliation between such a claim and the self-exonerating public address of a doomed fanatic. Just as the judges and ministers of the era were reinventing law's proper mode of address by burying the vengeful oracles of the past, Brown developed a literature of critique by defining it against the emerging menace of the curse.

"*Wieland,*" as Laura H. Korobkin demonstrates, "is a novel obsessed with law, saturated with the vocabulary of evidence, testimony, proof, inference, corroboration, and judgment," and the crucial question posed by its plot is one of criminal culpability.[77] The law is more than a biographical or historical context for the interpretation of the tale. *Wieland*'s relation to criminal procedure is not, like its relation to national politics, an allegorical one. The tale is literally composed of a series of trials. It develops by staging scenes of confession and judgment, interrupting them at key moments to reconfigure the positions of relative authority. In this tale, legal institutions reach beyond the official halls of justice to compose the script of private exchanges and meditations. Even in their parlors, in their bedrooms, and in the wild spaces of their country estates, Brown's characters play the parts of defendants and judges. The genres of legal speech organize the very form of Brown's experimental performance.

The obvious example is Theodore Wieland's address to the court. In *Wieland,* as in Brown's source text, the account of the massacre is given in the form of a confession, in the murderer's own voice. The scene is the courtroom, where "thousands" have gathered to watch the trial. Speaking to his "judges and auditors," Wieland delivers enthusiastic vindications of his character and of his crimes. The defendant on the stand becomes radiant as he recalls "the blissful privilege of direct communication" with his God (159). "My deed was enjoined by heaven," he says; "obedience was the test of perfect virtue" (169). Fanatical in his adherence to the commands of an unseen spirit, which he sets above the laws of the land, Theodore makes himself the judge of the court. "Hide your audacious fronts from the scrutiny of heaven," he exhorts. "Ye may deplore your wickedness or folly, but ye cannot expiate it" (158). His confession becomes a curse.

For some time, critics have understood Theodore's performance as a fictionalized version of Yates's testimony or of Beadle's unpublished writings. But Brown did more than dramatize these well-known confessions. He revised them to emphasize the dynamics of public address and reception. Before Theodore describes his visions or narrates his crimes, he considers the audience before whom he has been called to confess. "It is strange," he says. "I am known to my judges and auditors. Who is there present a stranger to the character of Wieland?" The judge and jury are members of his community. They know his name, and they have had years to observe his habits and his conduct. "The task of vindication," before these familiar people, "is ignoble," and Theodore at first seems unwilling to undertake it (157). "I utter not a word to cure you of your sanguinary folly" (158).

After a moment, though, the defendant on the stand reconsiders the crowd, and he sees that "there are probably some in this assembly who have come from far." "For their sakes," he continues, "whose distance has disabled them from knowing me, I will tell what I have done, and why" (158). Theodore's performance is expressly designed for a public of strangers, and for this public alone. In this sense, his speech is shaped from the beginning by the conventions of print. It is broadcast toward listeners who have no personal ties to the speaker or to each other, and it seeks to refashion a fragmented, heterogeneous audience into a moral community through a ceremony of judgment. In those who "come from far"—and, beyond the courthouse, in the wider world where his confession will go on circulating—Theodore hopes to discover a tribunal other than the one that has already condemned him. His performance, he insists, is not for his friends or his family. It is an appeal to a court of public opinion, an imagined community that might understand his words as he does, as the inspired speech of a martyr.

With Theodore's confession, Brown made his contribution to the diagnosis of the disorder called enthusiasm.[78] The courtroom speech exposes the violent tendencies of a religious temperament, associated in the United States with the evangelical revivals of the eighteenth century, that rejects the mediating authority of established churches and of scripture. Theodore claims direct access to the will of God. But this claim, from his own perspective at least, serves as a rhetoric of exoneration, not as a symptom of enthusiasm. To be sure, Brown identifies Theodore's speech as the ranting of a lunatic, but he also uses it to emphasize the distinct form of oppression that his fictional performance will seek to undermine and to escape: the tyranny of law in the intimate, putatively private lives of families and communities. The opposition between the familiar community and the public of strangers, in *Wieland,* is also an opposition between the offender's obligation to confess and his opportunity to vindicate himself.

"If my testimony were without corroborations," Clara Wieland writes to her friends in the opening pages of her epistolary narrative, "you would reject it as incredible" (8). Theodore is not the only one, in this book, who is seeking vindication. Clara, too, is trying to clear her name. In the troubled weeks before the massacre, she recalls, "aspersions" were cast on her character, and she became associated with Carwin's vicious designs. The trouble began when her friend Henry Pleyel overheard a conversation between two voices in the night, apparently those of Carwin and Clara, which exposed her as "one of the most profligate of women" (106). Theodore is the first to confront her. "You speak before a judge," he says, "who will profit by any pretence to acquit" (105). Clara realizes that she has been cast in the role of a defendant at trial. She is startled that her brother's knowledge of her character, informed by decades of close companionship, is not enough to protect her from suspicion. "Do you deem a formal vindication necessary?" (104).

When she confronts Pleyel, she begins by setting the terms of her testimony: "I came hither not to confess, but to vindicate" (113). Again, she appeals to the faith in her character that her intimate friend should have built up over many years, and she chastises her accuser for abandoning this trust: "the tenor of my life, of all my conversations and letters, affords me no security; every sentiment that my tongue and my pen have uttered, bear testimony to the rectitude of my mind; but this testimony is rejected. I am condemned" (113). Pleyel, however, is unmoved by the performance; it seems only to provide "new proofs" of Clara's "wickedness" (114). He would like to sympathize with his old friend, he says. "I am not constituted thy judge. My office is to pity and amend, not to punish" (114). But the very utterance shows how difficult it has become for him to play any other role.

Theodore's address is a public vindication by a violent offender who claims to have broken the laws of the state in his obedience to the will of God. Clara's testimony is an act of private exoneration by the innocent victim of wrongful aspersions. Yet the two performances share a common understanding of their own compromised circumstances, a sense that personal, familiar attachments, which ought to protect the speaker against unjust accusations, have failed to do so. Long before the Wielands' miniature society is devastated by the combination of Carwin's verbal tricks and Theodore's inspired violence, it has already been transformed by the intrusion of the law; the boundary between the public ceremonies of judgment and the private dynamics of compassion has broken down. Carwin, the self-effacing, self-interested deceiver who speaks in the voices of others and of God, is the tale's figure for this tyrannizing incursion.

In the extended wake of the massacre and the trial, Clara produces her own written confession. This is the text of *Wieland* itself. "Listen to my narrative, and then say what has made me deserve to be placed on this dreadful eminence" (8). She traces her own disgrace and her brother's terrible crimes to the agency of Carwin, and she is willing to concede that their own "imperfect discipline" of thought may have exposed them to his power (7). Along the way, an unspoken intention of her letters is to distinguish her narrative from Theodore's fanatical cursing. First, she declines to invoke any higher law, to protest the injustice of her fate: "I address no supplication to the Deity" (7). Second, and more subtly, she addresses herself to a special kind of public, neither her closest companions nor the general public of print. The tale, as Brown indicates in his prefatory note, "is addressed, in an epistolary form, by the Lady, whose story it contains, to a small number of friends" (6). The reader, Clara says, is "a stranger to my misfortune," and the story "is not intended as a claim upon your sympathy" (7).

Instead, *Wieland* becomes a lesson in the subtle powers of deception and nonrational persuasion, the complexities of guilt, the unconscious motives and half-repressed desires that animate human lives, and other ambiguities that elude the grasp of any narrowly legalistic conception of responsibility—the "moral constitution of man," in Brown's phrase (5). But if Brown's performance opens a space for speculation about these mysteries, it does so by defining its literary project against the public cursing of an enthusiast. It aligns itself, rather, with the testimony of an innocent who wishes only to preserve her purity and her autonomy, in a circuit of address and reception at the margins of power. Thus *Wieland* locates literature's public address precisely in the semiprivate space that was already being vacated by legal authority. The tale's measured defense of private life and of the individual conscience was no attack on the institutions or the ideology of law. Instead, it preserved, even reinforced, the boundary between the duties of the citizen and the sentiments of the heart, between "public compassion" and private sympathies, which had been drawn by the ministers of justice themselves.

CHAPTER 3

Blasphemy "At the Court of Hell"

The anonymous author of an 1815 "Essay on Profanity" listened to his neighbors' voices with a mixture of fascination and repulsion. The devil seemed to be devising ever-craftier, ever-nastier ways to possess the human tongue. "Yes, with what malignity does the swearer pursue the name or the character of him whom he feels to be his enemy. He culls new modes of blasphemous speech, not content with the old and common ones, because they do not give sufficient sway to the devil within him. Every hour he strives to use a degree higher in the scale of blasphemy—that scale graduated at the court of hell."[1] Thus the polite idiom of civic virtue recognized its monstrous other, a factionalizing brand of performative speech that gave expression to a wicked, inhuman spirit. The old, common oaths had been abandoned, and new blasphemies were making their way into the world.

As the official bonds between church and state continued to unravel, as the popular press generated more and more scandalous material, as Andrew Jackson gathered the common people for an assault on the organs of power, American conservatives tried hard to preserve what they called order. "We take it for granted," Samuel Gridley Howe wrote in "Atheism in New England" (1835), "that every reasonable man, be he a Christian or a sceptic, will assent to the axiom, that religion of some kind, is favourable to, if not indispensable for, the order and morality of every large community." Not long ago, Howe remembered, it would have been unthinkable that blasphemy would be tolerated in the streets of New England. "But now, we find an extensive party . . . who openly and violently assail Christianity, and attack our system of morals." The end result, according to this panicked Whig, would be the division of the social world into irreconcilable camps. Looking into the future, he beheld the terrible prospects of heteroglossia and antagonism, already approaching in "the spirit of envy and malice, which the poor begin to manifest toward the rich."[2] Among the reasonable, with their shared commitment to property and customary authority, the disagreement between the pious and the skeptical might be carried on in peace. But if blasphemy spread to the laboring classes, the time for polite conversation would be over.

Troubled by these nightmares of a society at war with itself, American ministers and public officials set out to punish the new blasphemies of the nineteenth century. Immediately recognized as contests that would shape the future relations between church and state, the blasphemy cases were tried before James Kent in New York and Lemuel Shaw in Massachusetts, some of the most revered judges in the country. As they condemned the blasphemers, the courts bound legal customs, including common law traditions imported from England, to a view of the United States as a society held together by the people's shared faith. The defendants responded by appealing to the precious freedoms of opinion and expression that had been secured by postrevolutionary constitutions. In an era of disestablishment and free exercise, they argued, dissent from religious doctrine was no crime.

But the blasphemy trials were about more than the liberty of the private conscience. They were about the courts' capacity to defend the peace by publicly invoking the people's faith. And they were about the dangerously divisive power of blasphemous speech acts in the public sphere. This chapter explores the transformation of two genres of legal literature—the opinion of the court, in which judges spoke for, and thus conjured, the sovereign people, and the popular trial reports generated by the rising mass press. It shows how the blasphemy trials, as they were transmitted to the public in these genres, became occasions for the disciplinary regulation of both the court's public address and the offenders' self-exonerating appeal to the lawgiving people.

Blasphemy was prosecuted not only in the courts of law but also in the court of public opinion, and there, in the long run, the defendants have won a kind of vindication. Liberal historians have reclaimed the blasphemers as some of secularism's last martyrs, unjustly condemned by a judiciary that had not yet liberated itself from the superstitions of the old world. Blasphemy law, according to an influential critique by Leonard Levy, "was a vestigial relic of a dead age, and should have disappeared altogether after the American states became independent of Great Britain."[3] This interpretation of the blasphemy cases was widely available even as they were being prosecuted. An 1828 polemic against the blasphemy laws, for instance, argued that "there is no man, or set of men, on earth that has a right to make laws respecting the religious opinions of individuals"; "the law should take cognizance only of *immoral actions.*"[4] Such critiques of religious persecution carried on the Revolutionary era's assault on lawcraft. In a free and enlightened republic, they argued, the freedom of conscience was to be recognized as sacred.

From the point of view of legal authorities, though, the blasphemy that was condemned by the nineteenth-century courts was not exactly the kind of heresy that had been persecuted in darker times. More and more, prosecutions in the Anglo-American legal world focused on "style" rather than "substance," the manner of the utterance rather than the matter of the proposition.[5] At stake in these trials, Sarah Barringer Gordon shows, was "the crucial difference between religious and moral debate, on one hand, and vituperative and subversive rhetoric, on the other."[6] No longer a question of heretical beliefs or statements, blasphemy was being redefined as a violent act. No longer a sin against the church, it was an offense against the sovereign people. These cases were episodes in an ongoing conflict between traditionalists and freethinkers, between the authority of the governing classes and the clamoring voices of the common people—but they were also occasions for the courts to reconsider the changing character of the law's public sphere.

Indeed, the most notorious of the blasphemy cases served, paradoxically, to advance the project of legal rationalism. In punishing Howe's antagonist, the freethinker Abner Kneeland, in the 1830s, Shaw's court positioned itself as an institution devoted to the preservation of a polite, deliberative public sphere. The blasphemy statute, according to the opinion of the court, "does not prohibit the fullest inquiry, and the freest discussion, for all honest and fair purposes, one of which is, the discovery of truth."[7] The laws of Massachusetts were fully amenable to an elite culture of debate; they provided a secure space where reasonable discussions, including serious disagreements about theological questions, could be carried on in peace. The social stability required for such exchanges of ideas, the court suggested, was precisely what was threatened by the blasphemer's incendiary utterances. Or, as the minister Lyman Beecher put it, Kneeland was guilty of "creating and extending a poisonous leaven, which . . . shall undermine the faith and moral principles of the nation, and prepare society for dissolution."[8] His words were criminal deeds.

Defeated in the courtroom, Kneeland took his case to the public, identifying himself as "a martyr in the cause of truth": "Imprison me," he threatened his judges, "and long after each of our heads shall be laid in the dust, when all our prejudices, bigotry, superstition, and even religious hate . . . shall have received their quietus, my name and memory will be hailed with gratitude by future generations as a bold and fearless pioneer in defense of civil and religious liberty"; "the names of my persecutors, if remembered at all, will be remembered with execration."[9] The untold story of the blasphemy trials is the story of this curious reversal. Widely criticized for conducting an intolerant, theocratic inquisition, Shaw's court depicted itself as the protector of a reasonable deliberation which might submit even the most skeptical propositions to the test of truth. Kneeland, who liked to think of himself as an apostle of reason, was so infuriated by his own persecution that he called for insurrectionary action against the state, hurling curses at his judges in the pages of his newspaper.

As the controversy over Kneeland's case raged on, even the critics of the blasphemy statutes tried to distinguish the private freedom of conscience from the kind of public ranting that threatened to stir up a mob. The elite culture of letters saw how Kneeland had converted the mass press into a tribunal for self-exoneration through the invocation of higher law, and it played its part in the regulation of the curse. Thus blasphemy became a captivating problem not only for the defenders of a traditional order or the advocates of a more inclusive, pluralist one but also for the developing literary culture of the era. The ways of thinking about oracular address that preoccupied both the opinion of the court and the trial report were taken up in literary genres like the gothic tale and the book-length romance. The ideals of self-reliance and the autonomy of conscience were advanced by aspiring authors who perceived, from a wary distance, the power of the curse.

The Faith of the People and the Opinion of the Court

The first great American blasphemer of the nineteenth century, a certain Mr. Ruggles, shouted his curses in the streets of Salem, New York: "Jesus Christ was a bastard, and his mother must be a whore." Ruggles was apprehended, brought to trial, and found guilty of blasphemy. The court sentenced him to a term of three months and a fine of five hundred dollars. Ruggles appealed to the state Supreme Court. His defense, developed by an attorney named John L. Wendell, was that his words had not violated any legitimate law. There was no statute against blasphemy in New York State. The lower court had convicted Ruggles under the customs of English Common Law. Wendell knew that New York's constitution had provided for the enactment of some parts of the Common Law, but he pointed out that it had also guaranteed the freedom of religious exercise, explicitly voiding any Common Law customs relating to an established church. The punishment of blasphemy, Wendell argued, was a remnant of the old alliance between the king's law and the Church of England. Under the people's constitution of New York, the crime was obsolete.[10]

The state's supreme court was not persuaded. In 1811, it voted unanimously to uphold Ruggles's conviction. "There is nothing in our manners or institutions which has prevented the application or the necessity of this part of the common law. We stand equally in need, now as formerly, of all the moral discipline, and of those principles of virtue, which help to bind society together. The people of this State, in common with the people of this country, profess the general doctrines of Christianity, as the rule of their faith and practice; and to scandalize the author of these doctrines is not only, in a religious point of view, extremely impious, but, even in respect to the obligations due to society, is a gross violation of decency and good order."[11] The opinion of the court used the example of blasphemy to affirm that there was a deep, ongoing interdependence between customary jurisprudence and the will of a Christian people

Even in the twenty-first century, the Ruggles opinion continues to be cited as evidence of an alliance between religion and government in the early republic. This reading of the case is shared by today's conservatives and liberals. Those on the right applaud the court's description of a uniformly Christian nation. Those on the left denounce a lingering, theocratic lawcraft which awaited its defeat by an enlightened secularism. What each of these perspectives overlooks, more or less, is the instrumentalist rationality which animates the opinion. The court takes the trouble to distinguish a "religious point of view," not its own, from the state's interest in "the obligations due to society." There is a secularity that tends toward cynicism in the judge's description of the Christian faith as a "moral discipline" whose function is to preserve "good order." Already, religion has been grasped as a technology of statecraft.

For a poetics of justice, too, there is the question of how the court's own way of addressing the people contributes to the mode of governance it describes. Christianity, the court proposes, is the rule of the people's faith and practice, the medium of their belonging to a shared world, and the prohibition of blasphemy enforces the moral discipline that binds them together. But who speaks these lines? And to what public do they address themselves? The opinion of the court in Ruggles's case was delivered, and probably written, by Chief Justice James Kent, a titan of the early American legal world. According to Perry Miller, "Kent, for vastness of comprehension and for elegance of style, stood as *the* American Blackstone"—"the most revered, the most reviled, the most feared member of the American bar of his time."[12] Kent belonged to the generation which consolidated the power of the legal profession in the wake of the Revolution. He would serve not only as a state supreme court justice but also as the first professor of law at Columbia and, famously, as New York's Chancellor of Equity. His *Commentaries on American Law* (1826-1830) would become the most important legal treatise produced in the United States since St. George Tucker's edition of Blackstone. In delivering the opinion of the court in the Ruggles case, however, this domineering legal rationalist suppressed his own name and adopted the role of the oracle.

The conventions of the genre had been established by the U.S. Supreme Court under the leadership of John Marshall. Prior to Marshall's intervention, the Court had followed the English custom of *seriatim* opinions. Each of the several justices composed his own decision and read it aloud in the courtroom at the conclusion of the trial.[13] "When I deliver my sentiments from *this chair,*" James Wilson told his students in the lecture hall in 1791, "they shall by my honest sentiments. When I deliver them from the bench, they shall be nothing more."[14] According to some in the early republic, *seriatim* opinions had the virtue of presenting a range of arguments, allowing the public to weigh the merits of each judge's claims. "Seriatim argument," Thomas Jefferson observed, "shews whether every judge has taken the trouble of understanding the case, of investigating it minutely, and of forming an opinion for himself."[15] Every judge was responsible for his own view of the case, accountable to the public and to the political authorities who held the power to impeach him. Jefferson's position on *seriatim* opinions reflected his commitment to a deliberative public sphere and to the strong power of elected officials, who might divest judges of their offices in the name of the sovereign people.

Indeed, it was precisely the Jeffersonian matrix of critical deliberation and popular sovereignty that Marshall's Court would seek to transcend, most famously in the landmark case of *Marbury v. Madison* but also through its ongoing efforts to secure the authority of the judiciary against the anti-Federalist challenge. By refashioning the generic conventions of the opinion of the Court, as Paul Kahn shows, Marshall redefined the law's relation to the sovereign people. No longer identified with the thoughts or sentiments of any particular judge, the new genre spoke for the people themselves: "Because the opinion does not belong to the individual judge, it can appear to belong to all. It must appear to be what any citizen would say and thus what all would say together. A well-crafted opinion aims to speak in the voice of 'we the people.' It reminds us of that mythical moment when we all first spoke in a common voice."[16] This "moment," of course, is a retrospective illusion, produced through the self-authorizing magic of performative address. "The sovereign people do not make law as a representation of themselves. Rather, the Court makes the sovereign people it purports to represent through the creation and maintenance of an appearance: the opinion."[17] Masking his own authorship, the judge invites the public to hear his voice as its own, to become the collective power that authorizes the ongoing rule of law.

In the Ruggles case, the opinion of the court declared that blasphemy encroached on the norms that gave all laws their meaning and their binding force. Blasphemy did violence to the very spirit of social cohesion, and the "vilification of the gospels" could therefore be punished as "an attack on the moral foundation of law."[18] To explain why, the court recalled that public officials and witnesses at trial were routinely required to swear an oath while touching the Bible. This verbal ritual would become meaningless, an empty form, if the speaker felt no reverence for the sacred text. At the same time, too, the opinion was leading its readers through another kind of ceremony. It was blessing its decision with a religious sanction and with the assent of the people. The opinion in *People v. Ruggles* took its generic conventions from the Marshall Court, but it took its ideology from such judges as Nathaniel Chipman and Jesse Root. Identifying the common law with higher law, the court could invoke the shared norms that bound the people together as a community.

The advocates of free exercise and free expression attacked the court's decision against Ruggles as a piece of theocratic tyranny. Some in the New York legislature proposed revising the constitution to invalidate common law precedents relating to blasphemy and other religious crimes. But the reform failed, in part because the opinion of the court had done its performative work in the public sphere. As it circulated in the press, the opinion was seen to gather "widespread public support" for Kent's Christian version of common law. "The popularity of the Ruggles decision," Gordon observes, "grew over time. Evangelicals frequently reprinted the opinion as a prooftext of the fundamental Christianity of their unruly Republic."[19] By 1815, the opinion had been picked up by such newspapers as the *Weekly Recorder*. In their prefatory remarks, the editors anticipated the reception of this important text: "men of real information and piety, though opposed to the establishment of religion by law, will rejoice in the consideration, that what is usually denominated Common Law, is in force in our country, and, if duly carried into operation, would give a powerful check to blasphemers in their impious and heaven-daring course."[20] The court was an oracle of the unwritten law that was professed in common by the people; its enforcement of moral discipline was an occasion for popular rejoicing.

In its 1824 decision against the blasphemer Abner Updegraph, Pennsylvania's Supreme Court followed Kent's lead in making itself the mouthpiece of a Christian people. In this case, too, the court gave special attention to its own style of public address. "Christianity is part of the common law of this state. It is not proclaimed by the commanding voice of any human superior, but expressed in the calm and mild accents of customary law. Its foundations are broad and strong, and deep; they are laid in the authority, the interest, the affections of the people."[21] Even as it pronounced its verdict against the blasphemer, the court insisted that no "human superior" was addressing the public in a "commanding voice." Instead, the punishment expressed the "mild" spirit of a Christian people. Here again was the self-effacing rhetoric of lawcraft. The opinion enlarged the authority of the court's decision by inviting readers to imagine themselves as its original authors.

Ruggles and Updegraph receded into history, but the controversy over blasphemy was not over. It came to its climax—and to a decisive transformation—in Kneeland's trial for articles published in the *Boston Investigator* in December of 1833. Reviled by some as a dangerous charlatan, defended by others as a champion of enlightenment, Kneeland was "first and last . . . a preacher, in the pulpit and out."[22] Born in 1774, he had started out as a Baptist lay preacher, then joined the Universalist Church, where he became an itinerant minister and, in time, the leader of congregations in Pennsylvania, New York, and Massachusetts. After several crises of faith and conflicts with church leaders, he gave up the ministry to pursue a secular career as a lecturer and journalist. A notorious agitator against New England's traditional ruling powers, he promoted the creed he called "pantheism" and the radical social causes of the Jacksonian period—an expanded franchise, the abolition of slavery, poverty relief, women's rights, and birth control. Among his intellectual heroes were Voltaire and Thomas Paine. His circle of reformers included

Robert Owen and the "female champion of atheistic liberty," Frances Wright.[23] Kneeland's lectures attracted huge, unruly crowds, mainly from the laboring classes, and the *Investigator* had over two thousand subscribers.[24] As the conservative Howe noted with alarm, the number gave only a partial indication of Kneeland's popularity: "The Boston Investigator strikes off two thousand impressions weekly, which are eagerly taken up, read, and handed from one to another."[25] From the beginning, the dangerous power of Kneeland's words was amplified by their rapid and far-reaching circulation.

In 1833, at the invitation of Thomas Whittemore, publisher of *The Trumpet,* Kneeland composed a short letter that explained his dissent from the tenets of the Universalists, his former brethren. "Universalists believe in a god which I do not; but believe that their god . . . is nothing more than a chimera of their own imagination."[26] The deity of the ministers, Kneeland said, had no substance. They were calling their congregations to bow down before a mystifying fiction. Kneeland's letter would soon be read as an affront to the foundations of the Christian faith and the moral and social stability of the state. As Roderick Stuart French argues, the prosecution represented an effort by Massachusetts Whigs to reassert the bond between orthodoxy and social order in an era of secularization and a rising populism: "Kneeland's amalgam of religious skepticism, sexual liberation, and appeal to the alienated worker threatened the synthesis of the sacred, the status quo, and sexual inhibition precisely at the moment New England's proud theocratic experiment was crumbling. Disestablishment in Massachusetts in 1833 was no more than a belated, painful sign of that fact."[27] Kneeland's group, the "First Society of Free Enquirers" was asked to leave its meeting-place at Julien Hall. The blasphemer was arrested, indicted, and brought to trial.

As the case unfolded, the court scrutinized the language of Kneeland's open letter to Whittemore. Had the defendant merely expressed his own opinions, according to his rights, or had he committed the criminal act known as blasphemy? The prosecution based its case on common law customs and on a 1782 statute which provided for the punishment of anyone who "shall wilfully blaspheme the holy name of God, by denying, cursing, or contumeliously reproaching God, his creation, government, or final judging of the world." The Commonwealth argued that Knee-land was guilty according to the letter of the law—he had denied the existence of God. But the defense asked if any such law could legitimately be enforced. The Massachusetts constitution protected the freedoms of conscience and expression: "no subject shall be hurt, molested, or restrained . . . for worshipping God in the manner and season most agreeable to the dictates of his own conscience; or for his religious professions or sentiments; provided he does not disturb the public peace, or obstruct others in their religious worship." Given this constitutional guarantee of religious liberty, Kneeland proposed, the blasphemy statute reflected an obsolete union between the powers of church and state. Certainly Kneeland's text was just the kind of speech that the constitution had been designed to protect—"the expression of a sincere and honest belief, and nothing more."[28]

Those who took Kneeland's side in the press argued that the state had no business with the private faith of its citizens. It should concern itself only with criminal actions against the public peace. "We cannot look with equanimity upon the resuscitation of ecclesiastical tyranny," declared an 1838 editorial on the case; the persecution of blasphemy belonged to "the days of witchcraft."[29] The force of this objection was weakened, however, because the prosecutors and the courts had been careful, all along, to make the same distinction. The Massachusetts Attorney General James T. Austin, who represented the Commonwealth before the Supreme Court, drew the line this way: "It is not because [the defendant] entertains erroneous opinions that he is subjected to prosecution. . . . It is because by his conduct, he has committed high treason against the vital interests of society, that society demands his punishment."[30] Austin had strong opinions about the incendiary potential of the press; this was the same man who had recently celebrated the mob that murdered the abolitionist printer Elijah Lovejoy out in Illinois, and he saw Kneeland as another enemy of the public peace. The blasphemer had not offended the Universalist church, a private party. He had done violence against the sovereign people of Massachusetts. The Kneeland case went through two mistrials, a conviction, and an appeal, and it "inspired torrents of legal eloquence, and floods of sermons, and agitated oceans of print."[31] Through it all, though, the two sides would share a single understanding of the central issue: the distinction between dissenting opinion and criminal action.

Nearly five years after the publication of the offensive article, in 1838, the state Supreme Court upheld Kneeland's conviction, and he was sentenced to sixty days in the Common Jail of Suffolk County. The opinion of the court was delivered by Chief Justice Lemuel Shaw. It began by acknowledging "the intrinsic difficulty attending some of the questions raised in the case"; the justices were divided, and it had taken an unusually long time to arrive at a decision.[32] The court recognized that it was obliged to safeguard the constitutional liberties of conscience and of the press. In the end, though, it found that the statute against blasphemy did not violate those protections. Even the nonbeliever, the court suggested, "may announce his doubts publicly, with the honest purpose of eliciting a more general and thorough inquiry, by public discussion, the true and honest purpose being the discovery and diffusion of truth. None of these constitute the willful blasphemy prohibited by this statute."[33]

Blasphemy, according to the court, was not the kind of speech that was uttered by reasonable people in serious, sober debates. The blasphemer was after something other than the truth. He sought to weaken the social power of religion. This was the court's definition of the crime, derived from the statute and from common law precedent: "blasphemy may be described, as speaking evil of the Deity with an impious purpose to derogate from the divine majesty, and to alienate the minds of others from the love and reverence of God."[34] Blasphemy could be pronounced in many modes. It might even take the grammatical form of a proposition—a statement that there is no God—but its real design was performative, diminishing the cohesive and disciplinary power of a common faith. Coming around to its decision, the court reinforced the distinction between dissenting opinion and blasphemous action. The law against blasphemy "is not intended to prevent or restrain the formation of any opinions or the profession of any religious sentiments whatever, but to restrain and punish acts which have a tendency to disturb the public peace."[35] Understood this way, the blasphemy law was "entirely consistent" with the spirit of the constitution.

Shaw's court cited Kent's decision against Ruggles as one of its oracles, but its own interpretation of blasphemy law departed from precedent in a significant way. The Massachusetts court had taken Kneeland's own argument for the liberties of conscience and the press as the very logic by which it condemned him. The punishment of blasphemy, the court argued, did not compromise the freedom of religious exercise; it protected the proper space of that freedom. The deliberative public sphere, with its characteristic idiom of reasonable inquiry and polite discussion, would be secured through the suppression of the disturbing speech act known as blasphemy.

The Martyr's Trial Report, or Dispatches from Hell

And what, in the meantime, would be the fate of the blasphemer? In Edgar Allan Poe's 1840 tale of religious persecution, "The Pit and the Pendulum," the anonymous narrator is cast into a dungeon and subjected to an elaborate series of terrors. Condemned by the Inquisition for his firm assertion of a dissenting opinion, caught between the vast depth of the pit and the descending blade of the pendulum, he becomes a wretched, dehumanized creature with only the most tenuous grasp on reason: "By long suffering my nerves had been unstrung, until I trembled at the sound of my own voice, and had become in every respect a fitting subject for the species of torture which awaited me."[36] Poe's tale turns on this reversal: religious persecution transforms a reasonable citizen into a depraved, "unstrung" figure. Punishment, rather than proceeding as an effect of the convict's character, remakes that character into the offensive "subject" who deserves to suffer. There is some of the same irony in the story of Abner Kneeland.

After the death of his attorney, Kneeland had represented himself on appeal before the Supreme Court. He had floated various theories, some of them mutually contradictory. Sometimes he claimed that he had not committed blasphemy, according to the letter of the law. He had rejected only the Universalist God, not belief in general; the court would understand this if it read his text closely enough to observe that there was no comma in the phrase "Universalists believe in a god which I do not." Sometimes Kneeland suggested that there was no such thing as blasphemy; it was "an imaginary crime." Sometimes he made the case that atheists were incapable of blasphemy, since one "cannot

curse or contumeliously reproach a nonentity." In his final address to
the court, though, Kneeland abandoned these various technical arguments. Against the legitimacy of statute and common law, he appealed
to a higher standard. "The subject" of blasphemy, he said, "is entirely
above the capacity of man to judge, or the power of man to punish": "the
law has no right to say what is or is not religion, what is or what is not
blaspheming against God." Preparing to hear his sentence of imprisonment, Kneeland assumed the crown of martyrdom and condemned the
court for the crime of "persecution." He would write, in a public letter to
Chief Justice Shaw, "I have just as good a right to judge you as you have
to judge me."[37]

Kneeland was hauled off to the Suffolk County Jail. He was past sixty
years old, and the long ordeal of his trial had exhausted and enraged
him. His wife and infant son had died; he blamed his persecutors for
their death. After a brief stay in a debtor's cell, he was unceremoniously
removed and required to serve his sentence among the common criminals—another indignity. His keepers permitted him to read and write,
however, and his letters from the jail were published in the *Investigator* and elsewhere. Soon, he had collected his various writings on the
case, with related documents, into the *Review of the Trial, Conviction,
and Final Imprisonment in the Common Jail of the County of Suffolk, of
Abner Kneeland, for the Alleged Crime of Blasphemy, Written by Himself.*
Here, Kneeland adapted the style and structure of the trial report, one of
the era's major genres of lawcraft, to the purposes of his own vindication.

"Though only a few trial accounts were printed in America before
1750," Karen Halttunen notes, "by the end of the [eighteenth] century
they were being published in numbers comparable to execution sermons.
And in the first decades of the nineteenth century, their volume swelled,
swamping all other forms of narrative and demonstrating the historical
triumph of the legal discourse [of crime] over the theological."[38] Unlike
prerevolutionary crime genres, the trial report was not ordinarily preoccupied with Biblical themes or the state of the convict's soul. It took up
scientific and legal problems: forensics, psychology, criminal procedure.
It also redistributed the authority of judgment. In this secular, often polyvocal genre, according to Daniel Cohen, "the truth was no longer baldly
asserted . . . by an authoritative spokesman, whether minister or lawyer,

but was mediated . . . through the autonomous judgment of the community itself, as represented by jurors and, by extension, readers."[39] The trial report invited modestly educated, marginally enfranchised readers into the ceremony, cultivating their capacity to weigh evidence and to form opinions about guilt and punishment. In this way, the genre continued to shore up the authority of the law, even as it gradually abandoned the invocation of scriptural authority or a divine sanction.

But Kneeland was the rare defendant who had access to his own press, and he used it to turn the trial report into a kind of protest literature. In the dispatches from the prison he called "Hell," he no longer represented himself as a defendant seeking legal exoneration or leniency. He sought to turn the reading public against the statute book and the courts that enforced it. He opened his *Review of the Trial* with this dedication to the reading public: "It is the right, and should be the privilege, of each and every individual who has been accused of any heinous crime, . . . as a dernier resort,—to appeal to the public. And it is believed . . . that the public when correctly informed, will do each and every individual justice to the full extent of its power."[40] Kneeland had taken his case from the Supreme Court of the Commonwealth to what he saw as the higher, more enduring court of public opinion. The convicted blasphemer had accepted the role of the martyr. Writing from the scene of his disgrace, he would turn to the idiom of the curse.

Whether Kneeland had committed blasphemy back in 1833, or whether he had been a voice of reason against superstition, in his letters from the Suffolk County Jail he unleashed a spiteful verbal violence. "Thousands who have been kept back by your hellish arts and stratagems," he wrote in an open letter to the Massachusetts clergy, were about to "come out boldly"; "No longer *shall* you bear the rule over the minds and bodies of our fellow citizens." Kneeland would wield his "tongue" and his "pen" against irrational laws, but he warned that reasonable deliberation was liable to give way, under the pressure of persecution, to revolutionary action: "Though he be a king on the throne, the governor of a state, a priest in the pulpit, a judge on the bench, or an attorney general at the bar, if he be a tyrant, his office will not protect him. Oppression may . . . be endured long before a reaction can take place; but the longer it is endured, so much the more severe will be the vengeance when it comes; and come it will, sooner or later."[41] Kneeland had gone far beyond his advocacy for freedom of conscience and expression. He had turned to a menacing, incendiary speech. He provoked the public to civil disobedience, asking his readers to cleave to conscience against the unjust law.

At least once, Kneeland uttered a threat of revolution. "To destroy tyrants," he wrote, "will require something more than words." "Do you understand me?"[42] Here, the blasphemer crossed the crucial threshold between speech and action. Persecution had converted him from a rationalist who loved the free exchange of ideas into a self-styled martyr willing to call for insurrectionary violence. His prophesies of doom against the tyrants he saw everywhere in Massachusetts were surely more threatening to the public peace than his mild-mannered dissent from Whittemore's Universalist creed. Beyond its meaning for Kneeland's biography, too, his cursing against the state calls for a revised interpretation of his role in the law's public sphere. What if, as a sympathetic editorial in the *Universalist Watchman* suggested, Kneeland was not an "apostle of Reason" but an "illiberal" writer who threatened the peace by addressing the public in an "enthusiastic" mode?[43]

There is an unresolved problem in the logic of the opinion in Kneeland's case. It arises from the court's distinction between expression and action. The court makes it clear that the honest expression of religious sentiments is protected by the constitution. Only speech acts that diminish public reverence for religion and disturb the peace are punishable as blasphemy. And yet, as Kneeland pointed out again and again, with a rising exasperation, the words for which he was convicted were clearly the expression of his own opinion. "Universalists believe in a god which I do not." How could such a sentence be redefined as something more than a proposition, as a blasphemous act? In his dissent from the majority opinion, Associate Justice Marcus Morton would see this as the decisive question in the case. A "mere denial" of the existence of God was not enough to count as blasphemy. The crime "must have reference to other men and consist in a malicious purpose to infringe their rights, to destroy their peace of mind, or to disturb the good order of society."[44] Morton could not grasp how Chief Justice Shaw and the majority had interpreted Kneeland's words as such a transgressive act.

Some answers might be found in the court's peculiar treatment of the medium in which Kneeland had published his denial, a cheap newspaper for the mass public. The court's official position was that the medium, speech or print, made no difference. Shouted in the streets or circulated in the press, blasphemy was the same crime. But the prosecution and the legal profession itself were preoccupied, throughout Kneeland's trial, with the rise of the mass press and the mass public. Attorney General Austin almost certainly saw the connection between Kneeland and Lovejoy. S. D. Parker, the attorney for the state in one of the lower court trials, had defined this as a case about the new danger of blasphemy in the channels of the mass media. There had been "other infidels" in the generations before Abner Kneeland, Parker told the jury, "but the works of these persons were read only by men of literary habits—necessarily a few." In the case of Kneeland's *Investigator,* "here is a journal, a newspaper, cheap, and sent into thousands of families. Where one man would be injured by Hume, Gibbon, or Volney, a thousand may be injured by this newspaper, so widely circulated, so easily read, so coarsely expressed, so industriously spread abroad."[45]

At the same trial, Judge Peter Thatcher cited an English precedent and reminded the jury that, "Of all human beings. . . , the poor stand most in need of the consolations of religion, and the country has the deepest stake in their enjoying it, not only from the protection which it owes them, but because no man can be expected to be faithful to the authority of man, who revolts against the government of God."[46] These were ominous lines. The poor appeared as a desperate body, precariously swaddled in a religious faith which restrained as it consoled. If the ties were loosened by blasphemous language, this mass might rise in revolt. It was the obligation of the state to keep the bonds of consolation in place; this was the manner of "protection" it offered to the poor. Just a year before the Massachusetts court decided Kneeland's case, a Delaware court had established that "a written publication of blasphemous words, thereby affording them a wider circulation, would undoubtedly be considered as an aggravation of the offense, and affect the measure of the punishment."[47] The special danger posed by Kneeland's article had something to do with the cheapness, the coarseness, and the wide circulation of his paper among the poor. It was in constituting a counterpublic that dissenting words became blasphemous deeds.

Shaw's Supreme Court had recognized that the difference between propositions and speech acts, between personal opinion and criminal blasphemy, was, in part, a matter of reception. It involved the response of audiences whose minds could be alienated from religion. Just below the surface of the court's distinctions between words and deeds was a worried recognition that, if the poor could be addressed in print, by way of a cheap newspaper like the *Investigator*, they might come to imagine themselves as a faction with its own claim to sovereignty. The very boundaries of the public sphere would be opened up to include a new population, with its tendency to "revolt." Perhaps the courts really were becoming what they had claimed to be all along—the defenders of a deliberative public sphere that had depended, for a century or more, on the regulatory supervision of all but the privileged "few," with their "literary habits."

As for Kneeand, he was not so much an apostle of reason as the pied piper of the counterpublic that was pressing on this public sphere, and making its claim to sovereignty, from the outside. The *Investigator*, under Kneeland's editorship, had become a rare forum where the poor and the unrefined could publish their opinions. In the letters from subscribers that were printed in the paper, French suggests, "one often detects a sense of pleasure in writing for publication; no doubt it was a privilege novel to [the authors] as individuals and to persons of this standing in society in general." As an example, French cites a sympathetic letter from a young female correspondent, calling herself Eliza, who flaunted her contempt for men and for all traditional authority, slandering Massachusetts as a "Priest and Witch-ridden State."[48] Kneeland's case might thus be understood to reveal how an elite political culture, with its restricted model of a deliberative public sphere, reacted against the rise of a radical press whose audience was the unruly, uneducated masses. As the court drew its labored distinction between reasonable speech and blasphemous action, its real design was to police the boundaries between the bourgeois public sphere and the anarchy of the mass press.[49]

But even this formulation may undervalue how much was hanging in the balance. The prosecutors of blasphemy perceived that the mass press was doing something more than providing a new forum for the voices of subjects who had enjoyed no access to the older public sphere of refined opinion. As Joss Marsh argues in a study of English cases from the 1840s, "blasphemy was not a denial but an *assertion* of community."[50] The circulation of blasphemous language had an interpellative effect—in addressing a new kind of public, it helped to summon that public into being. Recognizing this capacity, antiblasphemy rhetoric developed a critical poetics of the mode of address that called the mass public to the cause of justice, in opposition to the law. The peculiar blasphemy of the Jacksonian era was conceived from the union of the penny press and the summoning power of the curse.

The prospect disturbed not only conservatives like Samuel Gridley Howe but also the leaders of New England's moderate reform movements. Under the leadership of the liberal Unitarian minister William Ellery Channing, the reformers drew up a petition for Kneeland's pardon. Like Kneeland, they were ready to consign the blasphemy laws to an unenlightened past. "The assumption by government of a right to prescribe or repress opinion has been the ground of the grossest depravations of religion, and of the most grinding despotisms." The decision to punish Kneeland, they wrote, was "at variance with the spirit of our institutions and our age." Unlike the imprisoned freethinker, however, Channing and his circle expressed their concern that this rabble-rousing fanatic "should, by a sentence of the law, be exalted into a martyr, or become identified with the sacred cause of freedom."[51] An article in the *Evangelical Magazine* made the same point: "[Kneeland's] persecution will . . . give him tenfold influence and importance."[52] Much like Howe and Shaw, these liberals watched nervously as the mass press transformed the traditional culture of letters, and they had no desire to see the public sphere opened to the cursing of fanatics. The best way to diminish Kneeland's power, they suggested, was to leave him alone.

Kneeland was savvy enough to see that a pardon would weaken his position in the public sphere. He told his followers not to sign the petition. "*I* should ask for no pardon," he wrote. "The current of public opinion is turned so much against this odious persecution, that every iota of suffering which I shall have to endure . . . will help the cause in which I am engaged."[53] Kneeland seems to have recognized that the very terms in which the reformers were advocating for the toleration of blasphemy—the freedom of conscience, a private matter of no interest to the institutions of the state or to the sovereign community—would also have consigned him to obscurity and impotence. He presumed to reject their offer of a tranquil oblivion. He wished to address the public from a position of martyrdom.

The Miserable Multitude

Channing's circle of liberal ministers and writers adopted a complicated stance on the Kneeland case. They opposed the persecution of religious speech, even of Kneeland's pantheistic nonsense. They wanted to see the prisoner released, the law reformed. But they also wanted to distance themselves from the blasphemer and his mob. Channing's most famous disciple, Ralph Waldo Emerson, delivered his controversial address to the graduating class of Harvard's Divinity School in 1838. In the same year, he signed the petition for Kneeland's pardon. As Robert E. Burkholder demonstrates, some ministers linked Emerson's address, with its attack on the cold formalism of the Universalists, to Kneeland's blasphemies. Emerson was never arrested. He was protected, to some degree, by his connections to privilege. But Emerson's security was also a measure of his harmlessness. Next to the "eminently more dangerous" editor of the *Investigator,* "Emerson was not much of a problem: his influence was limited to a small group of mostly Harvard-trained intellectuals, almost all of whom had some ties to the conservative establishment themselves, and to those who attended his lectures and who had bought and read *Nature.*"[54] To question orthodoxy in the presence of such company, men who knew what they believed and could publish their own learned, well-reasoned responses, was offensive. To blaspheme before the multitude was criminal.

Emerson was insulated not only by his social position but also by the genre of his address, by the limited orbit of its circulation, and by the circumspection of his own rhetoric. His early career showed how a dissenter in New England's culture of letters might take up a martyr's cause in a cautious way, defining the freedom of conscience while tacitly opposing the incendiary cursing of a fanatic in the combustible context of the mass press. But the complex relations among the theocratic past, the secularizing present, and the character of blasphemy's counterpublic received their most vivid treatment in the work of another author, a Massachusetts Democrat who would learn that, for better or worse, his destiny was tied to Kneeland's party.

Nathaniel Hawthorne's "Alice Doane's Appeal" was published anonymously in *The Token* in 1835, midway through Kneeland's five-year ordeal. Hawthorne never formally acknowledged the early tale as his own; it appeared in none of the bound collections produced during the author's lifetime.[55] For the few critics who have returned to "Alice Doane's Appeal," its interest has been in Hawthorne's development as a revisionist critic of the Puritan past. Michael Colacurcio, for instance, understands the tale as an exercise in moral historiography, emphasizing its engagement with the problem of "specter evidence," the power of the devil to manipulate the forms of the living, that preoccupied the witch trials of the 1690s.[56] Hawthorne's source was Charles W. Upham's *Lectures on Witchcraft,* delivered in Salem in 1830 and published the following year.[57] Hawthorne shared Upham's view of the episode as an "execrable" crime, and he praised the lectures as a work of "that better wisdom, which draws the moral while it tells the tale" (111). But one of the didactic lessons of "Alice Doane's Appeal" is that the sins of the past continue to haunt the present. The "mournful gaze" of the living upon the "shame" of "our fathers" is also a look of recognition, of kinship, that claims an enduring heritage (111). "Alice Doane's Appeal" engages New England's public culture of justice in its own 1830s, exploring how the condemned might invoke a higher law in acts of performative self-exoneration.

Much like Charles Brockden Brown's *Wieland,* Hawthorne's tale composes a gothic portrait of a family circle violated by an outsider who wields a dark verbal magic, ruining an innocent woman's reputation and driving her brother to murder. The setting is seventeenth-century New England. The protagonists are Alice and Leonard Doane, siblings who have lived together in a peculiar intimacy since their parents were killed in fighting with the local Indians. Their virtuous lives are disrupted when a mischievous wizard contrives to bring a third, unknown sibling into their village. Walter Brome seduces his own estranged sister and taunts Leonard with "indubitable proofs" of her "shame" (116). Possessed by a jealous fury, Leonard murders Walter and leaves his body half-buried beside a frozen lake.

What follows are two acts of ceremonial, quasi-legal speech. The first is Leonard's "dreadful confession" to the wizard (117). The murderer describes the tormented condition of his mind and the details of his crime. The wicked hermit, however, gives Leonard no justice. His only answer is a ghostly laughter that might be mistaken for the wind. "Wretched" with guilt for their twin crimes, the siblings make a midnight visit to the village cemetery. This time Alice is the one to speak, addressing the heavens and pronouncing her "appeal." Again, Hawthorne attends less to the speech act than to its reception, as Alice's plea for justice seems to summon specters from their graves: "the dead of other generations, whose moss-grown names could scarce be read upon their tomb stones, and their successors, whose graves were not yet green; all whom black funerals had followed slowly thither, now re-appeared" (119). The tale concludes when Leonard and Alice, guilty of murder and incest, are recognized as morally innocent by the ghostly assembly that Hawthorne calls a "miserable multitude" (120).

Hawthorne's description of the miserable multitude is elaborate and weird. He identifies a range of historical types—colonial founders dressed for imperial warfare; ordained ministers in postures of devotion; children and old maids; the dead of distant generations and of recent memory. "All, in short, were there" (119). Midway through this passage, though, comes a curious turn: "Yet none but souls accursed were there, and fiends counterfeiting the likeness of departed saints" (119). All the dead seem to have been summoned, but the appearance is an illusion. This is really a congregation of the damned, some of whom have impiously taken the forms of the saved. "Had the pastors prayed, all saintlike as it seemed, it had been blasphemy" (119).

This "counterfeiting" is Hawthorne's most explicit reference to the colonial controversy over specter evidence. Describing the graveyard scene as a "parody" of the mystifications and injustices at work in the colonial courts, Lauren Berlant notes the cruel irony of Alice's position. The defendant submits her testimony to the spirit of Walter Brome, who is both "the accuser and the jury."[58] But Brome is not the only audience for Alice Doane's appeal. The scene is, emphatically, a public one, performed before a ghostly congregation. This audience is endowed with the power to recognize a moral and spiritual innocence, even in a case of legal guilt. If Hawthorne's scene is a gothic restaging of a witchcraft trial, then, it rearranges the players in an important way. The spectral forms are not those of the accused or of the afflicted. They are an assembled public, a collective body called into being by an extra-legal plea for justice.

Perhaps, then, the relevant sources for the tale's historical context include not only Upham's *Lectures* but also the self-exonerating convict narratives, trial reports, and polemics that were beginning to circulate in the mass press of the 1830s. Much more clearly than either the reactionaries or the reformers of his time, Hawthorne perceived the poetics of justice in these texts—how they sought to summon into being the audience that they seemed to take for granted. Writing from a position of abjection, the author of an appeal attempts to constitute a normative community in opposition to the one that grants legitimacy to the institutions of law. Hawthorne's special concern, though, is not with the rhetoric of these speech acts. The words of Alice's appeal do not even appear in his tale. Instead, Hawthorne devotes his attention the damaged, excluded character of the public that answers the offender's call. The miserable multitude has no class identity. It is a socially heterogeneous assembly whose only unity is in its common sense of estrangement from the circle of the elect. This is a counterpublic, buried beneath the community and cast out from the heaven of sovereignty.

"Alice Doane's Appeal" is one of the most vivid representations of the curse produced in the Jacksonian culture of letters. But it is also an exercise in literary regulation. As he depicts the performative magic of the blasphemous appeal and the ghostly character of the counterpublic, Hawthorne takes a series of steps to distance himself from his own ominous vision. One displacement has already been enacted in the shift between the tale's two offenders. It is not the guilty murderer who is granted the power to exonerate himself; it is Alice, the victim of deception and seduction, who takes center stage. She is vindicated only by disavowing her own desire and autonomy. As in *Wieland,* the appeal is dissociated from the violence of a brother's crime and linked to a sister's innocence. It seeks not to justify a transgression but to restore a lost purity.

Hawthorne drew a boundary, too, between the public character of Alice Doane's appeal and the semi-private world of his own literary endeavor. As readers know, the tale at the heart of the piece is framed by a sketch that describes the circumstances of its performance. The gothic plot of Walter Brome's murder, Leonard Doane's confession, and Alice Doane's appeal is disclosed in fragments and summaries by an anxious narrator who is preoccupied with its style and its reception. Here, the setting is "a pleasant afternoon in June," and the author is strolling with two lady companions through the Massachusetts countryside, leading them, in time, to Gallows Hill, where the witches of Salem were hanged in 1692 (110). He takes a manuscript from his pocket and begins to read, opening with the description of Walter Brome's abandoned corpse.

Throughout his reading of the tale, Hawthorne's narrator will take the time to reflect on its form and technique, and especially to consider its effects on his little audience. As he delivers a "fantastic piece of description," intending like a wizard "to throw a ghostly glimmer around the reader," he remarks, "I paused, and gazed into the faces of my two fair auditors." Never is his satisfaction more intense than in this moment, when he sees that "their bright eyes were fixed on me; their lips apart" (118). Elsewhere, though, the narrator is less confident in the power of his tale. He confesses that it has "no conspicuous merits" (113). He mentions that it belongs to a series written some years ago and that, in a fit of artistic dejection, he burned most of the other manuscripts—a distinctly modern, private, and literary bonfire of the vanities. Worst of all, at the climax of the narrator's performance, the moment of terror and illumination, his companions are unmoved. When they ought to tremble, they begin to laugh. The writer's aspirations are withered once again.

What has gone wrong? Hawthorne's narrator analyzes the pedagogic (and erotic) failure of his tale in terms of the historical consciousness of his listeners. The terrible story of Alice Doane, he thinks, "would have brought even a church deacon to Gallows Hill, in old witch times," but the consumers of secular, sensational fictions in his own era have no such reverence for the authority of ancient superstitions (121). Standing on Gallows Hill, a place "blasted" by a "physical curse," the narrator is troubled by how lightly his neighbors seem to take the past: "we are a people of the present and have no heartfelt interest in the olden time" (111). He concludes with a call for a "monument" carved from "dark, funereal stone," to memorialize the "crime" of the witch trials (123). Like the historian Upham, Hawthorne's narrator wishes to educate his listeners into a more solemn appreciation of history, drawing a moral about their own frailty as he tells his gothic tale.[59]

Thus the narrator makes an experiment in genre: "a trial," as he puts it, "whether truth were more powerful than fiction" (121). Recalling the history of the witch trials, he draws on all his powers of eloquence to describe the somber procession of the doomed from the village to Gallows Hill. He depicts the martyred witches and the persecutors who had "disgraced an age, and dipped a people's hands in blood." He singles out the name of Cotton Mather, "the one blood-thirsty man, in whom were concentrated those vices of spirit and errors of opinion, that sufficed to madden the whole surrounding multitude" (122). And, as he recounts the dark procession to the scaffold, he is delighted to see that his rhetoric does its seductive work. "Here my companions seized an arm on each side; their nerves were trembling; and sweeter victory still, I had reached the seldom trodden places of their hearts, and found the well-spring of their tears" (123). The penetration promised earlier by the listeners' open mouths is consummated here. Moral education and erotic conquest come together, indistinguishable.

Hawthorne's narrator, then, salvages fiction from the fallen condition of sensationalism by identifying it with moral historiography. He insists that the tale is not an amusement for the frivolous consumer but a serious literary reckoning with the past, backed by "good authority" and designed to awaken its listeners to the enduring significance of their own collective burdens. Like the defenders of Abner Kneeland, the narrator feels that the legacy of the witch panic is alive and well in Massachusetts. Like Brown's Clara Wieland, too, he understands himself to be involved in the work of moral pedagogy. He is teaching his readers about the vulnerability of undisciplined hearts to corruption by a malicious, self-interested but self-effacing authority, in this case the hypocrite Mather. The sketch becomes a critique of priestcraft and lawcraft, but its protest is in the service of an exhortation to vigilant self-discipline—a lesson about the "infirmity" of the "human heart" (123). Identifying its public as an intimate circle, outside the scene of sovereignty, "Alice Doane's Appeal" is no curse.

The conspicuous attention paid by Hawthorne's narrator to his own failure, to the poverty of his literary efforts and to his personal obscurity, was characteristic of the posture that the author would adopt for most of his career. Indeed, the persona of the neglected artist became part of Hawthorne's marketing strategy.[60] Even after he had become a commercial success, Hawthorne continued to identify himself as an obscure, unimportant scribbler, and especially to denigrate early magazine pieces like "Alice Doane's Appeal." According to some critics of his politics, these gestures of withdrawal from the public world are signs of his failure to involve himself in the struggles of his time. According to some defenders of his artistry, the same retreat was necessary to the development of a morally serious critique of consumer society: alienated from the dominant culture, the Romantic writer endeavors to redeem consciousness from its subjection to ideology.[61] The relation of "Alice Doane's Appeal" to the law's public sphere, however, does not conform neatly to either of these accounts. Instead, the tale is animated by its ambivalence about the power of the curse. It does define its project in terms of moral pedagogy, a concern to preserve the modern self against mystification and corruption, but at its heart is a compensatory fantasy of world-transforming public address, idealized in the appealing figure of martyred innocence.

Thus Hawthorne's peculiar conception of literature, even in an early tale like "Alice Doane's Appeal," committed him to a renunciation of the incendiary politics of cursing even as it gave him an occasion to theorize that power, not least as a fantasy of the self-constituting authority that could be wielded by the condemned and the disenfranchised. Some years later, as he began to reinvent himself, to emerge from putative obscurity and to take his place as an author on a national stage, he would return to Alice and the wizard, building a revised version of their story into the structure of *The House of the Seven Gables*. In Chapter 1, I sketched the romance's depiction of a judge who refashions lawcraft for a democratizing modernity—or, as Hawthorne puts it, "an ambitious demagogue, who hides his aspiring purpose by assuming the prevalent hue of popular sentiment."[62] Now, with the beginnings of the curse in view, it becomes possible to see how the same book handles the revenge of the martyrs and, in the process, imagines its own immunity from the charge of an incendiary blasphemy.

Maule's curse, in *The House of the Seven Gables,* is a lingering, shape-shifting thing. It begins as a speech act. The dispossessed wizard, with the noose around his throat, gazes at his persecutor and prophesies that "God will give him blood to drink!" (7). The speaker claims no agency in restoring justice. God, not Maule, will carry out the retribution. And while his "enemy," Colonel Pyncheon, does not flinch at the wizard's words, there is another audience, a circle of unnamed "village gossips," which takes them more seriously (7, 8). To the gossips, the curse signi-fies a corruption in the foundations of the Colonel's mansion, a haunt-ing presence that "would darken the freshly plastered walls, and infect them early with the scent of an old and melancholy house" (8). In time, these predictions about the Pyncheon house seem to come true. The well-water turns to poison. The family line degenerates. The Pyncheon patriarchs die mysteriously, with bloodstains on their beautiful shirts.

The curse is a terrible fate, somehow both beguilingly subtle and monstrously excessive. Each new manifestation is peculiar enough that the gossips' belief in a single, all-corrupting curse can still be dismissed, by skeptics, as a superstition. Yet the very structure of Hawthorne's romance seems to confirm the gossips' view. The book gives a retrospec-tive unity to the various ills endured by the Pyncheon house by por-traying them as expressions of a single curse, persisting down through the generations. Maule himself is an undead presence, and every Pyn-cheon patriarch seems to meet his counterpart in a new wizard, come to take revenge. The inset tale entitled "Alice Pyncheon" is a reworking of "Alice Doane's Appeal," but it is also one of several internal repetitions in *The House of the Seven Gables* itself.

This time, the patriarch is Gervais Pyncheon, grandson to the origi-nal Colonel. And the Maule is another Matthew, descended from the first martyr. Hawthorne emphasizes that Pyncheon courts his antagonist, inviting Maule into the mansion in the belief that the wizard can dis-close the whereabouts of the family's apocryphal title to a vast territory in Maine. Maule is a proud craftsman, and he refuses to bow or scrape, but after some reflection he leads the old man to believe that he does, in fact, have the power to recover the document. In exchange, he demands the house of the seven gables, rightful reparation for his grandparent's dispossession. And he asks, ominously, for one more thing. "The only chance of acquiring the requisite knowledge," he says, is "through the clear, crystal medium of a pure and virgin intelligence" (143). Maule wants to use Pyncheon's maiden daughter, Alice, in his occult operation.

Dreaming of a baron's splendor, Pyncheon consents to Maule's terms. As the wizard works his magic, though, it becomes clear that he is not going to retrieve the lost legal paperwork. His trick, instead, is to bewitch Alice, to take mastery over one who looks down on the plebian carpenter with aristocratic contempt: "But alas, for the beautiful, the gentle, yet too haughty Alice! A power, that she little dreamed of, had laid its grasp upon her maiden soul. A will, most unlike her own, constrained her to do its grotesque and fantastic bidding. Her father, as it proved, had martyred his poor child to an inordinate desire for measuring his land by miles, instead of acres. And, therefore, while Alice Pyncheon lived, she was Maule's slave, in a bondage more humiliating, a thousand-fold, than that which binds its chain around the body" (149). In this case, it is not the swindled laborer but his addressee, the maiden Alice, who is the martyr, stripped of honor and autonomy.

Hawthorne's romance identifies this act of wizardry as an extension of the first Maule's curse, but it is a repetition with a difference. Where the original Maule repudiated his own agency, attributing the power of restorative justice to God, his descendant is involved in the "grotesque" assertion of a self-interested will. With the reincarnation and refashioning of the Pyncheon patriarchs, Hawthorne had exposed the corrupt self-interest of oracular authority. With the transformation of Maule's curse, he showed how a lowly carpenter's assertion of his natural rights might tend toward a revolutionary claim to power. What the antiblasphemy polemics called "the spirit of envy and malice, which the poor begin to manifest toward the rich," is fantastically realized, in Hawthorne's story, as a vengeful tyranny more absolute, and more humiliating to its enemies, than that paradigm of unjust domination in antebellum America, the slavemaster's possession of the enslaved body. This is the secret unity, in *The House of the Seven Gables,* between the oracle and the curse. And if the book seeks to unmask the oracles who have enchanted the people into abdicating their proper sovereignty, it also wishes to assure its readers that it repudiates the wizardry of the Maules.

As in "Alice Doane's Appeal," Hawthorne enacts this regulatory self-discipline by reflecting, at length, on the similarities between a wizard's bewitching of the afflicted and a writer's seduction of his audience. Hawthorne attributes "Alice Pyncheon," the inset tale, to the "lawless mystic" Holgrave, the artist who boards in the Pyncheon house (162). Holgrave is a daguerreotypist, a political journalist, and an author who publishes stories in *Graham's Magazine* and *Godey's Lady's Book*. One sunny afternoon, he unfolds a manuscript and reads it aloud to the lovely and cheerful Miss Phoebe Pyncheon. Like the anonymous narrator of "Alice Doane's Appeal," Holgrave is exquisitely self-conscious about his reputation and about the charms of his art. He makes a dismissive joke about the fleetingness of "literary fame," and he promises that he is capable of sensational effects—"as for pathos, I am as provocative of tears as an onion!" (133).

By the time Holgrave has finished his performance, his story has begun to work a wickeder magic on his listener. "It was evident that, with but one wave of his hand and a corresponding effort of his will, he could complete his mastery over Phoebe's yet free and virgin spirit; he could establish an influence over this good, pure, and simple child, as dangerous, and perhaps as disastrous, as that which the carpenter of his legend had acquired and exercised over the ill-fated Alice" (150). The enslaving magic dramatized in the tale threatens to take hold in the scene of its telling. Holgrove, the descendant of the Maules, seems to be enacting their revenge, once more. The wizard's ancient curse, already reimagined as his grandson's mesmeric spell, is about to be reanimated once again, this time as the aesthetic power wielded by the author of a sensational fiction.

In the end, though, it does not happen that way. The cycle is broken when the author performs a difficult act of self-restraint. For an artist like Holgrave, "there is no temptation so great as the opportunity of acquiring empire over the human spirit," but this wicked impulse is overmastered by the daguerreotypist's "rare and high quality of reverence for another's individuality." Holgrave "[forbids] himself to twine that one link more, which might have rendered his spell over Phoebe indissoluble," and she is released from his possession (151). The spell is broken, Maule's cruelty is safely buried in old witch-times, and the manuscript of "Alice Pyncheon" is consigned to the flames.

As Hawthorne's narrator takes over from Holgrave, returning to the antebellum present and the main plotline of *The House of the Seven Gables,* he marks the transition, right away, by recalling the genre of his own book. Describing the evening landscape, he observes that the Pyncheon house's "common-place characteristics—which, at noontide, it seemed to have taken a century of sordid life to accumulate—were now transfigured by a charm of romance" (151). We have departed the world of the magazine tale and passed, it seems, into a finer atmosphere. With this passage, *The House of the Seven Gables* announces its renunciation of sensational fiction and its aspiration toward the subtler aesthetic of the romance, whose true concerns, as Hawthorne writes in the Preface, lie with "the truth of the human heart" (3).

Yet the same gesture reveals how Hawthorne's romance requires the presence of these other genres, how it produces its own self-understanding by performing their suppression and regulation. As Meredith L. McGill argues, "*The House of the Seven Gables* depends on the literary forms it tries to disavow," and the sensational power to seduce and manipulate a public, which the book associates with the lower genres of magazine fiction, is "carried forward . . . by the force of its repudiation."[63] For McGill, the crucial aspect of these dynamics is the special kind of authority that Hawthorne can claim for the high art of the romance through his rejection of sensational fiction, including his own earlier productions. The author's self-positioning as an outsider to mass culture enables him to subject it to a humiliating critical analysis. Hawthorne writes from an attitude of "suspended animation" which is best understood "not as powerlessness or even power-in-restraint, but as . . . producing the author as a figure of exemption from a culture it nonetheless is empowered to critique."[64] The posture of repose makes Hawthorne immune from complicity in the world's injustices and, at the same time, negates his responsibility for the political consequences that might attend his public indictments of them.

As McGill shows, then, it is less the sovereign "individuality" of a reader like Phoebe than the autonomy of a literary author which is at stake in the framing of "Alice Pyncheon." Revisiting Hawthorne's reflections on the literary regulation of the curse, a poetics of justice can perceive, as well, how the author reimagined and amplified, in retrospect, the seductive power of the sensational and freely circulating magazine fiction against which he defined his romance. In the case of Hawthorne, whose earlier "Alice Doane's Appeal" was so disparaging of its own sensational effects, it might even be claimed that such power was attributed to magazine fiction precisely in the act of its renunciation. Not until he had forsworn any effort to mesmerize his readers did the author acknowledge that his tales could ever have been capable of that bewitching magic.

When, later, Hawthorne did endow popular texts with the power to dominate "the human spirit," he did so from a safe distance. He had made a categorical distinction between low and high genres, not unlike the boundary between the mass press and the elite culture of deliberation which had been drawn in the blasphemy trials. And even this carefully erected firewall seems not to have been secure enough to satisfy Hawthorne. He took the trouble, in his Preface, to lay out his own project of self-regulation. The author of a romance, he wrote, "will be wise, no doubt, to make a very moderate use of the privileges here stated, and, especially, to mingle the Marvellous rather as a slight, delicate, and evanescent flavor, than as any portion of the actual substance of the dish offered to the Public. He can hardly be said, however, to commit a literary crime, even if he disregard this caution" (3). With its reference to the "laws" of art and "literary crime," the Preface has often been cited as evidence of Hawthorne's interest in the legal culture of his era. In using these legal metaphors, though, Hawthorne clearly seeks to displace law, in the formal sense, as a standard of judgment. He presumes that his public is involved in consumption and appreciation, like the guest at a supper, and perhaps in some musing appraisal of the writer's fidelity to "the human heart."

This way of imagining literary address and reception is not confined to the Preface. It governs the many scenes of literary performance which are staged in the body of the romance, too. Phoebe reads aloud, in the garden, to the devastated Clifford. Holgrave's voice works its magic on a listener, not a reader. In these passages, the public circulation of literature is halted and domesticated, recast as intimate address. Hawthorne, then, did not only remove himself from the public worlds of law and politics, claiming a margin of aesthetic autonomy. He went so far as to identify his readers as a distinctly literary and privatized circle, indifferent to questions of public justice. Even if the Preface is read with suspicion, as a kind of alibi, and even if the romance subverts these aesthetic "laws" and claims the authority of critique, it remains a mystery where or when its protest will find a public capable of assenting to its call, unless in some indefinite future.

CHAPTER 4

Evil Speaking,
"A Bridle for the Unbridled Tongue"

Who speaks the curse, and who responds? In Hawthorne's *The House of the Seven Gables* the speaker is a laborer, resentful of the Pyncheons' wealth and privilege. The listener, the one bewitched, is the innocent maiden Alice. This choreography of intimate possession departed from Hawthorne's earlier version of the story. In "Alice Doane's Appeal," the heroine's occult cry for justice had summoned the "multitude" of the damned. In the 1835 tale, perhaps, Hawthorne was interested not only in women's exposure to seduction but also in their public exercise of nonrational persuasion. Here, again, "Alice Doane's Appeal" touched on the antiblasphemy discourse of the age. In the press and in the pulpits of the 1830s, women's public speech was depicted as an unholy, spellbinding magic. For her strong assertion of women's rights, including the right to public address itself, Fanny Wright was indicted in the newspapers as "a bold blasphemer, and a voluptuous preacher of licentiousness." Refusing even to listen to a lecture by the antislavery activist Abby Kelley, the Reverend Henry Ludlow denounced the speaker as a latter-day witch: "I will not sit in a meeting where the sorcery of a woman's tongue is thrown around my heart!"[1]

Abner Kneeland's blasphemy trial had begun as a conflict between a court system allied with established religion and a freethinker committed to the reasonable exchange of skeptical ideas. Before it was over, the two sides had virtually traded places: the court portrayed itself as the protector of rational inquiry, and the imprisoned editor of the *Boston Investigator* played the martyr, calling the mob to riot and rebellion. At the same time, a parallel reversal was being enacted in the evangelical churches, which confronted another kind of fanaticism. Disturbed by unordained exhorters and embarrassed by lay preachers who claimed to know the mind of God, church leaders undertook to regulate the disorder they called enthusiasm. They did so by way of formal and informal policies of repression, by excommunicating the defiant, and by putting their members on trial for such offenses as "evil speaking." Evil speaking was the sinful and slanderous utterance of judgment against a fellow Christian, especially against a clergyman. "Let us . . . never defile our tongue or our pen with this abomination," the Methodist minister Elijah Hedding preached in a discourse on the subject in 1837.[2] The true Christian would be known by his self-restraint: "His passions and propensities are in proper subjection to reason."[3] Thus the revivalists set themselves up as the defenders of a rationalized, well-disciplined faith.

If the main axis of opposition in the blasphemy cases was that of class, the persecution of enthusiasm, unordained preaching, and evil speaking seems to have been waged most aggressively as a war between the sexes. The Christian imperatives of humility and piety were used to stigmatize the feverish public performances of women who lacked the formal education of the ministers. Chastised for their errors and excommunicated for their sins, some would respond by appealing to the court of public opinion. They produced an intriguing genre of popular narrative, a hybrid of the trial report and the spiritual autobiography, which sought to restore their good names. In these texts, the unfolding of a pilgrim's progress toward salvation was infused with the logics of disinterested justice and reasonable persuasion that characterized the deliberative public sphere. Thus the controversial lay preacher Sally Thompson, in telling the story of her 1830 church trial for evil speaking, among other offenses, assured her readers, "My design is not to prejudice the public in favor of either side. All I ask is a fair and candid perusal."[4] The rationalist Kneeland had abandoned deliberation for an insurrectionary call to arms. The exhorter Thompson moved in the opposite direction, from the fiery judgment of her enemies to the dispassionate presentation of evidence.

On the surface of things, a servant of God like Sally Thompson might appear to have almost nothing in common with a freethinker like Abner Kneeland or an antitheocrat like Fanny Wright. The evangelicals wanted to save souls, not to enlighten minds, and the freethinkers looked on their revivals as absurd, superstitious carnivals. The old antipathy lives on, too, in much of the recent scholarship. Studies of the blasphemy trials have mainly understood them as episodes in the rise of secular reason, of enlightenment liberating itself from the shackles of theocracy. Cultural historians of enthusiasm, by contrast, have identified it with the struggles of women and other disenfranchised subjects to make their voices heard in public. To condemn enthusiasm was to practice exclusion in the name of rationalism. Where the first camp identifies reason with the freedom of the press, then, the second sees it as a rhetoric of repression, a way to police the boundaries of the bourgeois public sphere. Scholars have gone to the archive of exhortation and prophecy to reclaim voices which were too radical to be tolerated, in their own time, even by an enlightened liberalism.

A comparative study shows that, in the legal public sphere of the mid-nineteenth century, there was no single, fixed relation between modes of address and power relations. Reason, an endlessly contested value, could be an armature of either oppression or resistance. The self-abnegating invocation of the will of God might be used to justify authority, or to raise hell against it. Both blasphemy and evil speaking were identified as incendiary styles of public address that threatened to rend the moral community into factions. For a poetics of justice, the task of reading the two kinds of cases together is to discover what kinds of connections might lie beneath the apparently incommensurable surfaces—to see what fantastic powers were attributed to blasphemy and evil speaking by writers who disavowed them and, along the way, to understand the polite modes of persuasion which were protected, perhaps even created, through the regulation of these two enemies.

Harriet Beecher Stowe, a writer well-versed in the period's controversies over women's public address, saw the poetics of enthusiasm with some clarity when she described the response of a listener at a camp-meeting this way: "Mr. John Gordon . . . gave himself up, without resistance, to be swayed by the feeling of the hour. He sung with enthusiasm, and wished he was a soldier of somebody, going somewhere, or a martyr shouting victory in the fire."[5] In this scene, enthusiasm has a distinctive speaking style and a peculiar effect on its audience which are unrelated to its doctrines. Stowe marks the lack of any theological content with the empty pronouns "somebody" and "somewhere," placeholders for an absent creed. What remains, for the listener, is a formal feeling, a sense of having been summoned. John Gordon has not been convinced of the truth of a proposition. He has been called to imagine his own belonging to an oppositional faction, his place on the side of the martyrs in a dynamic of antagonism. Thus the novel points toward a hollowed-out structure of address and reception, a poetics that precedes the assertion of any particular proposition.

The rise of prominent literary evangelicals like Stowe helps to explain, as well, why the evil speakers' appeals to a rationalist court of public opinion could not fully exonerate them. Out of the conflict between reason and fanaticism, a generation of reformers was developing a third way, a kind of persuasion that would come to be known as "influence." Conceived by the evangelical press and perfected in the sentimental protest novel, influence was a mode of nonrational but nonviolent public address, associated with women's voices, that would be received as if it were heard in private. Influence pretended to wield its persuasive power in a zone of intimate entreaty and moral improvement that defined itself against law's public sphere. Thus the same social movements and literary innovations that regulated enthusiasm also worked, in a semi-clandestine way, to open a space for Stowe's protests against an unjust legal system. Retreating from the cold propositions of an implicitly masculine rationalism, but also from the factionalizing performances of enthusiastic exhorters, the evangelicals discovered the period's favorite conception of polite literature.

Enthusiasm's Evil Speech

Reflecting on the ideal of "true religion," the model of reasonable and well-disciplined faith promoted by mainstream Protestant denominations in the antebellum United States, the historian John Lardas Modern observes "a process of normalization at work." True religion was defined against illegitimate faiths and unacceptable practices. For this reason, Modern writes, public discussions of true religion are best understood "in light of their exclusionary processes," which helped to fortify social hierarchies. But some of these exclusions, he goes on to suggest, "were also inscribed upon the bodies who performed the prescriptions of Protestant normativity."[6] The creation of true religion, and of its distinctive styles of public address, involved two related but different kinds of suppression: At one level, the silencing of the unlettered, the undisciplined, and the lowly; at another level, the authorizing self-regulation of those who spoke the truth.

In an 1827 letter, widely reprinted in newspapers, the New England minister Lyman Beecher warned that the evangelical movement was getting out of control. The revivals, he wrote, had become possessed by "a spirit of fanaticism, of spiritual pride, censoriousness, and insubordination to the order of the Gospel, which, if not met by the timely and decided disapprobation of ministers and churches, threatens to become one of the greatest evils which is likely to befall the cause of Christ."[7] Beecher's efforts to preserve the legal bond between the state of Connecticut and the Congregationalist Church had been defeated in 1818, but in the wake of disestablishment he had aligned himself with the moderate evangelicals, seeking to rekindle the public's devotion to God. Soon, disestablishment came to seem less like a marker of religion's decline than an opportunity for its revival. The ministers turned their attention to securing the voluntary commitment of every believer.

Beecher's ambition was to cultivate a Second Great Awakening that could save the nation from a moral degeneracy whose symptoms included slavery, intemperance, and the smoldering resentments of the laboring classes. He was no hidebound reactionary. As Daniel Walker Howe shows, "in the world of his time he was a moderate reformer and practiced the arts of compromise."[8] But Beecher was convinced that some of his brethren were going too far. He pointed, in particular, to New School evangelists like Charles Grandison Finney and Nathaniel Beman, with their impassioned preaching style and their wild camp meetings. As Beecher contemplated Finney's controversial "new methods," he worried "that Satan, as usual, is plotting to dishonor a work which he cannot withstand"—in other words, that the unruly kinds of worship on display in the revivals would drive respectable people away.[9] The spirit of fanaticism would be the disgrace of the churches.

To make sense of the trouble, Beecher recalled the tragic history of the first Great Awakening. Almost a century ago, evangelicals had allowed themselves to hope that the Holy Spirit was sweeping through their world. New Lights like Jonathan Edwards saw their churches joined by members who recounted their conversion experiences with passionate intensity. Itinerant ministers like George Whitefield attracted massive crowds that greeted their direct, forceful eloquence with weeping and swooning. "It seemed as if all the World were growing Religious," Benjamin Franklin recalled, "so that one could not walk thro' the Town in an Evening without Hearing Psalms sung in different Families of every Street."[10] In all kinds of public spaces, the voices of women and the poor, American Indians and African Americans, were heard testifying to the presence of the Spirit.[11]

Almost as quickly as it had blossomed, though, the Awakening had withered and died. Revisiting the familiar story, Beecher saw a single case as the turning point. In the early 1740s, the young minister James Davenport had created a scandal when he left his church in New Haven to pursue an itinerant career. Davenport traveled through Connecticut and Massachusetts, preaching to excited crowds. (Among his many converts, he could count a young Mohegan Indian named Samson Occom.) Davenport's performances included a 1743 bonfire in New London, where the learned works of Congregationalist ministers were consigned to the flames, and he infuriated senior clergymen by publicly pronouncing judgments on the state of their souls—the most heinous kind of evil speaking. Leading the counter-attack, the Reverend Charles Chauncy of Boston laid aside such terms as "awakening" and "revival." He used the keyword *enthusiasm*.

In "Enthusiasm Described and Caution'd Against" (1742), Chauncy began by acknowledging that "the word, from it's Etymology, carries in it a good meaning, as signifying *inspiration from* GOD." The prophets of the Old Testament were enthusiasts in their way, oracles moved by the Holy Spirit. "But the word," Chauncy continued, "is more commonly used in a bad sense, as intending an *imaginary,* not a *real,* inspiration."

In this modern usage, enthusiasm signified a kind of disease, "a bad temperament of the blood and spirits" that produced "a sort of madness."[12] The disorder, according to Chauncy, threatened to corrupt the most cherished institutions of eighteenth-century society. Property would be redistributed. The bonds of marriage would be loosened.[13] The laws of God themselves would become uncertain, as factions made their irreconcilable appeals to divine authority. The enthusiasts of Chauncy's day were "blasphemers of God, and open disturbers of the peace," throwing church and state into confusion.[14]

The minister's task was to diagnose this condition and to inoculate his congregation against its malign power. What made preachers like Davenport so dangerous, Chauncy wrote in his *Seasonable Thoughts on the State of Religion in New England* (1743), was that they "rather aimed at putting [the people's] Passions into a Ferment, than filling them with such a *reasonable* Solicitude, as is the Effect of a just Exhibition of the Truths of God to their Understandings."[15] As Ann Taves shows, Chauncy's sermons brought him into an intellectual alliance that looks unfamiliar to those of us who have come to think of reason as the antagonist of religion: The Old Light Congregationalist found himself in the company of John Locke and David Hume, using the language of modern science to explain the beastly convulsions and dehumanized speech of the enthusiasts.[16] But Chauncy's campaign against Davenport was also something more than a debate about the relation between faith and passion. Enthusiasm, as Chauncy imagined it, upset the proper distribution of goods and power by redefining the conditions of public address.

A reasonable Christianity, the minister argued, would speak a disciplined language. A well-governed church would restrain the tongue. In making these claims, Chauncy showed a special concern for the common people's reception of enthusiastic address. The appearance of inspiration, he said, "gains [enthusiasts] a great reputation among the populace; who . . . commonly harken to, and revere their dictates, as tho' they really were, as they pretend, immediately communicated to them from the DIVINE SPIRIT."[17] Enthusiasm, according to Chauncy, severed manner from matter, form from content. The assent of the audience had little to do with the truth of the speaker's doctrines; it was summoned through the "mighty Energy" of his performance.[18] Enthusiasm was a malign paradox, self-aggrandizement in the form of self-abnegation. "Men may make an appearance, as if they were acted by the SPIRIT, when, all the while, they have no other view . . . but to serve themselves."[19] The apostles of enthusiasm gained the power to summon and command a faction of the public precisely by seeming to yield all control, and Chauncy did his best restore them to a subjectivity that could be held accountable for its errors.

The analysis of enthusiasm was carried one step further, perhaps, by Chauncy's colleague Benjamin Doolittle. Doolittle's "Enquiry into Enthusiasm" (1743), also published in the wake of Davenport's visit to Boston, shared many of the views of the other antirevivalist ministers. It diagnosed enthusiasm as a disorder that turned the public against the institutions of church and state. It linked the delusion to the passions and the sensations of the body, especially the female body, tracing its origins to the "curse" of Eve. It prescribed the curative power of reason. But Doolittle's inquiry took him beyond this received wisdom. Pondering its long history, from Biblical times down to the colonial present, he allowed himself to admit that enthusiasm was a shifting, uncertain thing—"such a *Proteus,* that Satan can put it into all Manner of Shapes."[20] Enthusiasm was not a stable object of analysis; it took on the appearance of consistency only through the process of its diagnosis and suppression.

Doolittle understood, too, that the danger could not be explained in terms of the social stratifications that had organized the world before the utterance of enthusiastic speech. Enthusiasts, he remarked, "value not high nor low rich nor poor, or any Person whatever, but such as entertain, or are favourable to their Enthusiasm." The circularity in these phrases—enthusiasts are drawn to enthusiasm—suggests the minister's inability to identify the social formation called together by enthusiastic performance. There seems to be no name for it. According to Doolittle, preachers like Davenport did not simply mobilize the lower classes against the wealthy and the powerful. They created unpredictable new factions. Once kindled, enthusiasm "*suddenly* takes with [men], and like *Wild-Fire diffuses* itself every where."[21] This menacing mode of speech, in Doolittle's analysis, was stripped of virtually all its doctrinal and social content. Enthusiasm was factionalizing performativity, purified.

As for the evil speaker James Davenport, he was soon apprehended and censured by the colonial assembly at Hartford. In 1744 he published his "Confession and Retraction." In this sad document, the most radical of the New England evangelicals humbled himself before the power of the orthodox ministry. One by one, he recanted his errors. Under the influence of a fever and a "false spirit," he confessed, he had fallen into enthusiasm. He had emboldened the common people to overstep the bounds of their proper authority, *"encouraging private Persons to a ministerial and authoritative Kind or Method of exhorting."* He had compromised the dignity of his office by *"Singing with others in the Streets."* He had presumed to accuse some ministers of being unconverted enemies of God, "making my private Judgment, the Ground of public Actions." Worst of all, Davenport feared that his transgressions had become "great Blemishes to the Work of God."[22] Intending to contribute to the Awakening, he had unwittingly tainted the New Lights by turning revivals into spectacles of delusion and perversion.

This was Beecher's account as well. "In the indiscretion of Davenport may be traced not only the suspension of the revival in this city [Boston] 80 years ago, when he came here and began to denounce the ministers as unconverted men; but those indelible prejudices against revivals which made old Calvinists formal, Semi-calvinists Arminians, Arminians Unitarians, and Unitarians Universalists." As Beecher saw it, Davenport's scandalous performances had led the ministry and the public to seek a cool, rational style of worship. Moderates like Edwards, Beecher's hero, struggled to dissociate themselves from enthusiasm, and they never fully recovered from the scandal. In time, the reaction against Davenport had led to "the great Eastern defection"—the disorder of factional strife, the triumph of a bloodless formalism, and the fall of the established churches.[23]

Thus the problem for the evangelicals on the eve of the Second Great Awakening, as Beecher understood it, was to promote the renewal of faith while avoiding the scandal of enthusiasm. His solution was a series of informal regulations for the movement. Ministers, Beecher proposed, should balance their threats of divine punishment with assurances of Christian mercy, since "the human mind is *more* affected by kindness than by severity." They should not be too quick or too harsh in their judgments of the unconverted; evil speaking against others was itself a reprehensible sin. And they should guard against an overzealous public address, which tended to provoke imitation among men and women who lacked the proper "moral power." The wrong kind of preaching, full of fire and condemnation, was likely to be taken up by false prophets for their own self-promotion, or by followers who were unable to distinguish "harsh and provoking epithets" from the mild truths of the gospels.[24] The specter of Davenport might be lurking anywhere.

The Gender of Authority

As he developed his evangelical program, Beecher gave special attention to the problem of "female prayer in promiscuous assemblies." Promoted by the New School preachers, this spectacle was grotesque and unnatural to Beecher's eyes. It violated the standards of feminine virtue that he saw as essential to social order. "There *is* generally, and *should be* always, in the female character, a softness and delicacy of feeling which shrinks from the notoriety of a public performance. It is the guard of female virtue, and invaluable in its soothing influence on man; and a greater evil, next to the loss of conscience and chastity, could not befall the female sex or the community at large, than to disrobe the female mind of those ornaments of sensibility, and clothe it with the rough texture of masculine fibre."[25] This obscene performance, as Beecher imagined it, stripped a woman of her proper "ornaments," only to expose an unwelcome surprise—the "rough texture" of a man.

Many others shared Beecher's sense of panic. An 1833 polemic reported, with alarm, that it had become common "for elderly women to deliver, in an excited and incoherent manner, an exhortation to the people"; the "feverish and unnatural state of feeling" that led such women to their "public labors" was a "shame," "to be deplored." For the Presbyterian who wrote these lines, the image of the ranting exhorter became the other against which a model of femininity—"discreet, good keepers at home, teachers of good things"—could be defined. As the churches suppressed women's public religious performances, associated with "strong fanatical impulses" and an "absence of scriptural knowledge," they circumscribed the "range of appropriate female duties."[26]

The conservatives in the older denominations had no monopoly on this kind of prudery. In a cultural history of American women's preaching, Catherine A. Brekus describes the "sweeping backlash that took place during the 1830s and 1840s."[27] Evangelical sects like the Methodists and Baptists were building large congregations, acquiring new kinds of respectability, prestige, and social power. In the process, they began to abandon some of the controversial practices of their earlier, more freewheeling days. "Female preachers were shunned as enthusiasts and forced out of the pulpit," Brekus writes. "Unlike men, they lacked institutional authority, and they had been allowed to preach only because individual clergymen accepted their claims to divine inspiration."[28] Once encouraged by the ministry, itinerants like Sally Thompson and Elleanor Knight were now being persecuted by the churches. The source of their authority, the claim of access to the voice of God, was discredited, and many who presumed to speak in public found themselves cast out and shamed.

Although they made various arguments with reference to scripture and church history, both sides in the conflict over women's evangelism also understood it as a conflict over access to publicity itself. Thus the disgraced exhorter Knight described her persecution as the painful suppression of her voice: "There is no worse oppression [than] to press the word of the Lord within, and hinder those from speaking that long to seek."[29] According to her narrative, published in 1839, Knight was the daughter of a Justice of the Peace from Cranston, Rhode Island. When she was nineteen, she married the unfortunate Harding Knight, Jr., who soon fell into "intemperate habits."[30] Seeking consolation in religion, and inspired by the example of the female preacher Sarah Thornton, Elleanor Knight began a brief career as an itinerant exhorter. On a few occasions, she preached from the gospels. These performances, Knight recalled, had reclaimed souls for Christ. But they had also brought infamy on her name.

Recounting her "Trials and Labours," Knight attempted to defend herself against those who condemned her as a fallen woman and a fanatic. "Reports were put in circulation concerning me, and I felt the necessity more and more of trying to defend my character by writing." The phrase "Read and then judge" was printed across the title page of Knight's text. Accused of irrational, incendiary speech, she sought to distance herself from fanaticism by adopting a cool and moderate tone. "I thought it was best to let the world know the truth, and then they would be prepared to judge for themselves."[31] The task of the narrative, it becomes clear, is to demonstrate the author's conformity to certain standards of reasonableness and self-effacement. She wants the public to understand that hers is a disciplined faith.

As part of her self-exonerating narrative, Knight defines herself explicitly against the arrogance and delusion of enthusiasm: "[I] met with those strange brethren; about six of them had long beards; they walked along the broad aisle and holla'd very loud; they jumped and stamped and shook terribly. I thought *I* saw the effects at this time of not trying the spirits by the word of God. It appeared according to the best information I could gain that those brethren were truly converted to God, but they had embraced the idea that they might follow every impulse of feeling." Knight went on to diagnose the disorder that had taken hold of these wayward souls: "They manifested but little love or charity for others. They had run into enthusiasm."[32]

Thus Knight showed that she could speak the language of true religion, distinguishing her own sense of a Christian calling from the enthusiasm of the "strange brethren." She went on to link the struggle of women preachers to antislavery and other progressive causes: "while we try to free the slaves, do not try to hold your wives and sisters in bondage."[33] If Knight had been condemned because she had violated the rationalist norms of true religion, then perhaps she might reclaim some legitimacy by conforming her discourse to those norms.

Knight was the victim of gossip and ridicule, but in other cases the condemnation of female preachers took on the formal character of a legal ritual—a hearing, a trial, an excommunication. In 1830, Sally Thompson appeared before a Select Committee of the Methodist Episcopal Church in Cherry-Valley, Massachusetts, on charges of insubordination, immorality, and evil speaking. The charge of insubordination concerned her organization of public meetings without the endorsement of church leaders. The immorality in question was lying to them about her evangelical labors. Her evil speech consisted of a series of judgments uttered against her adversaries: she was accused of calling one preacher "a spy," another "a snake in the grass," and a third "an enemy to the work of God."[34]

According to the trial report that was published in Thompson's name, she had begun her career as an evangelist in Boston, where she had the support of her husband and of respected ministers. She looked to the example of early Methodists like Mary Bosanquet Fletcher, whose biography, by Henry Moore, was reprinted in several American editions in the early nineteenth century. Thompson's travels took her into New York State and then to Cherry-Valley, where she became the subject of controversy among the clergy. There were some who encouraged Thompson to speak at meetings, and even to preach from the gospels, but there were others who felt that she was a dangerous character. As one circuit preacher put it, she was "useful in moving in her proper sphere; he thought that she moved in too large a sphere."[35]

In a classic sermon on evil speaking, well known to American Methodists, John Wesley defined his topic this way: "evil speaking is nether more nor less, than speaking evil of an absent person."[36] The sin went by such names as back-biting, tale-telling, and whispering. It might be committed with a malicious heart, or it might be performed out of a false sense of obligation. It might be lies, or it might be the truth. The crucial thing was that evil speakers broke the Christian's commitments to humility and neighborly love, presuming to judge others when their duty was to hold their tongues.

To Wesley, evil speaking was an "extremely common" sin, committed "among all orders and degrees of men."[37] For the American evangelicals of the 1830s, though, the offense came especially to be associated with public utterances of judgment, rather than private gossip, and above all with the spiritual pride of unlettered enthusiasts. Evil speaking, the minister Horatio Wood told his congregation in 1844, was committed out of "ignorance,—a want of that cultivation of mind and of that general intelligence, which enlarge the intellect and elevate it above trifles."[38] "Christians! You would convert the world," thundered the Methodist circuit-rider Israel Chamberlayne. "You invoke the *power* of religion. You do well; for an unbridled tongue makes loud proof that you need it."[39]

Chamberlayne was a hardline evangelical who wanted to exclude from church membership anyone who had not experienced a spiritual conversion. His pamphlet, *Evil Speaking, or, A Bridle for the Unbridled Tongue* (1849) may be the antebellum ministry's most vehement discourse against improper speech. It is certainly one of the most elaborate and searching. For Chamberlayne, the rising menace of evil speaking provoked a consideration of the very nature of human language. "Speech was the crowning gift of all the other gifts of God to man," he wrote in his opening pages. "Unperverted by sin, it was to have been the endlessly diversified medium and instrument of the highest social happiness." In a fallen world, however, language was corrupted, becoming an instrument of deception and violence: "this perverted faculty wears the hellish honor of having achieved the enthrallment and ruin of our race." The unbridled tongue was the devil's plaything.[40]

Not content to scold the evil speakers, Chamberlayne dramatized their appearance at the supreme tribunal of judgment, foretelling their damnation: "You are preparing to meet [the divine Judge], not by demeaning yourself as a penitent and humble subject of the law, but by a bold infraction of it, in the condemnation of your fellow subjects; thus, practically, denouncing, as unjust, not only the law itself, but the Lawgiver and the Judge."[41] Here, evil speaking was recast as the violation of a divinely constituted legal order. The offender was one who set herself above the law, whose judgments against her fellow subjects were implicit affronts to the authority of God himself. The blessing of speech had become a curse.

Publicly tried for this abominable crime, Sally Thompson was acquitted by the Select Committee in Cherry-Valley, but the verdict was reviewed by a Quarterly Conference of Methodist leaders in Worcester and, after a meeting behind closed doors, the evil speaker was excommunicated. Disgraced, Thompson took her case, in the form of a trial report, to the court of public opinion. "In addressing myself to the public, I do it not with the spirit of rebellion or censure," she assured her readers. "I do it not for self aggrandizement, but that the world may know that I do not wish to screen my conduct from the public eye."[42] Thompson reproduced the minutes of the Select Committee meeting that had exonerated her, and she included letters from respected ministers who testified to her good character. She hoped that readers would recognize her innocence.

Thompson's central theme, however, was that she had nothing to hide. "My whole course has been open to the world," she wrote. "I have studied no concealment, and have enveloped my conduct in no mystery.

Could I under these circumstances say that I had done wrong?"[43] To demonstrate her innocence, in short, Thompson insisted on the publicity of her performances. There was some pathos, or it may have been irony, in her repeated declarations of her own visibility. After all, it was precisely her full exposure to public view that seemed most to disturb her fellow evangelicals. Thus the author and reformer Catherine Williams recorded her disgust at the spectacle of Thompson's preaching: "Her mouth, usually of sweet and placid expression, from her efforts to speak out loud, was absolutely disfigured."[44] Public address, as Williams described it, had turned Thompson's pleasant mouth into a hideous, distorted organ. In the end, the evil speaker had really been condemned for the offense of publicity itself.

The Westford Circuit's reply to Thompson's pamphlet was prepared by the Reverend Matteson Baker. Right away, the author apologized for the unpleasant work that had fallen to him. He assured his readers that he would have preferred to say nothing at all about the case. "Were the limits of Westford circuit the bounds of Mrs. Thompson's singular movement, or the misleading errors of her pamphlet, we should have been spared the small pains . . . of giving the public an answer." It would have been best for everyone, Baker suggested, if the whole affair had been kept within the familiar confines of the local community. But Thompson's self-vindicating appeal was freely circulating, "tending to give a wrong bias to the public mind abroad, and to lead those in want of better information, into the peculiar evils of disaffection, and perhaps ruin." In Baker's account, Thompson's pamphlet was carrying on the verbal mischief that her preaching and evil speaking had begun. "She has labored to disaffect the minds of persons towards, not only the ministry, but the general government of the *Methodist Episcopal Church,* by crying out, as . . . other factious parties have done, against its *Episcopacy.*" The end result would be the corruption of her followers' eternal souls and a factional struggle for power in the present. Baker did what he could to point out the distortions in her story and to discredit her authority.[45]

In reaching its verdict against Sally Thompson, Brekus suggests, "the Methodist hierarchy decided that female preaching was unacceptable under any circumstances." Imposing "restrictions on [women's] religious speech," the churches of the 1830s consigned women to a private world.[46] From this point of view, the persecution of female evangelism can appear to be just one link in a larger chain. The ideology of the nineteenth-century Republic, according to Mary P. Ryan, "held that the female sex embodied those uncurbed human passions that inevitably subverted the self-control and rationality required of citizens." Such a view "inscribed gender differences on the public as a principle of exclusion."[47] Excluding a class of subjects whose very bodies were supposed to make them incapable of reasonable deliberation, the suppression of enthusiasm reinforced the line between "women's proper place" and the public arena of rational exchange.

Yet this story is incomplete. It is true that, in the nineteenth century, as in the eighteenth, enthusiasm was identified with the dissolution of the family and the unnatural stimulation of the passions. Old Lights like Chauncy had recoiled from the wild voices and contorted bodies of the enthusiasts—"bitter *Shriekings* and *Screamings; Convulsion-like Tremblings* and *Agitations, Strugglings* and *Tumblings,* which, in some Instances, have been attended with Indecencies I shan't mention."[48] The orthodox ministry posed a stark choice between fanaticism and reason, the seduction of the passions and the discipline of the mind. Such, at least, were the terms (however distorted) in which Lyman Beecher and his colleagues recollected the enthusiasm crisis of the First Great Awakening. But the aim of their reform project was precisely to prevent their own era from confronting the same impossible choice. They meant to develop a style of worship that would chart a middle way between an incendiary enthusiasm and a soul-numbing rationality.

By the 1830s, the evangelicals had come to control much of the infrastructure of public address in the United States—printing presses, pulpits, meeting places—and they could simply refuse to grant access to the unruly. At the same time, they required the elaborate performances of self-discipline even by those who were given the speaker's privilege. Thus the Reverend Matteson Baker, in attacking Sally Thompson on behalf of the Methodist episcopacy, promised that he had "studiously endeavored to avoid all unnecessary and extravagant remarks, as tending more to irritate than to convince."[49] The task was not just to exclude an enthusiast from public address; it was also to repudiate the evil speaker within—to refine and to domesticate the practice of exhortation. And a special kind of moral persuasion, associated with women's voices, would be essential to the endeavor.

Indeed, the same movement that suppressed women's preaching and exhortation—sometimes, as in the case of Catherine Williams, the same writers who condemned the likes of Sally Thompson—also created a vast, unprecedented arena for women's public address. To be sure, according to the ideology of polite evangelism, the "domestic" was the "sphere" where "female graces chiefly shine," but for its persuasive power and its very sense of a common purpose, the movement depended on the medium of print and on the creation of far-reaching networks of transmission and circulation.[50] The evangelical reformers' appeals to the personal conscience and the private sphere, in other words, were carried out by way of an aggressive intervention in the field of public address.

The very notion of the private, Elizabeth Dillon argues, "is constructed in the print public sphere," as the cherished fantasy of domesticity is staged, over and over again, for reading publics.[51] The evangelical press, with its religious and educational literature, its temperance and reform pamphlets, and its popular sentimental novels, made women authors some of the most renowned public figures of the antebellum decades. There was a good deal of exclusion, but there was also a highly nuanced kind of regulation. The product was a disciplined mode of persuasive writing which strategically disavowed its claim to publicity and, in the process, acquired a peculiar sort of power.

Influence, or The Higher Law at Home

The name for the kind of power attributed to women's speech was *influence*. An 1829 article, "Christian Females Exhorted to Use their Utmost Influence in Favor of Christianity," made the difference perfectly clear: "this influence is possessed by females, and was doubtless bestowed upon them by a wise and benevolent God, as a counterpoise to that authority with which He has invested men."[52] Drawing this distinction, the evangelical press, intimately connected to a rapidly expanding women's literature of domestic life, established one of the antebellum period's most cherished commonplaces. It expressed the conception of gendered power that Ann Douglas calls the "doctrine of influence": men's rational authority, exercised in public, was to be balanced by "the cloistered and untested virtues of the non-participant."[53]

The regulation of enthusiasm played a special part in the evangelical movement's public creation of privacy. Everywhere in sentimental culture, men's power in government and business was said to be softened by the humanizing influence of their wives and mothers at home. In the polemics against women's preaching and exhortation, though, the proper exercise of influence was defined against a kind of speech whose publicity itself monstrously disfigured the feminine subject. As Beecher saw it, women's "soothing influence on man" was inseparable from the "softness and delicacy of feeling which shrinks from the notoriety of a public performance." If the opposition between influence and *authority* could elsewhere seem to exclude women from public address altogether, this second distinction, between influence and *enthusiasm,* defined the varieties of public address in which women might engage. And it did so, ingeniously, by disguising them as something other than public address. Through the restraint of the grotesquely embodied, masculinized exhorter, the evangelical press introduced a mode of mass-mediated persuasion that would seem to have been performed in intimate seclusion.

No one represented the paradox of domestic influence in print better than the daughter of Lyman Beecher who became the most famous American author of the nineteenth century, Harriet Beecher Stowe. A passage from her best-loved novel, *Uncle Tom's Cabin,* is often cited as a parable of the doctrine of influence. In this familiar scene, an Ohio senator comes home. A business-friendly pragmatist who hopes to preserve the peace between North and South, he has just convinced the legislature to pass a fugitive slave law, providing for the re-enslavement of runaways who are captured in the free states. When his wife learns the news, she scolds him for facilitating a wicked compromise. Her protest, as Gregg D. Crane has argued, express the "clear conflict between the positive law of the state and the ethical commands discerned by the moral sense."[54] "My dear," the Senator says, "let me reason with you." "I hate reasoning," is Mrs. Bird's reply.[55]

The Birds' conversation is interrupted by a commotion in the kitchen. The runaway Eliza, traveling with her young son, has come to seek refuge at their house. The senator and his wife listen to the fugitive's terrible story, and Mrs. Bird's eyes well up with tears. Here, the cold rationality of the political game meets the warm, embodied reality of human suffering. It is as if Mrs. Bird has summoned Eliza to expose the emptiness of her husband's arguments. An hour earlier, the abstract "idea of a fugitive," for the senator, "was only an idea of the letters that spell the word"; now, "the magic of the real presence of distress" is worked on him (77). The man of public authority has abandoned the logic of political compromise and market negotiation. The moral power of women's appeal to the sympathetic heart, exercised in the private space of the kitchen, has made him weep with regret and give his money away in charity. He donates ten dollars to Eliza's cause and, in a secret act of subversion against the law he helped to establish, arranges her fugitive passage north.

On one hand, Stowe's story clearly segregates influence from authority along a conventional, gendered boundary: the moral persuasion exercised by women at home is distinguished from the political power of the men who make the laws. As Brook Thomas suggests, the "conflict between Senator and Mrs. Bird" marks the distinction between "the calculating, rational, public world of business presided over by men" and "the private realm where moral values and religion were taught [by women]."[56] The ideology of separate spheres is firmly in place. On the other hand, though, the same story plays out a fantasy of the transformative capacities of sentimental discourse itself—a discourse whose true audience, as Stowe knew very well, was a reading public.

The development of a mode of nonrational but persuasive public address that would be received as if it had been spoken in private—this is one of the signature achievements of evangelical literature, and *Uncle Tom's Cabin* is one of its monuments. Behind it, as the animating impulse of this mode of address, was a double retreat, a differentiation from two forms of public performance. The first was the rational argumentation associated with the critical public sphere. Sentimental influence made no pretension to the kind of impersonal, bloodless reason that characterized learned debate. For this reason, among others, it could seem to express a feminine modesty. "Her husband and her children were her entire world," Stowe writes of Mrs. Bird, "and in these she ruled more by entreaty and persuasion than by command or argument"

(68). At the same time, though, sentimentalism took the side of influence against authority out of a tacit recognition that deliberative reason had forfeited its prestige. Pervaded by the interests of a ruthless capitalism, the public sphere had entered the era of its disintegration. The exercise of deliberation among learned elites was either corrupt or obsolete: "I hate reasoning."

This moral critique of a disintegrating public sphere received one of its most extreme formulations in the autobiography of another, less famous evangelical, Zilpha Elaw. Born near Philadelphia to a free family of color, Elaw answered the call to preach and pursued a remarkable transatlantic career of itinerant evangelism that took her throughout the Northern states, into the plantations of the South, and eventually to England, where she published her *Memoirs* in 1846. Elaw's claims to a divine authority explicitly invoked legal discourses of evidence and rationality; to authenticate her vision of an angel, she wrote, "Seldom do the juries of our criminal courts establish their verdicts on evidence equally abundant and express." As for the men who attempted to silence and discredit her, she denounced them as the agents of the devil: "The principalities and powers of evil spirits. . . , by blinding and infatuating the sons of men, inspired them with a hostile zeal against me." Perhaps no nineteenth-century American preacher made a more forceful declaration of her own right to public address, in opposition to such entrenched patterns of exclusion.[57]

Yet Elaw introduced her *Memoirs,* curiously, with a sustained attack on the print public sphere: "Take heed what you read: as a tree of knowledge, both good and evil, is the press; it ofttimes teems with rabid poisons, putting darkness for light, and light for darkness; extolling earthly grandeur and honour, spurious valour and heroism; fixing reputation and character on a false basis; and frequently appearing as the panegyrist of the rankest principles, and the basest vices." Thus Elaw's story, published in pamphlet form and circulated on both sides of the Atlantic, began by announcing its own suspicion of "the press." It aligned itself with an evangelical counterpublic which stood in opposition to a secularized, corrupt public sphere: "Above all, shun an infidel, obscene or disloyal newspaper press." And it addressed its readers not as a mass public of strangers but as an intimate circle of "Dear Friends," joined together in prayer.[58]

In taking up the posture of private address, Elaw, a forceful advocate of women's right to speak the truth in public, cannily negotiates with the logic of her own exclusion. For the second kind of performance from which even Stowe's brand of sentimental literature withdrew was that of the grotesquely embodied (gendered, racialized) public exhorter. As any reader knows, there is a great deal of religious speech by unordained characters in *Uncle Tom's Cabin*. Little Eva becomes the "little evangelist": Jesus, she tells the slave girl Topsy, "will help you to be good; and you can go to Heaven at last, and be an angel forever, just as much as if you were white" (246). Tom carries the gospel to others in bondage: "The Lord hasn't called us to wrath. We must suffer, and wait his time" (344). Mrs. Bird exhorts to her husband and, occasionally, seems almost to pronounce a curse against the state: "It's a shameful, wicked, abominable law, and I'll break it, for one, the first time I get a chance" (69).

Indeed, *Uncle Tom's Cabin* has been interpreted as a fantasy about the democratic distribution of religious authority to the subjugated and the disenfranchised—"a utopian vision in which individuals who share responsibility for one another's moral and religious well-being have superseded professional preachers."[59] But this vision remains utopian, this democratizing tendency is everywhere contained, because of the novel's organizing distinction between the public and the private. The novel explores several types of black expression and stages various models of black resistance, but there is no one like Zilpha Elaw in its pages. As for Mrs. Bird, she is surely no enthusiast—her exhortations are spoken in the kitchen, addressed to her husband and infused with the memory of her lost child. The audience of influence, in *Uncle Tom's Cabin*, is never a crowd of strangers; it is always a circle of intimates.

And in these versions of private exhortation or "entreaty," Stowe identified a model for her own address to readers. A number of commentators, in the antebellum period and in recent scholarship, have remarked that Stowe's authorial voice sometimes takes on the cadences of the jeremiad, but her own afterword to the novel asked the public to imagine the scene of reading as a private one. Referring to the serial publication of *Uncle Tom's Cabin* in the *National Era*, Stowe writes:

> The "Author of Uncle Tom's Cabin" must now take leave of a wide circle of friends, whose faces she has never seen, but whose sympathies, coming to her from afar, have stimulated and cheered her in her work.
>
> The thought of the pleasant family circles that she has been meeting in spirit weekly has been a constant refreshment to her, and she cannot leave them without a farewell.
>
> In particular, the dear little children who have followed her story have her warmest love. Dear children, . . .[60]

As the passage develops, it defines the relation between author and audience as one of increasing closeness. The "wide circle of friends" becomes "pleasant family circles," which become, in turn, so many "dear little children." Elsewhere, Stowe may have adopted the authoritative voice of the minister, or even the enthusiastic one of the exhorter. Here, as Dawn Coleman observes, the author "retreats . . . to the feminine authority of maternal affection."[61] Her afterword is an exercise in domestication.

For Elleanor Knight, exhortation meant, first of all, the opportunity to address a public of strangers. She insisted on stepping out of the private sphere to which the norms of polite religion would have confined her, and she made the difference explicit: "I felt it was my duty to talk to the church as well as the children, and to the world as well as the church."[62] For Stowe, by contrast, scenes of private persuasion were the ideal—the very conception of the literary medium that *Uncle Tom's Cabin* sought to transmit. Publication gave authors like Stowe (and perhaps Elaw, too) the freedom to adopt a range of voices, to enact a variety of performances, but the premise of this freedom was that the page was a private space. Discovering its own identity in contrast to the monstrous figure of the exhorter, sentimentalism instructed a reading public to imagine itself not as a crowd, not even as a public, but as so many discrete persons, each a private heart to be watched over and cultivated towards right feeling. In the process, the evangelical movement devised a peculiar new conception of literature: the circulating text, once the paradigmatic medium of address and critique in the public sphere, became a zone of private entreaty and moral persuasion. Casting out the enthusiasts, the literature of sentiment domesticated print.

The disavowal of public exhortation, though, was a peculiarly productive and legitimating kind of repression. It enabled the evangelicals
to define their interventions in the public sphere, including their invocations of higher law, as literary and pedagogical endeavors to redeem
(not to rend) the national community, one conscience at a time. In *Uncle
Tom's Cabin,* the rationalist public sphere of civil society has been
eclipsed. The morally abhorrent slave code is so neatly aligned with the
logic of private property that the economic interests of private citizens
have lost their critical distance from the oppressive policies of the state.
The most vital idiom of critique is now the sentimental, with its appeal to
the heart. Thus the gendered organization of the world into public and
private spheres, as Stowe represents it, becomes the premise not for the
silencing of women's voices but for their triumph over a fallen, masculine
reason. This was the subversive lesson of the doctrine of influence: Separate from the state, and therefore able to measure the law's legitimacy
against its own, nonlegal standards of justice, a domesticated religious
sentiment rises to displace critical reason from its place of privilege in
the public sphere.

CHAPTER 5

The Curse of Slavery

S towe's tendency to recast public address as private influence in *Uncle Tom's Cabin* might be measured against the militant religious and political speech that shakes the South in another antislavery novel from the same period. This book does not shy away from the intensities of public exhortation. The African American lay preacher who is martyred in its pages does not talk, as Uncle Tom does, in the idiom of humble entreaty. He is a lonely fanatic, haunting the swamps—"there was no recurrence of every-day and prosaic ideas to check the current of enthusiasm"—and he rants with an apocalyptic fury.[1] "The Lord is against this nation!" he shouts. "The Lord shall utter his voice from Jerusalem, and the heavens and earth shall shake! In that day I will cause the sun to go down at noon, and darken the whole earth! And I will turn your feasts into mourning, and your songs into lamentation!"[2] A mixed crowd of slaveholders and the enslaved, petty sinners and pious folk, listens to these words with a growing terror. Some hear the voice of delusion, but others recognize a harsh, old-fashioned justice. Beyond their settled towns and planted fields, at the margins of the community, an insurrectionary force is gathering.

The book is *Dred: A Tale of the Great Dismal Swamp*, by Harriet Beecher Stowe. The difference between Dred's dark prophesies and

Uncle Tom's modest entreaties is remarkable. It is not just a matter of a heightened intensity, the author's growing rage against the national sin of slavery. Stowe has turned from the private scene of moral instruction to the public performance of condemnation, from the sweet whisper of influence to the thunder of the curse. She aligns herself with radical orators like David Walker, William Lloyd Garrison, and Frederick Douglass: far from conceding the disintegration of the public sphere, she attempts to recreate it as a space of prophetic resistance. "The author," Stowe writes in her preface, "felt that no apology was needed for endeavoring to do something towards revealing to the people the true character of [the system of slavery]."[3] Her reading public is not coddled into picturing itself as a circle of children. It is expected to understand itself as a sovereign national community, capable of shaping its own legal and political history.

Stowe's purpose in *Dred*, by her own account, is to judge the laws of the land against a divine standard: "God in his providence is now asking the American people, Is the system of slavery, as set forth in the American slave code, *right?*"[4] The crucial setting of *Uncle Tom's Cabin* was the auction block, where economic rationality corrodes the integrity of the family. *Dred* fixes its attention, instead, on a courtroom scene, where the speech of the judge activates the law's punishing force. Directly engaging the legal public sphere, Stowe places the exhortations of her title character in opposition to a specific kind of juridical performance. At the center of the novel, the crisis event that sets in motion its characters' destinies, is an appellate court's decision, delivered from the bench.

Stowe took her text from the North Carolina Supreme Court's opinion in *State v. Mann,* as decided by Chief Justice Thomas Ruffin in 1829. She probably chose this document, well known and much debated in the antebellum press, because, as Laura H. Korobkin notes, it crystalized "the cold-blooded, rationally approved cruelty of the South's slave law."[5] The question before the court was the criminal culpability of a white man who had viciously wounded an enslaved woman. Had he done harm to a person whose security was guarded by the laws, or had he merely damaged a piece of property? Did the shelter of the law, in other words, extend to the enslaved? The court decided that no crime had been committed. To explain why, it reflected on the nature of the master-slave relation. "The end is the profit of the master, his security, and the public safety; the subject, one doomed, in his own person and his posterity, to live without knowledge, and without capacity to make anything his own, and to toil that another may reap the fruits."[6] Under the slave codes, natural law and social customs are suspended. The logic of instrumentality, of profit and toil, governs everything. To compromise the master's absolute dominion would be to imperil the public safety.

Thanks to *State v. Mann,* Robert Cover observes, "Judge Thomas Ruffin would become the most eloquent spokesman for a doctrine of stern necessity, requiring an unflinching, conscious disregard of natural justice."[7] The mode of legal thought and speech associated with this doctrine makes no claim to the sanction of a higher law. It categorically expels such claims from the courtroom. Reproducing Ruffin's most notorious opinion, Stowe emphasizes that the judge speaks in a "passionless, clear, and deliberate" voice as he performs his own submission to the rigors of legal reasoning. "What I see, I must speak, though it go against all my feelings and all my sense of right." The only response from the assembled public is a "dead silence."[8] The contrast to the exhorting and inspiring speech of Dred, with his appeal to the vengeful heart, could hardly be more perfect.

Stowe allowed herself some creative liberty as she transformed the historical Thomas Ruffin, a staunch defender of the plantocarcy, into the humanely sensible Judge Clayton, caught between the incommensurable obligations of conscience and of law. In the process, she suppressed what most people following the legal debates over slavery would have known: that the Southerners had their own higher-law arguments for their peculiar institution. Proslavery rhetoric, in the courts and in the press, could wildly violate the norms of dispassionate reason to which Judge Clayton subjects himself. Still, Stowe's fiction was true to some aspects of elite legal culture in the antebellum period, especially in the North. *Dred* dramatizes, in its way, the final stage in the transformation of the public culture of justice between the Revolution and the Civil War.

In the early national period, the judiciary had been associated with the mystifications of priestcraft and the common law. Judges like Jesse Root had invoked an all-governing, universal justice, written upon the table of our hearts, and reformers like William Sampson and Robert

Rantoul had sought to dispel this subtle spirit by subjecting the courts to a rationalist critique. By the 1830s, in Stowe's account, the relation was perfectly inverted. The courts had become the "passionless" agents of political and economic rationality, duty-bound to enforce a slave code that made no claim to a higher justice. Abandoned by the legal profession, the invocation of divine law had been left to the opponents of legal authority, reformers who appealed to the heart and, in extreme cases, insurgents whose "wrathful denunciations" called down the vengeance of the Almighty. For Judge Clayton's sensitive son, there is no hope left in a legal career. Hearing his father describe the iron bond between slavery and the law, he renounces the profession. The straight path away from a corrupt legal system seems to be the only one open to "a Christian man."[9]

This story about the secularization of law and the spiritualization of resistance, the corruption of the public sphere and the retreat into conscience, has an attractive elegance. It harmonizes the self-understanding of the antebellum judiciary, as expressed by many of its leading intellectuals, with the protest against judicial quietism developed by such abolitionist luminaries as Stowe, Garrison, and Wendell Phillips. It describes the withering of legal formalism, from the expansive version enunciated by Christian jurists like Blackstone and Root to the restrictive one of Justices Ruffin and Shaw, helplessly constrained by statutes they sometimes claimed to despise. A compelling tale of the ruses of power, it shows how the critical force of reason could be wrested away from reformist attorneys like Sampson and Rantoul, becoming an instrument of oppression. And it explains why the evangelical abolitionists abandoned the public arena of legal struggle and turned to the Christian conscience as the court of last appeal.

Most of the stories I have been telling, in the preceding chapters, have conformed to the general contours of this narrative. In the two chapters that follow, I wish to bend its clean lines by unsettling two of the key distinctions that give it shape. The first is the opposition between the rationalism of the antebellum judiciary and the obsolescent oracularity of lawcraft. Cover is right to say that distinguished judges like Ruffin and Shaw refused to invoke higher law against the authority of the slave codes. But the defenders of slavery, in courtrooms and especially in the popular press, did not always show such restraint. In some cases, the slaveholding order was aligned with a transcendent ideal of justice, beyond the letter of the law, and the sovereign communities of Southern states, even of the nation itself, were called to reconstitute themselves through the ceremonial condemnation of antislavery offenders. The emergence of the radical abolitionists' higher law crusade responded, perhaps, to a hardening of formalism in the courts, but it also provoked a revival of oracular justice in the public sphere. It was precisely in relation to these reactionary performances that the judges in the high courts were able to position themselves as the custodians of polite reason, elaborately demonstrating their own refusal to indulge in lawcraft.

On the other side of the conflict, the abolitionists distinguished their effort to influence public sentiment from the incendiary public exhortations of insurrectionists like Dred. They took the side of humble entreaty against righteous enthusiasm, of the domestic interior against the public forum, of moral and legal reform against rebellion. As Gregg Crane puts it in a discussion of *Dred*, "Stowe's polemic of dangerous sentiment . . . is long on sentiment and short on danger." Yet the very gesture of disavowal led the abolitionists, again and again, to call the figure of the martyr before the court of public opinion. They depicted men like Dred as the limit, the reckless extremism in which they would not indulge, but their acts of repression also betrayed their affinity with the enthusiasts. Indeed, the literary regulation of the curse contributed, in subterranean ways, to the conception and augmentation of its power. Crane sees a failure of the political imagination in *Dred,* owing to the "unresolved tension between expiatory sympathy and revolutionary wrath," but the very possibility of a "sympathetic revolution," as he calls it, became conceivable as a fantasy about the transformative power of the higher law's public invocation.[10] In time, even those works of martyr literature that repudiated violence and enthusiasm would find a militant reception. Such were the afterlives of the oracles and the martyrs in the crisis years of the struggle over slavery. This chapter traces them in a Virginia trial report and in an abolitionist poem whose speaker promised not to curse.

The Trials of Nat Turner

As antebellum readers would easily have recognized, Stowe's source for the character of Dred was Nat Turner, the exhorter who helped to organize the Southampton, Virginia, slave rebellion of 1831. The uprising has been called "the largest and most consequential act of slave resistance in American history."[11] Speaking from another point of view, Governor John Floyd of Virginia would refer, instead, to the collective trauma endured by the slaveholders—a "melancholy subject which has filled the country with affliction, and one of the fairest counties in the Commonwealth with mourning."[12] Turner and his followers killed more than fifty whites, and in the weeks that followed, as violence swept across the South, untold numbers of enslaved and free blacks were put to death, tortured, and otherwise mortified. The rebellion brought the half-submerged violence of slavery into the open, provoked a new set of repressive laws, and widened the divide between North and South. It also raised deep questions about language and power. According to an apocryphal account by William Wells Brown, Turner made these exhortations to the rebels on the eve of the uprising: "Remember, ours . . . is a *struggle for freedom*. Ours must be deeds, not words."[13]

The Southampton rebellion quickly became the topic of speeches and debates. It gave rise to a tradition of folk tales and long-form literary adaptations ranging from *Dred* to William Styron's controversial novel about Turner in 1967.[14] The most fascinating and contested version, though, is still the pamphlet entitled *The Confessions of Nat Turner,* composed by the Virginia lawyer Thomas Ruffin Gray and first published a few days after Turner was put to death, in November of 1831. Now a canonical text for studies of American history and literature, reprinted in multiple editions and contexts, the *Confessions* continues to provoke new ways of imagining the relationship between language and power, words and deeds.[15]

Historians have tended to approach the text as a record of the Southampton rebellion, to be studied for its accuracy and detail—"a definitive account of the event, attributable to the rebel leader himself."[16] Literary critics have been preoccupied with the question of authenticity, the presence or absence of Turner's original voice.[17] In an influential reading,

Eric Sundquist synthesizes two apparently antagonistic approaches to describe the *Confessions* as a dialogic text: the pamphlet features the "disciplinary discourse" of its white editor, Thomas Ruffin Gray, but "Nat Turner's voice remains strongly present" in its pages.[18] Approaching the *Confessions* in these terms, Sundquist is able to answer the challenges posed by others who have read it as an apology for the slaveholding order, and to recognize Turner as an autobiographical subject.

But the *Confessions* belongs imperfectly to the genres of historical or autobiographical narrative.[19] The pamphlet opens with a certificate of authenticity, signed by six of the justices who heard Turner's case. It closes with what claims to be a transcript of the court's proceedings. The man who produced it had served as defense counsel for some of Turner's followers; Gray was an attorney and a minor public official who "was well aware of the power of legal forms and jargon."[20] The pamphlet, it should be clear, is a trial report. It addresses itself to the public culture of justice, and its power, whether radical or reactionary, was in its performance of the ritualized speech acts of religion and the law.

The question of the genre of the *Confessions* is more than a matter of antiquarian curiosity or theoretical nuance. It concerns the modes of address in which justice claims are made before reading publics and the modes of reception that might organize such publics behind or against the laws of states. Whereas Sundquist is concerned with the "intricate antagonism between slave's voice and master's voice," for example, a poetics of justice attends instead to another kind of dialogue—the performances of the judge and of the offender, the oracle and the curse, each suppressing his own voice so that a transcendent, impersonal authority can appear to speak through him.[21] According to the period's own fantasies about words and deeds, the crucial audience for these acts of self-negation is not the private, sympathizing reader but a normative community called together by its common assent to, or dissent from, the justice of the law.

The prosecution of Turner and the dozens of others brought to trial after the Southampton rebellion was a delicate matter. Even as authorities mobilized to put down the rebellion, they were scandalized by the outbreak of vigilante justice. Newspapers reported over a hundred African Americans dead in and around Southampton County; many more would be killed, wounded, and tortured as the violence spread to other slaveholding states.[22] A Northern witness to the scene was appalled by the torture of a black man he identified as "a Methodist minister among his brethren": "They burnt him with red hot irons—cut off his ears and nose—stabbed him, cut his hamstrings, stuck him like a hog, and at last cut off his head and spiked it on the whipping post for a spectacle and a warning to other negroes!!!"[23] Even the *Richmond Whig* reported "the slaughter of many blacks without trial and under circumstances of great barbarity." Brigadier General Richard Eppes, called in to restore order in the region, published a statement expressing "his deepest sorrow" that these "act[s] of atrocity" had "dignified the rebel and the assassin with the sanctity of martyrdom."[24]

The Virginia courts, as Stephen B. Oates argues, committed themselves to restoring the rule of law: "For the justices, all leading citizens of the county, the slave trials would demonstrate the integrity of their system, proving that in Virginia even mutinous slaves got a fair trial, that in all the heat and hysteria of the moment, the law would prevail."[25] Governor Floyd had written to the clerks of all county courts involved, requesting "the utmost accuracy . . . in the taking down and certifying the evidence."[26] In the cases of two alleged co-conspirators, the charge of treason was dropped because, according to Virginia law, only free subjects of the Commonwealth, not slaves, could be prosecuted for that high crime. In other cases, lower courts declined to try free persons of color because their jurisdiction in capital cases extended only to the enslaved. For Turner's trial, the court increased its usual number of justices and brought in armed guards to keep the defendant out of the hands of the mob.[27] The rebel was not going be dignified with the sanctity of martyrdom.

Recovered and published by the historian Henry Irving Tragle, the court's official record of the proceedings is not a verbatim transcript, but it does include the charges and the plea ("not guilty"), summaries of witness testimony, and the verdict and sentence that were pronounced. Given the high crimes in question, the evidence against the defendant was very slight.[28] Only two witnesses were called. Levi Waller, whose family had been butchered in the insurrection, testified that Turner "seemed to command the party [of rebels] to 'go ahead' when they left

[Waller's] house." Samuel Trezevant told the court that he and another justice, James W. Parker, "examined" the defendant, who "admitted he was one of the insurgents engaged in the late insurrection, and Chief among them." Trezevant ended by noting that Turner "detail[ed] a medley of incoherent and confused opinions about his communications with God."[29]

Trezevant's testimony was roughly consistent with what would be reported in the *Confessions,* but the trial record makes no mention of Thomas Ruffin Gray or his interview with Turner. Indeed, as Tragle notes, "There is no indication . . . that Trezevant, or anyone else, read any statement to the Court, but rather that Trezevant was speaking for himself and was telling the Court what he and Justice Parker learned from their own interrogation."[30] As far as the court was concerned, there was no such text as the confession of Nat Turner. In this and other ways, the document known as the *Confessions* is far from a reproduction of the official record kept by the Court of Southampton County. The substantial differences between the two texts reveal much about the widening divide between official legal procedures and the public culture of justice in the era of the curse of slavery.

Based on the testimony of Waller and Trezevant, Turner was convicted of conspiring to rebel and making insurrection. The trial record concludes with an unadorned recapitulation of the death sentence: "Therefore it is considered by the Court that [the prisoner] be taken hence to the Jail . . . therein to remain until Friday the 11th day of November instant, on which day between the hours of ten o'clock in the forenoon and four o'clock in the afternoon he is to be taken to the usual place of execution and there to be hanged by the neck until he be dead."[31] The sentence communicates the date and manner of the punishment, and little more. The key verb, "considered," suggests the dispassionate reflection involved in a routine judgment. The phrase "hanged by the neck until he be dead" appears in countless nineteenth-century capital trial records. This is the worldly discourse of enforcement, making no claim to the sanction of a higher power, no appeal to the restless souls of the dead or to the living spirit of the people.

When Turner was publicly hanged on November 11, Thomas Ruffin Gray was not there to see the spectacle. Gray has been something of an elusive figure ever since. During the interpretive controversies of the 1960s, historians had identified the man behind the *Confessions* as Captain Thomas Gray, "the son of a colonial planter-legislator" and the master of a "huge estate."[32] In 1978, Thomas C. Parramore discovered that this patriarch of the Old South had in fact died in September, 1831, weeks before Turner's trial. It was his son who published the *Confessions*. Nor had the younger Gray inherited his father's wealth or position. The reasons are unclear, but Thomas Ruffin Gray had recently fallen on hard times, losing his land and most of his fortune. His wife had died, perhaps in childbirth, and his father's will left him nothing.[33] Gray had interviewed Turner in his cell in the days leading up to the trial, then traveled to Richmond, looking for a printer who could produce 50,000 copies of the pamphlet he had prepared. He secured a copyright in Washington on November 10, and soon afterwards he found a printer in Baltimore. Before the end of the year, the *Confessions* was advertised for sale throughout the South and in such Northern papers as Philadelphia's *National Gazette and Literary Register* (December 1) and Connecticut's *Mirror* (December 17). The price was twenty-five cents.[34]

Parramore describes Gray as a broken and bitter young man, desperate for money, who may have identified, in some semi-conscious way, with his interlocutor: "On the face of the defiant black prophet, Thomas Ruffin Gray had read the mirror image of his own ravaged soul."[35] Gray's pamphlet did record his own troubled response to Turner's enthusiastic address. In a famous passage, he invited readers to imagine the prisoner in the darkness of his cell: "the expression of his fiend-like face when excited by enthusiasm, still bearing the stains of the blood of helpless innocence about him; clothed with rags and covered with chains; yet daring to raise his manacled hands to heaven, with a spirit soaring above the attributes of man; I looked on him and my blood curdled in my veins" (54–55). It is as if Gray feels himself seized by the "spirit" that makes itself heard through Turner. His reason rejects the exhorter as an enthusiast, yet his blood responds.

But if the pamphlet placed Turner into conversation with an antagonist, as part of the conventions of the trial report, it was not Gray. It was the chief judge in his case, Jeremiah Cobb. By contrast to the sentence documented in the official record, Gray's *Confessions* gives its readers a vehement oration that links worldly statutes to the law of God. "Nat Turner!" Cobb begins, "Stand up." The pamphlet stages the presence of two figures, a scene of address, and Cobb proceeds with an elaborate performance: "You have been convicted of plotting in cold blood, the indiscriminate destruction of men, of helpless women, and of infant children. The evidence before us leaves not a shadow of doubt, but that your hands were often imbrued in the blood of the innocent" (56).

Quoting from Gray's version of the confession, the judge uses Turner's words against him: "your own confession tells us that [your hands] were stained with the blood of a master; in your own language, 'too indulgent.'" As Cobb describes Turner's leadership, his power to wield a malignant verbal influence becomes the crucial issue. "I cannot but call your attention to the poor misguided wretches who have gone before you," Cobb says. "They were your bosom associates; and the blood of all cries aloud, and calls upon you, as the author of their misfortune." Again recalling Turner's confession, Cobb misrecognizes the defendant's appeal to a higher, divine justice as an excuse or a plea for mercy: "your only justification is, that you were led away by fanaticism" (56-57). The court aligns Turner with a long tradition of offenders condemned for crimes of enthusiastic violence, from William Beadle and James Yates on down the line.

Finally, the chief judge insists that the judgment he pronounces will express not his own sentiments but the impersonal conclusion of a legal process: "If this be true, from my soul I pity you; and while you have my sympathies, I am, nevertheless called upon to pass the sentence of the court." Here was the familiar distinction, at least as old as James Dana's sermon on the death of Joseph Mountain, between private sympathy and public compassion. Justice Cobb insists that he is not the author of the speech act he is about to perform. The authority of the law itself will be heard in his oracular voice. "The judgment of the court is, that you be taken hence to the jail from whence you came, thence to the place of execution, and on Friday next, between the hours of 10 A.M. and 2 P.M. be hung by the neck until you are dead! dead! dead! and may the Lord have mercy upon your soul." Cobb points to Turner as the "original contriver" of horrible crimes, but he claims that his own speech act originates elsewhere; the judge is passively "called upon" by the authority of the law (57). His conversion of Turner from the subject of crime to the object of punishment depends on his own conversion into the oracle of a law that comes from beyond himself. Once again the speaker of the confession is constituted as a subject, and the speaker of the sentence disavows his own subjectivity.

In this crucial passage, the *Confessions* invites readers to recognize the transcendent voice of the law as, in a sense, their own. Gray's preface indicates that his pamphlet "is calculated . . . to demonstrate the policy of our laws in restraint of [slaves], and to induce all those interested with their execution, as well as our citizens generally, to see that they are strictly and rigidly enforced" (41). The aim of the document, then, is to "induce" its public toward a more perfect identification with the slave codes. The ideological achievement of the *Confessions* is not, as some have suggested, that Gray's rhetoric transforms Turner from a political revolutionary into a gothic monster.[36] In fact, the text goes so far as to allow its readers—by way of the prosthetic figure of Cobb—the sentimental possibility of a private sympathy for the accused. But the *Confessions* also calls on its public to imagine itself as the moral community in whose name the death sentence is spoken. Thus the *Confessions* shows how a reactionary legal literature, in its effort to restore a sense of social cohesion after the trauma of the insurrection, might revive an oracular mode of address that had all but disappeared from the more refined legal culture of the Jacksonian period. It carried the ceremony of Turner's condemnation far beyond the Southampton courthouse, inviting a wide reading public to reconstitute itself as a sovereign community by recognizing the voice of the law as the medium of its own collective identity.

A review of the *Confessions* that first appeared in the November 25 *Richmond Enquirer* suggests how some of the pamphlet's earliest readers may have responded to its call. The piece was so widely reprinted that it became something like a standard commentary on the *Confessions*, appearing in such far-flung papers as the *New York Mercury* (December 21) and Maine's *Eastern Argus Semi-Weekly* (December 12). The anonymous reviewer begins by noting that the pamphlet "professes to give, from the Bandit's own lips, the circumstances which formed him a leader and a fanatic." The reviewer regrets that Gray's copyright prevents him from "mak[ing] copious extracts," but he proceeds to quote long passages, followed by interjections such as, "What wretches!"[37] In similar terms, the *Carolina Observer* pronounced that "the confession of Nat Turner bespeaks the character of a great fanatic."[38] In each of these reviews and many others, Turner's speaking voice was answered by the condemnation of the reader, a judgment which harmonized with and reinforced the death sentence pronounced by Justice Cobb.

With its righteous anger and its Old Testament cadences, the death sentence in the *Confessions* does much more than to authenticate or even to sensationalize the trial record for a popular audience. It transforms a rote legal procedure into a dramatic ceremony of justice. Like the old sermon-confession pamphlet, it seeks an extralegal sanction for the court's decision. Indeed, so strong was the influence of this long-standing genre, at least in New England, that an early review in the *Connecticut Mirror* mistakenly identified Gray as "the clergyman to whom [Turner] made [his confessions] while in prison."[39] But it was Justice Cobb, not Gray, who assumed the role once played by the execution sermons' oracles of God, inviting readers to assent to the verdict and the sentence, and to constitute themselves, retroactively, as the sovereign public from which the law originally emanated. In this way, the *Confessions* offered a much fuller, perhaps more satisfying record of responsibility assumed and justice executed than the one in the official trial record. It also rested on a different ideal of the relationship between language and power. Trafficking in performative magic, it exposed its audience to the curse of slavery.

"In the Sight of Many Who Reviled Us"

The Richmond reviewer did find "one defect" in the pamphlet, namely "its style." "The confession of the culprit is given, as it were, from his own lips," the reviewer remarks, "but the language is far superior to what Nat Turner could have employed—Portions of it are even eloquently and classically expressed." The style therefore "cast[s] some . . . doubt over the authenticity of the narrative, and [gives] the Bandit a character for intelligence which he does not deserve, and ought not to have received."[40] The long history of the critical interpretation of Gray's

Confessions, organized around the problem of authenticity, is already underway.[41] Perhaps, then, the very rhetorical forms and figures that the *Confessions* uses to achieve its gratifying effects may also create contradictions within its design.

Like the official trial record, the *Confessions* documents the charges of conspiracy and "insurrection," Turner's plea of "not guilty," and the testimony of two witnesses: Levi Waller and a "Col. Trezvant," here identified as the "committing Magistrate" in the case. The testimony of these witnesses, however, is not quoted. Instead, each is presented as a supplement to the printed confession. Waller's statement is described only as *"agreeabl[e] to Nat's own Confession."* Trezvant reads aloud the *"Confession as given to Mr. Gray."* In conclusion, the court asks Turner if he wishes to say anything in his own defense, and he replies, "I have made a full confession to Mr. Gray, and I have nothing more to say" (56). Unlike the official record, then, the pamphlet makes the important claim that Turner's own confession, as documented by Gray, was read aloud in the courtroom, before the judges and the assembled public, and that it was the key piece of evidence in his conviction.

In order to give a legitimate confession, Turner had to be heard as a speaking subject, as if uncoerced, in his own voice. In Virginia in 1831, the enslaved were not full legal persons, and their testimony was often excluded from court, particularly if it impugned a white defendant. An enslaved defendant's words and thoughts could be introduced, however, in the form of a confession.[42] As Saidiya Hartman argues, "the law's selective recognition of slave humanity . . . acknowledged the intentionality and agency of the slave, but only as it assumed the form of criminality."[43] In exchange for the capacity to speak, the offender was expected to acknowledge the legitimacy of the system that would judge and sentence him. Turner's voice did not "remain present"; the trial report elicited his speech as part of a ceremony of submission and judgment.[44]

Yet the speech reproduced in the pamphlet breaks with the generic conventions of the confession in significant ways. Like many other antagonists of the slave system, the Turner of the *Confessions* suggests that the slaveholding legal order rests on an unjust foundation. When Gray asks Turner, "Do you not find yourself mistaken now?", the defendant responds with a question of his own: "Was not Christ crucified?" (48). He presents himself not as a culprit but as a martyr, justified in the eyes of God. He concedes that the Virginia court has the capacity to load him down with chains and kill him, but he asserts that it does not have the legitimate authority to judge him. He awaits his redemption, and their damnation, in a world to come.

The Turner who speaks in the *Confessions* makes more than passing reference to a Christian justice. He represents himself as a prophet and an exhorter, communicating a message of divine justice that comes to him from elsewhere.[45] Indeed, Turner attends with care to the sources of his legitimacy as a leader among the enslaved. "The influence I had obtained over my fellow-servants," he claims, was acquired "not by the means of conjuring and such-like tricks," which would call attention to the conjuror, but "by the communion of the Spirit, whose revelations I often communicated." The men and women who responded to Turner's call, he insists, "believed and said my wisdom came from God" (46). Turner's style of address may have drawn from a variety of traditions, including the forms of lay preaching and conversion narratives common at revivalist meetings and some distinctly African or African American religious discourses.[46] He seems also to have had a feeling for the rituals of Anglo-American law. At times, he came close to mimicking the oracular sentence of the court, condemning his judges and appealing to an insurrectionary counterpublic.

As Turner recalls his youth, describing his acquisition of literacy and his first communications with the heavens, he tells the story of his encounter with a local white overseer and derelict, the wonderfully named Etheldred T. Brantley:

> it was plain to me that the Savior was about to lay down the yoke he had borne for the sins of men, and the great day of judgment was at hand. About this time I told these things to a white man, (Etheldred T. Brantley) on which it had a wonderful effect—and he ceased from his wickedness, and was attacked immediately with a cutaneous eruption, and blood oozed from the pores of his skin, and after praying and fasting nine days, he was healed, and the Spirit appeared to

me again, and said, as the Savior has been baptised so should we be also—and when the white people would not let us be baptised by the church, we went down into the water together, in the sight of many who reviled us, and were baptised in the Spirit—After this I rejoiced greatly, and gave thanks to God. (47)

Here, as elsewhere, the Turner of the *Confessions* explicitly disavows authorship of his visions, claiming that he is communicating a message revealed to him by God. He evacuates his own subjectivity and becomes the medium of a divine, inhuman agency. In the process, he anticipates and rewrites the script of legal justice. Like Cobb's death sentence, the revelations attributed to Turner bring about the violent transfiguration of his addressee; hearing his words, Brantley begins to bleed and to repent. The unorthodox baptism takes place before "many who reviled us," a public which, like the audience at a trial, constitutes itself through judgment. And the passage concludes with an invocation of divine sanction: Cobb's "may the Lord have mercy upon your soul" corresponds to Turner's "I rejoiced greatly, and gave thanks to God." The scene of Turner's communication, of Brantley's redemption, and of their mutual baptism might thus be understood as a restaging of the courtroom scene, but with a dramatically different effect: after the bloodletting, the white overseer and the black exhorter together are cleansed and sanctified.

Thus Judge Cobb's oracular performance of the death sentence is answered by Turner's prophetic dissent. Such a rhetorical subversion had no single, inevitable effect in the world. For some, the lines probably seemed to verify Turner's fanaticism, providing a pathological, not political, account of the rebellion. In the broader public sphere of the 1830s, however, another kind of reception was becoming available, thanks to the wide circulation of the pamphlet and to the efforts of antislavery writers like Walker and Garrison. Readers were learning to recognize the invocation of higher law as a mode of address that could summon a militant community in opposition to the statutes and customs enforced by courts. In staging Cobb's dramatic utterance of the death sentence, the *Confessions* enacted a ritual through which a reading public could reconstitute itself as the origin of legal authority, the sovereign community that gave its legitimating sanction to state violence. In composing Turner's confession as both an autobiographical narrative and a transcription of divinely inspired invocations of a higher justice, however, it had also made itself available to reception by counterpublics whose collective identities were mediated by a negative relation to the slave codes.

The incendiary power of Turner's confession, as it made its way into the public sphere, lay not only in the story he told about his life and crimes, but also in his appropriation of an oracular, nonrational and performative mode of address to a moral community. The rebellion, as Randolph Scully shows, "prompted a debate over the place of black religion, and particularly black men's religious authority, in Virginia society, and led to efforts to reconfigure the boundaries of religious legitimacy."[47] In December 1831, a few short weeks after the hanging of Nat Turner and the publication of the *Confessions,* Governor Floyd addressed the legislature on the subject of the recent violence. His administration, he promised, was devoted to restoring law and order in the Commonwealth. Though he never mentioned Turner by name, Floyd stated that "the most active . . . in stirring up the spirit of revolt, have been the negro preachers" who "have acquired great ascendancy over the minds of their fellows . . . [and] prepared them for the development of the final design."[48] A law passed in the same session commanded that "no slave, free negro or mulatto . . . shall hereafter undertake to preach, exhort or conduct, or hold any assembly or meeting, for religious or other purposes."[49] The punishment was thirty-nine lashes.

Through the winter of 1831–32, Virginia lawmakers continued to ponder the causes and consequences of the violence in Southampton, debating proposals for the gradual abolition of slavery and the expulsion of the state's black population. The slave law would survive, however, and Virginia would resort to a series of harsh measures designed to ensure the submission and immobilization of the enslaved. Cruel as these measures were, they also recognized the great capacity of black religion as a form of collective opposition to the slave system. To ensure the masters' security, it was not enough to put down the rebellion with arms, to enforce a stricter surveillance on the slaves, or to exile free blacks from the state. The voices of the exhorters had to be silenced.

Undying Sympathy

The persecution of incendiary speech, in the wake of the Southampton rebellion, did not end with the Virginia camp-meetings. It was carried into the public sphere of print, where its target was the higher law rhetoric of the rising abolitionist movement. In the years just before and after the rebellion, the abolitionists "introduced a distinct form of antislavery propaganda that," according to Jeannine DeLombard, "exploited the public's enthusiasm for legal spectatorship . . . as it appropriated the imagery of the courtroom to bring the 'crime' of slavery before the court of public opinion."[50] As their hope for victory in the courts of law withered, they were taking their case directly to the people, appealing to the justice of God.

The early 1830s were decisive years in the development of the higher law crusade. Walker had published his *Appeal* in 1829. Briefly jailed for libel, then hounded out of Baltimore, Garrison produced *A Brief Sketch of the Trial of William Lloyd Garrison,* designed "to rebut the defamation of [his] enemies."[51] In January of 1831, he brought out the first issue of the *Liberator.* In the same year, evangelicals gathered in New York, laying the groundwork for the American Anti-Slavery Society. Impatient with the halting efforts of the moderates in the colonization movement, they called for "immediate" abolition on the grounds that slavery was a "heinous crime in the sight of God."[52] Among their signature texts would be Lydia Maria Child's *Appeal in Favor of That Class of Americans, Called Africans* (1833).[53] Out in Ohio, the immediate abolitionists at Lane Seminary would stage their "rebellion" against the moderates in 1834. Three years later, the abolitionist printer Elijah Lovejoy was murdered by a mob as he tried to defend his press in Illinois.[54] By the end of the decade, the British reformer Harriet Martineau would be referring to this period in the antislavery struggle as "the martyr age of the United States."[55]

From Virginia to Massachusetts, *The Confessions of Nat Turner* was interpreted in relation to these transformations in abolition's public sphere, especially to the antislavery movement's invocations of higher law. Enraged by the Southampton rebellion, the Southern press was quick to associate the messianic visions of its leader with the religious extremism of the immediate abolitionists. It was widely claimed, though it was probably not much believed, that the rebels had been inspired by the works of Garrison and Walker. The Richmond paper's review of the pamphlet, for example, declared that the horrors recorded in its pages should "warn Garrison and the other fanatics of the North, how they meddle with these weak wretches."[56] The *Liberator,* according to this account, was no organ of moral or legal reform; it was an incendiary paper, crossing the line between personal conscience and political militancy, between reasonable words and violent deeds.

"Since I have had the charge of the Liberator, I have been freely branded a madman and an incendiary."[57] Garrison was in a precarious position. A committed pacifist, he professed that the tyranny of slavery and the brutality of insurrection were part of a single, soul-destroying cycle; each called forth the other as its counterpart. Garrison wanted to build a large-scale crusade against the slave codes, to gather dispersed legal challenges and acts of resistance into a social movement that could reform the law by democratic means.[58] He would revive the critical power of the public sphere by infusing it with a spiritual fervor, converting souls to the truth that the real source of rebellion, the untenable oppression of the slave system, had to be destroyed. Almost as soon as his campaign was underway, though, Garrison found himself associated with the bloodiest slave uprising in the nation's history. Thus the Southampton rebellion and its textual monument, the *Confessions,* provoked Garrison to reflect on the character of the law's public sphere, to define the reforming power of influence against the destructive force of the curse. Just as William Ellery Channing had endeavored to save the cause of religious freedom from the rabble-rousing of a blasphemer, and just as Lyman Beecher had set out to save the Second Great Awakening from the indiscretions of enthusiasts, Garrison found himself drawing a line between abolitionism's higher law crusade and the militant exhortations of Nat Turner.

Garrison's effort to regulate the dangerous power of antislavery discourse was not expended out of any respect for the rights or property of the slaveholders. It was a matter of self-exoneration. According to Garrison's account, the attack on his paper was being organized by his own rivals within the antislavery crusade. In 1831, he traced its origins to his break with the conciliatory moderates in the Colonization Society—once his allies in Baltimore, now his persecutors in the free North. "It was not until I began to expose the abominations of the American Colonization Society, that my life was sought, my character vilified, and my efforts denounced as incendiary."[59] The repression of incendiary public address was thus organized, in large part, by the internal antagonisms between competing factions of reformers.

When he received a copy of the *Confessions* in December, Garrison was quick to point out that, contrary to the accusations raised by his enemies, "it does not appear that [Turner] ever saw a copy of the 'infernal Liberator' or of 'Walker's Pamphlet.'"[60] Reprinting long passages from the defendant's confession, Garrison repeated the commonplace view that "Nat Turner was partially insane, and led astray by religious fanaticism." Once again, he called the insurrection a "dreadful tragedy." He made no mention at all of the oracular death sentence pronounced by Justice Cobb. "The intelligent population of New England," declared *The Liberator* in a related article, "abhor and reprobate the incendiary publications which are *intended by their authors* to lead to precisely such results (as concerns the whites) as the Southampton Tragedy."[61]

What set Garrison's review apart from virtually every other contemporary account in print, however, was his claim that the *Confessions* was itself a dangerous document, threatening the security of the slaveholders. "An edition of 50,000 copies has been printed at Baltimore, which will only serve to rouse up other leaders and cause other insurrections, by creating among the blacks admiration for the character of Nat, and a deep, undying sympathy for his fate. We advise the Grand Juries in the several slave States to indict Mr Gray and the printers of the pamphlet forthwith." These are odd, ambiguous lines. Considered in light of Garrison's ongoing effort to defend himself against charges of inciting rebellion, they are clearly colored by a defensive sarcasm; the abolitionist deflects the accusations made against his paper onto the presumably reactionary pamphlet.

Still, Garrison was one of a very few early readers who foresaw the kind of subversive reception which, over the course of a longer history, would give Turner the character of a martyr and a prophet. Here, perhaps, was another case of intricate antagonism. The abolitionist established the reformist design of his own publication against the violence of a militant enthusiast—but, in the process, he attributed an enviable, "undying" character to the rebel's words. To disavow a call for insurrection, after all, is to acknowledge that such a call might effectively be made in print, with tremendous effects. Garrison distances himself from the incendiary danger of the martyr's voice, yet he appreciates and magnifies its power.

From the Turner rebellion until John Brown's raid, the Garrisonians would hold the same vexed relation to militant public address. They continued to invoke higher law against the slave codes, and they continued to be charged with a reckless enthusiasm; they did what they could to distinguish moral influence from incendiary violence, and they found themselves associated with ranters and fanatics, murderers and insurrectionists. Meanwhile they also attended to the voices of the martyrs, especially of the enslaved, with a sympathy that tended toward reverence. Here they glimpsed the prospect of a performance whose addressee was not an aggregate of discrete, private consciences but a counterpublic that could be moved to violent resistance. Even in the act of defining themselves against the militants, the abolitionists were nurturing fantasies about the revolutionary power of the curse.

A vivid example of this double movement in abolition's relation to incendiary speech is "The Runaway Slave at Pilgrim's Point," written by the English poet Elizabeth Barrett Browning in 1846 and first printed in an American antislavery journal, *The Liberty Bell,* in 1848.[62] The text has been the subject of some debate in recent criticism, which takes it as a crucial text for appraising the politics of antislavery verse. On one side are those like Isobel Armstrong, who describes Browning's piece as a "successful analysis of oppression" and a work of radical protest.[63] On the other side, skeptical readers have emphasized the poem's reinforcement of a racialized and gendered hierarchy of speaking roles. According to Tricia Lootens's critique, for example, the poem manifests "the terribly flawed power of abolitionist radical sentimentality."[64] Finally, in a more fully contextualized study of the poem's political position-taking, Marjorie Stone shows how these tensions may have arisen from debates within the antislavery movement itself. Browning in "Runaway Slave" was "aligning herself with the Garrisonians" against the more moderate antislavery camps in England and the United States, Stone argues, and in the process the poet adopted "the Garrisonian reliance on moral suasion, deeply radical in some of its manifestations and conservative in others."[65]

Like the commentary that has taken shape around *The Confessions of Nat Turner*, these studies of "Runaway Slave" place the problem of subjectivity, of the self-expressive voice, at the center. Even Stone rests her case for the poem's radicalism on its presentation of "a black female martyr to the anti-slavery cause, speaking up for her race and articulating the curse that white slaveholders bring upon themselves."[66] If the poem is reconsidered in relation to the legal public sphere, however, the choice between agency and abjection appears less fundamental. Here, the peculiar genre of the poem comes into view: it is a Garrisonian abolitionist's experiment in the versification of popular legal forms like the criminal confession and the convict autobiography. The crucial problem is perhaps not the self-expressive capacities of a fugitive but the power that might be wielded by an offender's self-negating curse.

The poem is a dramatic monologue, set at Pilgrim's Point in Massachusetts, the site "where exile changed to Ancestor"—that is, where men and women in flight from persecution consecrated a new nation. The speaker introduces herself as another figure in flight, a fugitive from enslavement on a Southern plantation. She has made her way to this sacred place, she says, to invoke the pilgrims' ghosts. She plans to damn the slaveholders of the present in the name of their ancestors:

> And thus I thought that I would come
>   And kneel here where ye knelt before,
> And feel your souls around me hum
>   In undertone to the ocean's roar;
> And lift my black face, my black hand,
> Here in your names, to curse this land
>   Ye blessed in Freedom's, heretofore. (30)

In Browning's poem, as in Hawthorne's "Alice Doane's Appeal," colonial founders are imagined as undead specters who might be called to vindicate a victim of injustice. From the beginning, though, Browning's runaway slave describes the curse as an unrealized potentiality, a waning intention. Will she repress this dangerous impulse, or will she pronounce the curse? This is the mystery that gives the poem its plot.

As the several stanzas unfold, the speaker recalls the brutality she endured under slavery—the lashes at the whipping-post, the violation of her bond to an enslaved lover, her rape by white men. At the beginning, her role as the presumably innocent victim of this violence gives her a certain authority to testify against the slave system, even to pronounce judgment against it. In time, however, she makes a confession that reorients the public's relation to her authority. The runaway reveals that her crime, the transgression she means to justify, is not the theft of her liberty from her master. It is the murder of their child:

> And my own child—I could not bear
> To look in his face, it was so white:
> So I covered him up with a kerchief rare,
> I covered his face in close and tight!
> And he moaned and struggled as well as might be. . . . (37)

The confession does not end here. It goes on, lingering over the sensational details:

> And he moaned and trembled from foot to head,—
> He shivered from head to foot,—
> Till, after a time, he lay, instead,
> Too suddenly still and mute;
> And I felt, beside, a creeping cold. . . . (39–40)

The crime of infanticide is placed within the moral framework of the enslaved woman's struggle against her master, but it is not transmuted into allegory. Violating its prevailing, iambic rhythm with anapests that mimic the sound of struggle, the poem describes the thrashing of limbs, the expiration of breath—"He moaned and beat with his head and his feet"—and the turnings of the killer's thoughts. Drawing from the genres of popular crime literature, gothic as much as sentimental, it depicts a slow, embodied act of violence.

Having narrated the infanticide, the speaker returns to the question of the curse. "Whips! Curses! These must answer those!" (44). The curse, it becomes clear, is not only an appeal to the spirits of the pilgrim ancestors. It is a call to murderous violence: "lift your hands / O, slaves, and end what I begun." As Stone suggests, the runaway in these incendiary lines "calls . . . for a general slave insurrection."[67] In confessing her crime, she does not submit to the judgment of her auditors. She threatens to summon a counterpublic to recognize the killing as a legitimate act of resistance against an unjust order, and to carry on the struggle. Browning's speaker thus mixes certain allegorical types which were kept distinct in more conventional antislavery literature. She is akin to Stowe's Eliza Harris, the female fugitive who appeals to the sympathy of white benefactors, but also to Eliza's husband George, who makes his claim to autonomy and freedom by invoking the Revolutionary heritage. More militant still, she is about to call, like Dred, for a moral war against the oppressors.

In the end, Browning's runaway abandons this terrible prospect. She represses the urge to imprecation; she will not ask for blood in vengeance. "White men, I leave you all curse-free, / In my broken heart's disdain" (45). Uttering this benediction, she leaps from the cliffs into the sea. The drama of the poem ends in an act of self-sacrifice. To this extent, "Runaway Slave" is the story of one who chooses martyrdom, with the fantasy that liberty and equality might be waiting in some other world. In disavowing the curse, as Sarah Brophy suggests, Browning seems to have embraced the doctrine of influence, repressing a woman's public performance in favor of a private appeal that can only be acted upon by a masculine authority.[68] Yet the poet does so, in this case, not so much by identifying with the runaway slave, not so much by staging her suicide as a spectacular renunciation that forestalls political action in the present, as by developing a fantasy of the offender's curse. She imagines that this mode of address really might be capable of inciting a rebellion, answering violence with violence. The most unusual and compelling passages of the poem are not in its predictable final stanza but in its gothic middle sections, where a private confession becomes a public curse, an invocation of divine justice that reincarnates an undying revolutionary past in the living, rising hands of the present. Such is the incendiary mode of address in which, she assures the public, Browning will not indulge.

For many reasons, the revolutionary power of the curse—the capacity of an invocation of higher law to ignite a large-scale insurrection—was first imagined as a threat, not a promise. It was a nightmare disclosed by reactionaries like the Virginia authorities who set out to suppress black exhortation and to block the circulation of antislavery texts. Or it was a menace carefully and elaborately disavowed by reformers like Garrison and Browning who sought a nonviolent solution to the slavery crisis. In either case, though, it was also a fantasy. It was the dream of a discourse network which extended to the far-flung, disparate, often unlettered communities of the enslaved. It was the imagined prospect that a single utterance, a single curse, might summon them into a synchronized and coordinated act of rebellion.

It was, in other words, a vision of inspired resistance that involved a fantastic appropriation of the period's media infrastructure. Even when they depicted the curse as a spoken performance, these theorists of its power were clearly working within a social imaginary whose scaffolding was the large-scale network of publication and circulation, the mass medium of print. They were suggesting that the same communications systems which addressed and organized "the people" could be used to call a counterpublic toward revolution. To imagine the curse in this way, even in the process of disavowing it, was to introduce a fearsome prospect. It was only one more step, and perhaps a smaller one, from imagination-in-regulation to vengeful affirmation.

CHAPTER 6

Words of Fire

In the fall of 1859, the memory of Nat Turner's rebellion rose like a specter in the public sphere. Many readers returned to the *Confessions,* interpreting it against the grain of Thomas Ruffin Gray's prefatory instructions and Justice Jeremiah Cobb's oracular death sentence. Although most still repudiated Turner's violent means, some were beginning to see him as something other than a deluded enthusiast. When New York's *Anglo-African Magazine* republished the text of his confession in December, the editors remarked that the Southampton insurrectionist had exemplified "the mode in which the slave seeks freedom for his fellows." The struggle, the *Anglo-African* argued, would go on until the system of slavery was abolished: "The course which the South is now pursuing, will engender in its bosom and nurse into maturity a hundred Nat Turners, whom Virginia is infinitely less able to resist in 1860, than she was in 1831." Turner had sought "in the air, the earth and the heavens, for signs which came at last." More and more, he seemed like the prophet of an irresistible violence that was about to engulf the land.[1]

The position of the *Anglo-African,* like that of the *Liberator,* was that an unjust system, brutalizing to humanity and abhorrent to the laws of God, would provoke resistance without end. This was the curse of slavery. As an alternative to Turner's militancy, though, the *Anglo-African's* editorialist pointed, improbably, to the case of John Brown. "Nat Turner's terrible logic could only see the enfranchisement of one race, compassed by the extirpation of the other." Brown, by contrast, "believ[ed] that the freedom of the enthralled could only be effected by placing them on an equality with their enslavers." Where Turner had waged a merciless race war, Brown "is moved by compassion for tyrants and well as slaves." His heroic endeavor had been to redeem the slaveholders and to liberate the enslaved "without spilling one drop of blood." Brown was described, oddly, as a peaceable reformer who only wished to guide the enslaved to freedom, not to make war on Virginia.

Brown's trial was the last great crisis for abolition's public sphere. When he invoked the law of God to justify his crimes, he was drawing from three decades of antislavery sermons and pamphlets, especially from a radical tradition that developed in the 1850s. The Fugitive Slave Law of 1850, the Northern courts' decisions against runaways and their allies, the Supreme Court's racist definition of citizenship in the Dred Scott case of 1857—all of these had intensified the moral crusade against the slave system. To Unionists and Southern apologists, Brown's raid on Virginia represented an outbreak of fanaticism, a violent transgression against the rule of law that had taken antislavery exhortation to its nightmarish conclusion. To the Garrisonian abolitionists, it was a high-minded but doomed endeavor which had wrongfully resorted to violent means in pursuit of noble ends.

For the few who felt themselves most irresistibly summoned to Brown's cause, meanwhile, it seemed that a violent reckoning could no longer be averted. "The principles of God's law," the Reverend George B. Cheever wrote in *The Curse of God Against Political Atheism,* "cannot alter. Heaven and earth shall pass away before one jot or title of the law shall fail. As a standard of feeling and action, as a standard of right and wrong, as a standard of duty under all circumstances, and of judgment in every respect, it is unerring and unchanging. Its principles were given forth . . . to be obeyed, and carried into unfaltering execution."[2] Here was the righteous echo of the oracular address that had once been performed by common-law apologists like William Blackstone and Jesse Root; the invocation of a higher justice rebounded on the courts in the form of inspired and militarized dissent. "The great lesson" of Harper's

Ferry, Cheever preached, "is this: If the men of peace will not apply God's law against the sin of Slaveholding, in the shape of argument and earnest truth and the maledictions of God, the men of war will put it in the shape of bullets, and fight it out, and God will let them."[3] Even while Garrison and his circle tried to regulate the incendiary capacities of Brown's speech, then, there were some who were ready to move from supplicating words to violent deeds.

This chapter revisits the decade of crisis that began with the Fugitive Slave Law and ended with the outbreak of the Civil War, with *Scott v. Sanford* and *Commonwealth v. Brown* as ominous markers along the way. In these years emerged the most radical of the higher-law discourses, including a few sermons and other writings that openly called for violence. These were the militant companion-pieces to the visions of John Brown's martyrdom with which my story began. Here at the end, though, I take up two other works of antislavery literature, an autobiographical narrative and a serialized novel, which oriented themselves toward the law's public sphere. Both Harriet Jacobs's *Incidents in the Life of a Slave Girl* (1861) and Martin Delany's *Blake* (1859–1862) have been canonized in recent decades, and critics have attended with care to their aesthetics and their politics, including their critiques of legal institutions. What remains to be explored is the poetics of justice that was developed in and around these works. My premise is that we have not fully grasped either form or content, either the rhetoric of subversion or the force of critique, until we understand how the period came to endow these texts with the power to summon resistance in their own time. As it turned out, the *Anglo-African* would play a significant part in the cultivation of militant reading and the literature of insurrection—a public sphere aflame.

The Rights of Conscience

Locked up in his Missouri prison cell in the 1840s, the poet George Thompson reckoned that "the *law of God,* in slave states, is *null* and *void.*"[4] Not long afterward, with the passage of the federal Fugitive Slave Law of 1850, and especially after a series of crushing defeats for the antislavery bar in such contests as Thomas Sims's case, decided by

Lemuel Shaw in 1851, the slave system's mortification of justice seemed to creep far north of Mason and Dixon's line. Theodore Parker of Boston, in his trial report, described the encroachment with a vivid image: "This Anaconda of the Dismal Swamp wound its constricting twists about the neck of all your courts, and the Judges turned black in the face, and when questioned of law, they could not pronounce 'Habeas Corpus,' 'Trial by Jury,' nor utter a syllable for the Bible or the Massachusetts Constitution, but only wheeze and gurgle and squeak and gibber out their defenses of Slavery!"[5] The New England courts had once considered themselves the guardians of a justice ordained by God and enshrined in the people's customs. Now, according to Parker, they were so weakened by the compromises of federal legislators that they had abandoned their most ancient, most sacred obligations. The Christian jurisprudence of Jesse Root had been eclipsed by the weak, secularized formalism of Justice Shaw.

The staunchly abolitionist minister J. G. Forman, who was removed from his pulpit in West Bridgewater, Massachusetts, by a proslavery faction within his congregation, preached on the subject of "The Christian Martyrs" in 1851: "the Christian citizen reserves to himself the right to judge in every case whether the legislation of a government is consistent with the law of God."[6] Animated by the principle that the laws of the state had lost their legitimacy when they strayed from the commandments of God, the evangelical antislavery movement of the 1850s developed a more and more radical reform program, supplementing the persuasive power of exhortation with occasional acts of civil disobedience, especially against the Fugitive Slave Law. The organizing idea behind the campaign was that of higher law, or the duty of conscience in relation to the will of God, as distinguished from the citizen's obligations to the state. Invoked by the New York Whig William H. Seward on the floor of the U.S. Senate in 1850, the higher law soon became one of the most controversial topics of the antebellum period. An 1851 pamphlet described a civil society animated and factionalized along these lines: "It is agitated in clubs and coffee-rooms, in the cars and on the steamboats, in the street, the store and the market-place; everywhere where men go, goes with them this inevitable idea, of the conflict between the Rights of Conscience and the Obligations of Law."[7]

Both the advocates and the critics of higher law doctrine, however, knew that it was a dangerous idea, easily appropriated by enthusiasts, tending towards faction and strife. Warning against these destructive tendencies, the Illinois minister J. M. Peck attacked the evangelists of higher law not only on substance but also on "style": "What a catalogue of fanaticism, insubordination, criminality, and folly, is here given; and yet this is a true picture of hundreds of fanatics, and of the style and spirit of their address, in the northern States."[8] The minister John C. Lord, addressing New York's Union Safety Committee, foresaw an "abyss of ruin" opened up by the "fanaticism and treason" of the Garrisonians: "the spirit of disunion, once evoked, may extend its malign influences until . . . having accomplished its ruin of the South, the states at the North should divide, and each set up for itself."[9] Those who had introduced this malign force into the national community, he preached, were playing with a fire they could not control.

Even the defenders of higher law were wary of "false prophets" whose enthusiastic exhortations might bring on the horrors of war.[10] In the sermons and pamphlets that invoked the will of God against the statutes and the courts, therefore, they attempted to establish a set of regulating boundaries, managing the reception of higher law exhortations by an unpredictable public. The New York minister Richard S. Storrs, in an 1850 sermon, laid out the doctrine of higher law "in a single sentence": "It is the duty of each man to obey the Laws of the State, except where they conflict with the Law which God has given him; and on the reality of such conflict his Conscience must decide."[11] To the apologists of law and order, in the pulpit and at the bar, such a proposition seemed to lead toward anarchy. Every person would be set at liberty to decide if conscience required submission to the law. Each would say, with Henry Thoreau, "The only obligation which I have a right to assume is to do at any time what I think right."[12] The state's ideological hold over its subjects would be broken, and the character of authority would be exposed as mere force, the physical power to compel obedience and punish crime.

The evangelical abolitionists did not see things in the same way. For their antislavery crusade, in fact, the emphasis on conscience was a way to distinguish the private Christian's disobedience from the public performances of militant fanatics. In time, they hoped, the conversion of many and the martyrdom of a few would lead to reforms, and finally to the creation of laws that were worthy of a Christian's obedience. But the higher law doctrine was concerned, first of all, to redeem its adherents from their complicity in a legal system that seemed to require them to sin. (Thoreau's principle of civil disobedience was a Transcendentalist's adaptation of this evangelical doctrine: "Must the citizen ever for a moment, or in the least degree, resign his conscience to the legislator?"[13]) It was for this reason that the Fugitive Slave Law was so repugnant to those who valued the integrity of conscience above all else—more repugnant even than the Southern slave codes themselves. The men and women of the Northern states, who had once been able to imagine themselves as uncontaminated by the slave system, were now commanded by the government to capture fugitives and return them to their masters. There was a clear and painful contradiction between the ideal of purity and the reality of corruption, between the sacred rights of conscience and the obligations of law.[14]

In the last months of 1859, as John Brown's trial in Virginia became the defining mass media event of the season, the abolitionist press was exposed to renewed charges of stirring up rebellion with its reckless invocations of higher law. Pacifists like Garrison and Child found themselves accused of rabble-rousing, and they did their best to defend their position in the press. Not since 1850 had they made such a systematic effort to define the obligations of conscience in relation to the rule of law. They revisited the problem of civil disobedience, and they reflected with a new clarity on the modes of address through which they hoped to turn their public against the slave system. Indeed, while scholarship on higher law in the antislavery campaign has focused on the content of its arguments against the slave codes, discussions of the concept in the antebellum press attended with equal care to the performative force of its invocation—the style and manner of address.[15]

"Because [slavery] is a great sin, because it is a national curse, it does not follow that we have a right to say any thing . . . that we may happen to please. We certainly have no right to attack it in any manner that will gratify men's fancies or passions." The minister Henry Ward Beecher, the son of Lyman Beecher and the brother of Harriet Beecher Stowe, was one of several writers who set out to distinguish his antislavery principles from the spirit of Brown's doomed, fanatical raid. Beecher happily acknowledged that he had the "reputation," especially in the South, "of being a tolerably stout abolitionist." But he would not allow Brown's folly to represent the cause. Beecher described Harper's Ferry as a "miserable" piece of military incompetence, the "failure" of an enthusiast. Lingering over the old man's style of exhortation, Beecher accused Brown of evil speaking: "the *spirit* of rebuke," he reminded his congregation, "may be as wicked before God, as the spirit of the evil rebuked."[16] Nothing was to be gained for the antislavery cause, and much might be lost, in the divisive exhortations Brown was delivering in the courtroom and in the press.

Against the militant and fanatical spirit of rebuke, Beecher raised the call for "Christian quietness and patient waiting." He glorified the union as a sacred spiritual brotherhood, binding North and South in "a common national life." The best path toward emancipation, in Beecher's view, was not the "revolution" advocated by John Brown; it was "a change of public opinion in the *whole community*."[17] Brown's fiery rhetoric would provoke faction and strife. Beecher's conciliatory address, by contrast, would seek to improve the world without dividing it against itself. Despite the deep sectional division of the moment, he allowed himself to picture a national community capable of reforming itself through a slow process of reason and reflection, guided by the wisdom of a single God.

It is easy to imagine how Thoreau, not to speak of the insurgents who had fought with Brown, would have appraised Beecher's sermon. For James Redpath, Brown's first biographer and his faithful defender in the press, it was the supreme document of the Northern ministry's cowardice. After agitating with the radical English reformers known as the Chartists in the fiery struggles of 1848, Redpath had immigrated to the United States in 1849, and, as Albert J. Von Frank shows, he brought with him a militant style of revolutionary politics that divided him and his circle from the American abolitionists, even from the Garrisonians.[18] Reprinting Beecher's sermon in *Echoes of Harper's Ferry,* Redpath singled it out as an eloquent and influential piece of "that hypocritical cant which *talks* of sympathy for the Slave, and, at the same time, extinguishes all effective attempts to help him." "Pusillanimous preachers" like Beecher were willing to wring their hands and lament the slave system, but they refused to act.[19]

Redpath's rough distinction between words and deeds, however, did not quite account for the full range of Beecher's antislavery program. Beecher had his own thoughts on both language and action, and his own vision of how a moral force might bring down the slave system. Even in the face of the hostile response to Brown's raid, Beecher would not retreat entirely from civil disobedience. "If there were as many laws as there are lines in the Fugitive Slave Law," he declared, "I would disregard every law, but God's, and help the fugitive!"[20] Returning to the model of higher-law activism that had taken shape in 1850, echoing the Mrs. Bird of *Uncle Tom's Cabin,* he argued that resistance to such an unjust statute was obedience to God.

But Beecher was careful, after Harper's Ferry, to draw a clear boundary around the zone where such resistance should be practiced. In the North, the rights of conscience would prevail in 1860 as they had since 1850—but now the invocation of higher law became an occasion to redefine its boundaries, the limits of legitimate disobedience. "I do not believe we have a right to carry into the system of slavery exterior discontent." Beecher pictured a divided nation, a barricade running along its seam. "I stand on the outside of this great cordon of darkness, and every man that escapes from it, running for his life, shall have some help from me."[21] The free states might remain a field of action, but the South would await a different kind of moral force.

"There must be a Christian public sentiment," brought to bear not only in the legislatures but also in the plantation houses and slave cabins of the South. Indeed, Beecher advised, the work of abolition should begin not at the federal armory but in the domestic interior. Public sentiment should be awakened to the sanctity of the "three elements" at the heart of all civilized and Christian life: female chastity, domestic love, and the bonds of parental affection. "The moment a woman stands self-poised in her own purity; the moment man and woman are united together by bonds which cannot be sundered during their earthly life; the moment the right of parents to their children is recognized—that moment there will be a certain sanctity and protection of the Eternal and Divine government resting upon father, and mother, and children; and

Slavery will have had its death-blow struck!" The expansion of these three blessings to the enslaved was Beecher's alternative to Brown's militancy. Indeed, he offered himself up as a mouthpiece for the silent masses of enslaved women. "I stand up in behalf of two million women who are without a voice, to declare that there ought to be found in Christianity, somewhere, an influence that shall protect their right to their own persons."[22] A woman's voice, speaking up in favor of chastity, marriage, and the sanctity of the private family—this was Beecher's ideal of abolition's public address, his alternative to the apocalyptic exhortations of slavery's latest martyr.

Testimony from the Pit of Abominations

By the fall of 1859, Harriet Jacobs had come to doubt that her autobiography would ever appear in print. She had quarreled with Harriet Beecher Stowe, who condescendingly offered to write up some of the details of Jacobs's life for the *Key to Uncle Tom's Cabin*. She had traveled to London, seeking an English publisher, but returned to New York disappointed and embarrassed. According to Jean Fagan Yellin's biography, though, Jacobs was "shaken out of her melancholy" and inspired to finish her manuscript in October, when she learned the news from Harper's Ferry.[23] A few months later, she contacted the radical Boston publishing house Thayer and Eldridge, which had just brought out Redpath's *The Public Life of Captain John Brown* and *Echoes of Harper's Ferry*. In fact, Thayer and Eldridge was founded on John Brown; Redpath's biography was their first title and the investment on which they planned to stand or fall.[24] It was not a good bet. The firm produced the plates for Jacobs's narrative, then went bankrupt before publication was complete. The title page of *Incidents in the Life of a Slave Girl*, which was finally printed and bound in January of 1861, indicated simply that it had been "published for the author."[25] But Jacobs made the connection explicit when she composed, as her concluding chapter, "a tribute to Brown."[26]

As readers of *Incidents* know, the piece on the martyr of Harper's Ferry does not appear in Jacobs's book. Now lost, it was apparently suppressed by Lydia Maria Child, who, at the request of Thayer and Eldridge and their abolitionist friends, had agreed to edit Jacobs's narrative. Child gave her reasons, briefly, in a letter dated August 13, 1860: "I think the last Chapter, about John Brown, had better be omitted. It does not naturally come into your story, and the M.S. is already too long. Nothing can be so appropriate to end with, as the death of your grand mother."[27] Child explained her objections in terms of the organic development of Jacobs's narrative, and of a gendered propriety—but the revision clearly conformed to Child's larger design for *Incidents*. It was an effort to dissociate it from Brown's militancy and align it with the Garrisonian circle's program of nonviolent reform.[28]

Child had played a complicated and ambivalent role in the public conversation about Brown's case. "I sympathize with you," she wrote in an open letter addressed to the prisoner in the Charles Town Jail, "in your cruel bereavement, your sufferings, and your wrongs. In brief, I love and bless you."[29] She offered to travel to Virginia, to nurse him in his cell. Soon, she found herself publicly attacked for overstepping the bounds of feminine modesty, and she did her best to answer her critics. In a letter to the editor of the *New York Tribune,* dated November 10, 1859, she suggested that she had not intended for her correspondence with Brown and Governor Henry Wise to become public.[30] Elsewhere, she seemed to wish that she had never gotten herself associated with the Harper's Ferry raid at all, although her pamphlet on the case was a runaway best-seller, with over 300,000 copies in print.[31] In the end, she defended the rights of antislavery authors to make their case in the court of public opinion, but she also distinguished her own ethics from Brown's militancy. "Believing in peace principles, I cannot sympathize with the method you chose to advance the cause of freedom."[32] While she and Garrison disagreed with Beecher on the question of disunion, they shared his aversion to violence and his faith in the reforming power of moral influence. This was the perspective Child brought to her work on Jacobs's manuscript.

The scholarship on Child's suppression of Jacobs's final chapter emphasizes the editor's effort to make the narrative conform to sentimental conventions. As Albert H. Tricomi puts it, Child "directed [Jacobs's manuscript] away from the combustible militarism of [Brown's raid] . . . and foregrounded those melodramatic and sentimental parts illustrating the destruction of families and especially the sexual victimization of girls and women under slavery, along with the devastating effects this abuse brought to their grieving mothers."[33] Another study of the exchange, by Bruce Mills, suggests that such a revision was for the best. Tricomi instead attempts to reimagine the radical version that may have been destroyed in revision. But beneath this apparent disagreement is a deeper consensus: both critics maintain a categorical opposition between masculine militancy and feminine sentimentality. Both assume, as well, that Child accomplished her design—that *Incidents* became, under her guidance, a sentimental appeal for nonviolent moral and legal reform. Focusing on the vexed issue of Jacobs's self-expression, on the scene of writing and revision, they suggest that any militant aspects of *Incidents* would be recoverable only through an effort to reconstruct the author's "intentions" out of the incomplete record of her correspondence.[34] Another prospect comes into view, though, from a poetics of justice that turns from the scene of composition to the arena of circulation and reception, from the intentions of the author to the dynamics of the public sphere.

It would take one who had endured slavery, according to Jacobs, to bring its abysmal secrets to light. "Only by experience can any one realize how deep, and dark, and foul is that pit of abominations" (6). By 1861, the personal stories of fugitives and ex-slaves had become a familiar part of the abolitionists' crusade to move public sentiment against the slaveholders, but Jacobs's book offered the rare testimony of a woman, documenting the peculiar terrors of sexual vulnerability. An 1862 review referred to Jacob's book as "the first personal narrative in which one of that sex upon whom chattel servitude falls with the deepest and darkest shadow has ever described her own bitter experience."[35] Jacobs presented herself as a woman addressing other women, on behalf of her sisters in bondage. "There is no shadow of law to protect [the slave girl] from insult, from violence, or even from death; all these are inflicted by fiends who bear the shape of men" (45). At times, she drew from the conventions of the sentimental novel, appealing to the heart and to the public's appetite for sensation in hopes of reaching the widest possible audience—but she began by asking for God's blessing and by pledging to tell the truth: "Reader, be assured this narrative is no fiction" (5).

The men and women who worked with Jacobs to publish and promote *Incidents* were careful to represent it as an honest, uncoerced

account of her experiences, related in her own voice, and Yellin's biographical studies established that Jacobs's narrative had in fact been
"written by herself," as the original title page indicated, with relatively
minor revisions by Child.[36] Yet Jacobs's complicated relationship with
her audience—her efforts to navigate the sexual norms of the evangelical
abolitionists as well as the contested status of African American self-
expression—required elaborate techniques of encoding and displacement.[37] Although Jacobs insisted that her book was a sincere and factual
record, recent scholarship has emphasized the artfulness of its composition. *Incidents* has been canonized as a critique of the ideologies that
supported the enslavement of African Americans and the sexual subjection of women. In the most influential accounts, the interest of Jacobs's
work is in its capacity to expose and analyze structures of power that
would otherwise lie concealed within such notions as benevolent pater-
nalism, feminine chastity, and domestic love.[38] And the legibility of the
narrative as a work of ideology critique depends on the critic's respon-
siveness to its sophistication, the literary strategies through which it
exposes the violence of an unjust system.

Studies of the rhetoric and form of *Incidents* have demonstrated its
subtle complexities, establishing it as a literary work that demands close
reading as well as careful contextualization. In the process, however, the
analysis of Jacobs's ideological and legal critiques has tended to set aside
what Charles H. Nichols, in a pathbreaking study of the reception of
slave narratives, calls the "crucial problem" of the genre's "timeliness,"
its capacity to make a difference in its own time and place.[39] How did
Jacobs and her collaborators imagine that a reading public, in the crisis
years of 1859–1861, would respond to her protest? By what media and
by what means, in other words, might the critique of the slave codes be
expected to lead to their abolition? These are questions about the movement's conception of the law's public sphere. In order to address them, it
is useful to approach *Incidents* not as a work of critique but as a piece of
testimony. Jacobs famously described her desire to address the public in
this way: "I want to add my testimony to that of abler pens to convince
the people of the Free States what Slavery really is" (6). If critique is an
interpretive practice that seeks to disclose the operations of power within
normative discourses and institutionalized knowledges, testimony might

be defined, by contrast, as a ceremonial mode of truth-telling that is performed before a public invested with the authority to decide a question of justice. The distinction is imperfect, of course, but it does help to describe how the antislavery press understood its own project.[40]

Enslavement in Jacobs's narrative is not only a matter of physical domination. It is a condition of insecurity and exposure that follows from the law's refusal to recognize the validity of verbal commitments.[41] "No promise or writing given to a slave is legally binding," Jacobs writes (13). Loans made in good faith are never repaid. The last wishes of the dying are forgotten or ignored. Pledges of love are dishonored. Jacobs describes a whole range of swindles and betrayals, but she gives special attention to the problem of marriage. A wedding ceremony among the enslaved is "a mere form, without any legal value" (217). "The husband of a slave has no power to protect her," and the young narrator has no hope of entering "a home shielded by the laws" (59, 83). In such a world, the ordinary conventions of the romantic love plot have no place. Another kind of narrative will have to be told: "Reader, my story ends with freedom; not in the usual way, with marriage" (302). Thus the problem of legal promise-making gives the narrative its plot. Jacobs describes her flight from a corrupt territory of broken homes and empty oaths into a space of freedom where she and her interlocutors can commit themselves through speech acts.

Conceiving of her book as a kind of evidence against the slaveholders, Jacobs submitted it to the court of public opinion. She undertook "the painful task of confessing," and she addressed her audience as a tribunal of judgment in her case: "Pity me, and pardon me, O virtuous reader!" (83, 86). The offense to be expunged, however, was not her flight from her master's house, an act which, she assumed, would be recognized by an antislavery readership as legitimate disobedience. Giving a subversive turn to a phrase made famous by the Dred Scott case, Jacobs was openly, unapologetically defiant of the slave codes: "I regarded such laws as the regulations of robbers, who had no rights that I was bound to respect" (251). Her transgression, the crime to be delicately revealed and sympathetically viewed, was her decision to become the lover of the white man she called Mr. Sands, in hopes that he might help to protect her and her children from a cruel master.

The sacrifice of feminine virtue is a "painful and humiliating memory," but Jacobs makes no attempt to conceal it. She offers a full confession: "I know I did wrong" (86). She submits her case to the reader's judgment, and she asks for a pardon. In the process, she hopes to revise the terms in which her plea is decided. "The slave woman ought not to be judged by the same standard as others" (86). Indeed, the ambition of Jacobs's narrative is to transfer the burden of readers' moral condemnation from herself to the system of slavery. She will become, for them, the key witness to an otherwise secret knowledge. "Could you have witnessed that scene as I saw it, you would exclaim, *Slavery is damnable*" (38). Her testimony will provide a corrective to the public's incomplete vision, provoking a curse against the slaveholders.

In all of these passages, where Jacobs reflects on the genre and reception of her book, she attends not only to the hidden violence of slavery but also, with great care, to the public life of the law, with its ceremonies of performative speech and its rituals of justice.[42] Born in 1813, Jacobs had been a teenager at the time of the Southampton insurrection. She described the terror that came to her home town of Edenton, North Carolina, in its wake—vigilante mobs tearing through the houses of the enslaved; innocent men and women framed for conspiracy; confessions forced with the lash and the paddle. She devoted a chapter to the Fugitive Slave Law of 1850 and to the organized civil disobedience in the Northern states, pausing to praise a Massachusetts politician who had sheltered her for a time: "This honorable gentleman would not have voted for the Fugitive Slave Law, as did the senator in 'Uncle Tom's Cabin'" (292). (Here she carried on her feud with Stowe by insisting, again, on the difference between her testimony and the novelist's fiction.) In private correspondence and in the pages of her narrative, she lamented the U.S. Supreme Court's decision in *Scott v. Sanford* as an outrage against black humanity.[43]

Jacobs did seek to expose how the legal dehumanization and dishonor of the enslaved encroached into the nominally private scenes of domestic life. In narrating her delicate erotic negotiations with her master and others, she resisted the rhetoric of seduction which, in antebellum courtrooms, had recast white rapists as the victims of women's erotic designs. As Saidiya Hartman argues, Jacobs's story reveals that chastity, far from being a quality exercised by any transcendent, autonomous self, is a historically contingent value, secured by the structures of law and power; thus *Incidents* "historicizes virtue." What remains unhistoricized even in this account, however, is the relation between Jacobs's testimony and its reception by a reading public that might be persuaded by such an appeal. Hartman writes that *Incidents* "creates a dramatic vortex that engulfs the reader and vividly displays the relentless forces of sexual undoing; even the most obdurate reader cannot resist such entreaties."[44] This is an intriguing metaphor for nondeliberative persuasion. But the sense that Jacobs's narrative was an irresistible force, compelling the assent of every reader, seems to be projected onto 1861 from the perspective of a late twentieth-century interpretive community, where outrage against the slave system has become the norm, but where no specific strategy for resistance needs to be chosen. The task of critique ends with the reader's conversion to the truth.

The point is not the obvious one, that Southern and proslavery readers in 1861 did everything they could to discredit Jacobs's testimony. Rather, in the months of crisis leading up to the Civil War, there was a deep fissure within the antislavery campaign itself.[45] The audience before whom Jacobs testified was divided between two modes of fidelity to higher law, and its reception of her narrative was shaped by the disagreement. What sort of public might have been expected to hear Jacobs's testimony and to pronounce judgment against the slaveholders? Would readers carry their conviction to the public sphere of print, to the legislature, or into open rebellion? These questions, which preoccupied the antislavery press in 1859–1861, are basic to understanding how a narrative could have been imagined as an appeal to a contemporary public capable of reforming the law, or as a call to militant resistance. At stake in the forgotten struggle to shape the reception of *Incidents* was the power of literary testimony to call a sovereign community to transform the world.

Child's Introduction to *Incidents* recognizes that the "delicate" sexual matters explored in the narrative are likely to scandalize some readers, but the editor expresses her hope that this "monstrous" evidence will help to turn public opinion against the slave system. Child concludes with two calls to action. The first is for women: "I do it with the hope of arousing conscientious and reflecting women at the North to a sense of their duty in the exertion of moral influence on the question of Slavery, on all possible occasions." The second is for men: "I do it with the hope that every man who reads this narrative will swear solemnly before God that, so far as he has power to prevent it, no fugitive from Slavery shall ever be sent back to suffer in that loathsome den of corruption and cruelty" (8). Child's gendered vision of the narrative's reception recalls the familiar ideology of separate spheres. Women exercise their "moral influence." Men make binding oaths and take public actions.

What may be less obvious about Child's note is that it also circumscribes the field of masculine action. Implicitly distinguishing the politics of Jacobs's testimony from Brown's raid, Child calls for civil disobedience against the Fugitive Slave Law, but not against the slave system in the South. Much like Beecher's sermon on Brown, Child's introduction to Jacobs's narrative lays a cordon between the Northern field of masculine civil disobedience and a Southern "den of corruption" that awaits the redeeming influence of a woman's voice. Her men solemnly swear before God, but they do not join Brown in cursing the nation. They love and bless the wretched, but they do not quite say, with the readers Jacobs imagined for herself, *"Slavery is damnable."*

In the same letter that explained the suppression of the Harper's Ferry chapter, Child asked Jacobs for more details about the experience of North Carolina's enslaved people in the violent reprisal that followed Turner's revolt in 1831: "What were those inflictions? Were any tortured to make them confess? and how? Where any killed? Please write down some of the most striking particulars, and let me have them to insert." Child may have expected readers to understand these passages as oblique, coded reflections on the John Brown case.[46] But Child's express wish was for stories of black suffering, not of insurrection. Jacobs provided the terrible details: "Every where men, women, and children were whipped till the blood stood in puddles at their feet. Some received five hundred lashes; others were tied hands and feet, and tortured with a bucking paddle, which blisters the skin terribly" (98). Such passages guide the reader's vision away from the scene of armed resistance, toward the "particulars" of abjection and death.

In at least one letter, Jacobs expressed her regret that she had not been more closely involved in revising her own story: "I know that Mrs

Child . . . will strive to do the best she can more than I can ever repay but I ought to have been there that we could have consulted together."[47] Like Brown's "Address to the Virginia Court," the original conclusion of Jacobs's *Incidents* may have called on its public to enforce a judgment through violence. Certainly her models of civil disobedience include the benevolent gentlemen and ladies who shelter her from her master's agents, but she also takes the occasion to remember her brother, who responds to the news of the Fugitive Slave Law with a pledge of "stern hostility to our oppressors" (287). Since Jacobs's final chapter has not survived, it is impossible to know exactly how she handled Brown's case. In the early history of her critical reception, though, is some evidence that a resonance between her testimony and Brown's address was audible, at least to a few. However much Child may have tried to regulate the incendiary power of Jacobs's testimony, however much Jacobs herself may have seemed to shy away from militancy, there still seemed to be something of the curse about the book. It would be received, in some quarters, as a contribution to a circum-Atlantic project of black resistance, liberation, and uplift that traversed the boundaries of race and gender—indeed, as an incendiary call to arms.

The reviews which appeared in the antislavery press in the months following the publication of *Incidents* were almost all favorable; the movement welcomed Jacobs's testimony before the court of public opinion. Closer reading of these notices, though, reveals that the reviewers who praised the book found different ways of responding to its call. On one side were those who admired the pleasing style and lively plot. Thus the *National Anti-Slavery Standard,* a New York paper aligned with the Garrisonian cause of disunion, announced that "the book has a vivid dramatic power as a narrative, and should have a wide circulation."[48] The following week, the *Standard* reprinted Jacobs's Preface, Child's Introduction, and authenticating statements by Amy Post and George W. Lowther. The reviewer imagined how Jacobs's book might move its readers to action in the cause of reform: "If this narrative of the terrible experiences of a noble woman in slavery could be read at every fireside in the free States, it would kindle such a feeling of moral indignation against the system and its guilty abettors, and such a determination to resist and exterminate it by every legitimate and rightful means, as would put an end, once and forever, to all those projects of compromise by which politicians are now endeavoring to 'reconstruct' the broken Union."[49] The key phrase, "legitimate and rightful means," marks the limit of resistance. It draws the line between influence and enthusiasm, between a principled civil disobedience and a fanatical militancy, between the firesides of the free North and the fields of an abandoned South.

To another camp of readers, though, the fire kindled by Jacobs's narrative promised to burn through all such boundaries. This was the furious reaction of the *Weekly Anglo-African:* "No one can read these pages without a feeling of horror, and a stronger determination arising in them to tear down the cursed system which makes such records possible. Wrath, the fiery messenger which goes flaming from the roused soul and overthrows in its divine fury the accursed tyrannies of earth; will find in these pages new fuel for the fire, and new force for the storm which shall overthrow and sweep from existence American slavery."[50] In this review, there is no talk of "legitimate and rightful means." There is a prophecy of apocalyptic wrath against the curse of slavery. The fire in question is no domestic hearth in the free states but a militant campaign, raging into the South.

The *Weekly Anglo-African* and its counterpart, the *Anglo-African Magazine,* had been founded two years earlier, in 1859, by Thomas Hamilton. From the beginning, these periodicals served as a forum for extreme antislavery opinion. In its first year, the *Anglo-African* devoted substantial space and commentary to Brown's raid, trial, and execution, and it did not shy away from the prospect of armed intervention in the South.[51] It recognized that the mass press had made Brown's death an international spectacle, factionalizing public opinion around a ceremony of punishment: "'That sad hour from eleven till noon found concentrated on John Brown's gallows the attention, the sympathy, the hate, or the love of thirty millions of people! What an audience to gather, and how nobly taught!'" Emphasizing the heroism and sacrifice of the black men who had fought with Brown, the *Anglo-African* attacked Beecher's conciliatory sermon as a misrepresentation of the nature and the consequences of this historic crisis.[52]

In March of 1861, just two months after the appearance of Jacobs's *Incidents,* Hamilton sold the *Anglo-African* to an organization called the

Haytian Emigration Bureau. The group's mission was to resettle African Americans to the Caribbean island under the presidency of General Fabre Geffrard. Its principal agent in the United States was none other than the fierce disciple of John Brown, James Redpath.[53] When he took over the paper and the magazine, Redpath disagreed with some of his contributors, including the ex-slave Henry Highland Garnet, about the proposition of resettlement in Haiti, but he did his best to maintain his ties with them in the common cause of radical abolition.[54] If anything, Redpath took the publication in an even more militant direction. In the installment for April 13, 1861, alongside the review of Jacobs's *Incidents*, he printed one of many calls for rebellion: "Only through the Red Sea of civil war and insurrection can the sins [of the oppressor] be washed away."[55] The crimes of this guilty land would never be purged away but with blood.

It seems likely, then, that Redpath himself is the author of the review that harkens to Jacobs's "words of fire." The piece relates a vision of Jacobs's reception that has much in common with Redpath's preface to *Echoes of Harper's Ferry*. There, the editor described his intention in collecting public responses to Brown's raid as an effort to galvanize militancy. The use of antislavery texts was not to inspire Christians to exert their moral influence. It was to fire up an insurrection: "My desire to preserve these papers arises . . . from the hope that I may thereby fan the holy flame that their action kindled, until, becoming a consuming fire, it shall burn up, with thoroughness and speed, every vestige of the crime of American Slavery."[56] In their cadences, in their imagery, and in their political fury, the lines anticipate the "fiery messenger" of the *Weekly Anglo-African*'s review of Jacobs's *Incidents*.

What matters for a poetics of justice, though, is not so much Redpath's personal authorship of the review as its clear identification with the most uncompromising faction of the abolitionist crusade. Reading the two pieces together strongly suggests that the reviewer's endeavor was to join Jacobs's narrative to the body of radical writings on Brown, to enlist her and her readers into the cause of insurrection. The author may or may not have known, along the way, that Jacobs had made her own effort to forge the same connection. His conscription of Jacobs to the militant cause performed, perhaps unwittingly, an act of critical restoration.

"This Faithful Messenger"

In the years between *Scott v. Sanford* and the Civil War, the *Anglo-African* was also publishing one of the first novels by an African American author, Martin R. Delany's *Blake, or The Huts of America*. The text appeared serially in the *Anglo-African Magazine* in 1859 and then, after a pause of several months, in the *Weekly Anglo-African* from 1861 to 1862.[57] (During the interval, John Brown had been put to death in Virginia, and the *Anglo-African* had welcomed the appearance of Jacobs's *Incidents* as a renewed call to arms.) As readers know, Delany's story is divided into two parts. In the first, the hero travels through the slave states, sowing the seeds for a coordinated insurrection on a massive scale. In the second, he makes his way to Cuba, where he is reunited with his wife and conspires to plot an insurrection there. The revolutionaries plan to liberate Cuba from Spain and to repel the American planters who are trying to annex the island to the United States. Before the violence begins, though, the novel breaks off. The bloodthirsty curse "Woe be unto these devils of whites, I say!" is left hanging in the air (313).

Part 2 of *Blake* was serialized after the *Anglo-African* came under the official control of Redpath's Haytian Emigration Bureau, and its Cuban plot reflects the ongoing effort among antislavery radicals to develop a scheme of emigration under black leadership, distinct from the Colonization Society's missionary program (and, of course, in defiance of the annexation schemes of President Franklin Pierce and his Southern allies). But Delany's book is transnational in orientation, even in the early chapters, and its militancy is consistent from beginning to end. Page by page, it is concerned much less with emigration than with rebellion.

Although Delany sought the help of William Lloyd Garrison and others, in hopes of producing a book for sale, the chapters of *Blake* were not collected under a single cover until 1970. Then, Delany's fictional hero Henry Blake, like the Nat Turner of the *Confessions*, was hailed as an ancestor of the twentieth century's pan-Africanist militants and anticolonial revolutionaries. Indeed, Delany himself, as the historian Nell Irvin Painter observes, had been more or less "forgotten until his resurrection three-quarters of a century later as the father of black nationalism."[58] In the academy, his novel was canonized by scholars who were less interested in aesthetic value—even those who insisted on its importance tended to apologize for the awkwardness of its craft—than in reconstructing legacies of subaltern dissent and cosmopolitan radicalism. As a reviewer for *Phylon* put it in 1971, Delany did not "attain artistic immortality" with *Blake,* but he did deliver "one strident message," and the message was "insurrection."[59]

These critical efforts went some distance toward fulfilling Delany's own hopes for a bound edition of *Blake* (though a few missing chapters have never been recovered) and, in time, made possible a range of other interpretations. Eric Sundquist, for instance, reads the novel as a meditation on Southern expansion and a heroic expression of black militancy. *Blake,* in his view, showed how the same transnational economic and legal networks which sustained the system of slavery could also serve to organize a general insurrection that would radiate from Mississippi in the Deep South outward to Canada in the far North, to Cuba in the Caribbean, and to the distant shores of Africa.[60] In similar terms, Paul Gilroy recollects Delany as a key forefather for the tradition of black Atlantic radicalism which finds its unity not in the "roots" of a shared heritage but in the "routes" of migration and strategic alliance.[61]

What may have been obscured in Delany's retrospective conscription as a pan-Africanist "father," though, is the way his novel carved out a place for itself in its first context. A few preliminary distinctions have been drawn. Delany's brand of black nationalism has been read against the integrationist position of Frederick Douglass, with whom Delany waged a public debate in the 1850s, and his militancy has been contrasted to the sentimentalism of Harriet Beecher Stowe. Thus Gilroy describes Delany as "the progenitor of black Atlantic patriarchy" and a polemicist for whom "the public sphere was to be the sole province of an enlightened male citizenry."[62] In Sundquist's reading, likewise, Delany took the "example" of his hero "from Nat Turner rather than Uncle Tom."[63] Such a characterization puts *Blake* squarely at odds with the feminized politics of influence.[64]

For a poetics of justice, this gendered opposition is less significant, in the end, than the novel's literary intervention in the legal public sphere— its positivist critique of legal formalism, its skeptical and opportunistic use of religious protest, and its reconception of literary genres as weapons in a struggle over the foundations of authority. As the *Anglo-African*'s review of Jacobs's narrative makes clear, Delany's radical circle saw no necessary contradiction between militancy and the exhortations of a woman's voice. The significance of *Blake,* in my view, is that the novel takes the step from the imagination of the curse to its affirmation, from the regulatory disavowal of incendiary verbal action to its deployment in the service of revolution. Indeed, the novel can be read as the allegory of a militarized public sphere. Its hero serves as the medium of a synchronous address to the heterogeneous communities of slaves scattered around the Atlantic rim. In this way *Blake* braids together and gives a new twist to the three stories that have been developed over the course of my book—of the oracle, of the curse, and of an imaginative literature estranged from legal authority.

The vexed relation between black literacy and the antebellum legal system was fundamental to Delany's self-conception. His first biography, written by Frances Rollin with Delany's cooperation, recalled that his family had been driven from his home town—where else but the Charles Town, Virginia, made famous by John Brown's trial?—when his mother was prosecuted and threatened with imprisonment for teaching her black children to read.[65] The family moved to Pennsylvania, where Delany came of age, but his life continued to bring him into conflict with a racist legal order. His struggles to acquire a formal education, to protect his property rights, and to defend himself against charges of libel sharpened his insight into a system of dispossession that extended far beyond the borders of the South.[66] By the early 1850s he was making speeches and publishing articles against the Fugitive Slave Law. In 1857, he understood the Supreme Court's decision in *Scott v. Sanford* as the federal government's clearest, most brutally honest, disclosure of the foundations of legal authority in the country, North and South.

Chief Justice Roger Taney's famous decision in the case did not simply reject Dred Scott's claim to freedom, which was based on his long residency in the free states. The court denied that Scott had the right even to make such a claim—indeed, to make virtually any legal claim at all. The opinion argued that African slaves and their descendants had been categorically excluded from citizenship by the framers of the U.S.

Constitution. "Negroes of the African race," it said, were therefore not to be counted among the lawgiving people. They were not "constituent members of this sovereignty": they were "a subordinate and inferior class of beings," holding "no rights or privileges but such as those who held the power and the Government might choose to grant them."[67] These lines effectively blurred the distinction between enslaved and free persons of color. The court bound the legal dispossession of all African American subjects directly to their bodies.

In pronouncing its devastating opinion, the Taney Court staged the performance of its own paralysis: "It is not the province of the court to decide upon the justice or injustice, the policy or impolicy, of these laws. The decision of that question belonged to the political or lawmaking power, to those who formed the sovereignty and framed the Constitution. The duty of the court is to interpret the instrument they have framed with the best lights we can obtain on the subject, and to administer it as we find it, according to its true intent and meaning when it was adopted."[68] The court disavowed its discretionary power through two displacements. One emphasized the separation of powers: the authority to define the boundaries of the sovereign community was yielded to the representative assembly which had composed the Constitution. The other asserted the supremacy of the historical past over the present: the court was bound to interpret the Constitution according to the prevailing norms of the 1780s, the period when the document was written and ratified, not to consider the shifts in the people's sentiments which might have happened since. According to the specious originalism of the opinion, Taney and his fellow justices had no authority to "abrogate the judicial character of this court, and make it the mere reflex of the popular opinion or passion of the day."[69] Thus the court closed its doors against the living people of the present, with their fickle passions, and expelled, with them, the very question of justice.

In some ways, the opinion in *Scott v. Sanford* was repeating familiar gestures from the repertoire of oracular jurisprudence. The court's deference to the representative assembly and its presumed reverence for longstanding customs were at least as old as the formalism expounded in Blackstone's *Commentaries*. So, too, was the practice of changing the meaning of the law while projecting an illusion of custodial care. At the same time, though, the Taney Court was subtly redefining the function of legal formalism itself. The invocations of natural law and customs were now acknowledged as little more than ritualized, *ex post facto* justifications for the exercise of power in a context that was best understood as a struggle for domination. So-called rights, in the court's view, were little more than privileges granted at the discretionary whim of "those who held the power."[70] The depersonalized rule of law was just a pale cloak worn to battle in a race war.

It was this cynical oracularism, reducing the question of justice to the matter of power, that provoked and enraged Martin Delany. As Gregg Crane demonstrates, *Blake* develops an extended "dissent" from the opinion of the court, a "type of literary intervention in American jurisprudence" in direct opposition to "the official version of citizenship" expressed in *Scott v. Sanford*.[71] (Taney himself recognized that his opinion had gained a wide circulation, becoming the subject of "various comments and reviews" which had attacked the decision, and he published a "Supplement" to the official opinion in order to fortify and expand its arguments in the court of public opinion.[72]) Delany used the character of Judge Ballard, a Northern jurist with substantial investments in the slave system, as a mouthpiece for Taney's philosophy: "persons of African descent have no rights that white men are bound to respect" (61). Judge Ballard reckons this "a just construction of the law," but he takes pains to assure his Southern friends that his personal interest, not just his official duty, binds him to their side (61). Despite his Northern residence and his need to maintain the appearance of impartiality, "his interests . . . placed him beyond suspicion" as a protector of the slave system and a hunter of fugitives (5). This is a tie much deeper than any agreement about the finer points of constitutional interpretation, which are easily finessed to satisfy the wishes of the ruling class.

A little like Nathaniel Hawthorne in *The House of the Seven Gables,* then, Delany means to expose the hypocrisy of authorities who hide their own corrupt self-interest behind the mask of a self-effacing jurisprudence. A little like Stowe in *Uncle Tom's Cabin,* too, he shows how Northern and Southern business interests refashion the law to serve themselves, not the dictates of justice. But Delany marks his departure from these other literary critiques of law when he turns the same skeptical eye toward religion, which provided Hawthorne and Stowe with an alternative standard of judgment. "Don't tell me about religion!" Blake thunders. "What's religion to me?" (16). Delany's hero is ruthless in attacking the Christianity that props up the slaveholders with the myth of a divinely-ordained racial hierarchy. He goes on to reject that Uncle Tom-like faith, with its consoling promise of redemption in the afterlife, which seems to transfix the enslaved in their abjection. "If I ever were a Christian, slavery has made me a sinner," Blake says to those who would pray for his soul. "I feel more like cursing than praying" (103). In the end, he takes a skeptical view even of the curse—whose redemptive power, if it has any, will have to be proved in this world, not the next.

Delany's most sustained treatment of the problem comes in Chapter 24, "A Flying Cloud," where Blake visits the Conjurers of the Great Dismal Swamp. This band of maroons and veteran freedom fighters preserves the folk memory of a militant tradition that includes "General" Gabriel, Denmark Vesey, and especially Nat Turner. Carrying the torch of insurrection, Blake is hailed as the next prophetic leader in the line. By the time he leaves the swamp, Delany writes, "the old material extinguished and left to mould and rot after the demonstration at Southampton, was immediately rekindled, never again to be suppressed until the slaves stood up the equal of the masters" (116). There is no cautious disavowal here, no effort to restrain the incendiary capacity of revolutionary words or deeds. There is an open affirmation of the will to burn.

Blake comes around to this affirmation, however, only after subjecting the folk religion of the swamp to a thoroughly disenchanting investigation. The conjurers are not romanticized as the priests of a syncretic and subversive faith. They are exposed as charlatans. Thus, for instance, "Old Gamby Gholar, a noted high conjurer and compeer of Nat Turner," leads Delany's hero through a fortune-telling ceremony, using the scales of "innocent and harmless fish" for serpent's scales, a shard of bottle glass for a "blue stone," and a little bird's breastbone for the "charm bone of a tree frog" (112, 113). "Amusing enough it was to him who consented to satisfy the aged devotees of a time-honored superstition" (114). Throughout the passage, Delany focalizes the narrative through the protagonist's point of view, demystifying each object and deflating the authority of the conjurer.

Blake understands conjure as a means of raising funds for subsistence in the swamp and, especially, as a technique of self-authorization. As he explains later, "All that it does, is to put money into the pockets of the pretended conjurer, [and] give him power over others by making them afraid of him" (136). Blake agrees to be initiated into Ghamby Gholar's circle—but only because the title of conjurer "makes the more ignorant slaves have greater confidence in, and more respect for, their headmen and leaders" (126). It is worth remembering that the Turner of the *Confessions* had also disavowed conjure, insisting on the prophetic, rather than magical, origins of his authority. But Blake's appropriation of the supernatural is strictly instrumental—he treats conjure much as he treats a compass or a gold coin. He will invest himself in a mystifying authority if it serves the cause of insurrection, but he regards it all the while with an amused detachment. Here is the curse, coldly weaponized.

It is not only Delany's militancy but also his skepticism, then, which sets him in philosophical opposition to his best-known contemporaries in the antislavery crusade. Neither Stowe's divine injunctions nor Frederick Douglass's natural rights are coherently endorsed in *Blake*. Instead, Delany works from the premises of a positivistic realism. He understands concepts like higher law not as creeds to be believed but as tools to be wielded in the determined pursuit of racial self-interest. In this sense, the novel is less an inspired protest against the logic of Taney's opinion in *Scott v. Sanford* than its answer from the other side of the racial divide. With Delany's open "appreciation of the glittering trappings of power," Crane argues, *Blake* finally endorses the view that rights really are privileges granted by the powerful, and it imagines that the liberation and enfranchisement of blacks in the Americas can be achieved only through the revolutionary establishment of new nation-states under their own control.[73]

This reading, however, is left with an unresolvable contradiction between the rhetoric of justice and the politics of self-interest. It comes to this impasse because it naturalizes what the novel relentlessly problematizes: the unifying power of racial identification. For Delany, the idea that all black communities share a common self-interest cannot be taken for granted as a matter of heritage. It has to be produced through organization and coordination. As Gilroy writes, Delany's "anti-mystical racial rationalism required that blacks of all shades, classes, and ethnic groups give up the merely accidental differences that served only to mask the deeper unity waiting to be constructed not so much from their African heritage as from the common orientation to the future produced by their militant struggles against slavery."[74] The scattered and heterogeneous communities of color around the Atlantic have no sense, yet, of a common interest. They must be made to imagine themselves as a collective body. This is precisely the mission undertaken by Delany's hero, who becomes less the agent of a violent action (which is never carried out) than the medium of a unifying message.

Blake, who is called Henry Holland in most of Part 1, sets out on a journey that takes him throughout the slave and free states. Along the way he encounters black communities of many kinds. There are the house servants of Mississippi and the maroons of the Great Dismal Swamp. There are the comparatively well-treated laborers of Kentucky, so much more intractably enthralled, he observes, because of their complacency. There are the blacks of Arkansas, who maintain a secret communications network on a regional scale. There are the class-riven people of color in the eastern states, the creole congregations of New Orleans, and several others, too. Following this episodic or picaresque pattern, Part 1 of *Blake* is sometimes compared to an ethnographic travel narrative. One of its aims is to provide a panoramic and comparative study of black life in antebellum America. Henry's project, however, is not to observe these communities as he finds them; it is to reorient their self-understanding and, in the process, to bind them together in a new way. He calls his friends to see that their own salvation is linked to the revolutionary liberation of the race. "From plantation to plantation did he go, sowing the seeds of future devastation and ruin to the master and redemption to the slave, an antecedent more terrible in its anticipation than the warning voice of the destroying Angel in commanding the slaughter of the firstborn of Egypt" (83). Henry often describes his work in terms of demystification and enlightenment, but he is no disinterested ethnographer. He is a prophet and an evangelist.

Even as *Blake* disavows its faith in the slavemaster's Christianity and the petty tricks of conjure, then, it dreams of a linguistically mediated summoning on a far grander scale. Despite the professed skepticism of the novel's hero, Jordan Stein is right to observe that *Blake* builds its politics on a "messianic telos."[75] Here, too the same text which seems to deliver a cynical critique of the oracle and the curse begins to reveal its deeper imbrication in the antebellum period's poetics of justice. It is a story about the circulation of an incendiary prophecy, summoning a vast assembly of strangers into the faith that they belong to a moral community with one destiny—and it is a sustained reflection on the capacity of verbal performances, including literary performances like the novel itself, to do this work. In *Blake*, the autonomy of literature, its escape from and antagonism to legal authority, is not depicted as a withdrawal into the private sphere of conscience. A radical estrangement from the law endows the literary text with the power to stir up a revolutionary counterpublic.

The figure of the literary revolutionary in the novel is introduced in Part 2, in Blake's Cuban cousin and co-conspirator, the poet Placido. Delany based this character on the historical Gabriel de la Concepción Valdés, pen name Plácido, who was executed by the Cuban government for his alleged role in an insurrectionary plot of 1844. Delany's novel took part in an ongoing debate over the poet's legacy. Unlike many of Plácido's defenders, though, Delany was not concerned to prove the martyr's innocence. He meant to justify him as an insurrectionist. Delany's version of the poet has lived beyond 1844, into the 1850s, and his features have been blended with those of another Cuban poet and dissenter, Juan Francisco Manzano. Although Plácido's verse had been translated into English and circulated in the antislavery press, most of the poems attributed to the character in the novel were written by Delany's friend James M. Whitfield and, some speculate, by Delany himself. Rather than directly incorporating the historical figure, then, Delany created a composite who could embody the emergent literary radicalism of black intellectuals from around the Americas, writing in at least two languages.[76]

The novel gives special attention to the circulation and reception of a poem that begins this way:

> Were I a slave I would be free!
>> I would not live to live a slave;
> But rise and strike for liberty,
>> For Freedom or a martyr's grave! (195)

With the opening phrase, "Were I a slave," Placido performs a delicate act of identification. He acknowledges that he is not one of the enslaved, but he imagines his way into their position. Throughout the poem, the speaker exposes himself to degradation, then transmutes the shame of abjection into heroic self-assertion. "One look upon the bloody scourge," he goes on, "Would rouse my soul to brave the fight" (195). Placido's performance in the subjunctive mode—were I a slave, would I strike?—might be compared to Elizabeth Barrett Browning's dramatic monologue "The Runaway Slave at Pilgrim's Point." Unlike Browning and her Garrisonian friends, though, Placido ends by rejecting the constraints of pacifism—"Away the unavailing plea! / Of peace, the tyrant's blood to spare"—and commits itself to the "sabre" and the "vindicating brand" (196, 195).

Reading Placido's "stimulating appeal," Blake feels his spirit "kindled into a flame" (196). And as the incendiary poem circulates, through underground circles, among Cuba's dissidents, it seems to call many other readers to action. In fact, when Blake departs for Africa, apparently seeking to procure weapons and supplies for the struggle, it is Placido who takes over the task of organizing the Cuban rebels. Upon Blake's return, the poet tells him that "we have had our gatherings, held our councils, formed our legions, chosen our leaders" (241). Placido becomes less the author of self-expressive verses than a figure of circulation; the transmission of his words gathers and militarizes a counterpublic poised for revolutionary action. The poet does the work of summoning.

Delany introduces his two heroes, on the eve of the rebellion, as "Placido the cousin, adviser and counselor, and Henry Blake, the master spirit of the occasion" (252). On the surface of things, this characterization might appear to conscript the man of letters, as a subordinate, into the service of the man of action, his "master spirit." But *Blake* has devoted itself, from the beginning, to dismantling the opposition between words and deeds. Especially since the novel (at least in its extant form) never narrates the rebellion, Blake himself is best understood as a kind of medium—"this faithful messenger of his oppressed brethren," as Delany calls him (121). Indeed, the novel declines to reveal the full content of Henry's message, the signal which will coordinate the beginning of the rebellion. It focuses, instead, on the process of transmission.

As Henry makes his continental tour in Part 1, he comes to see that the real obstacle to a general insurrection is not the social death of the enslaved or the complacency of those who live under relatively soft masters. It is the absence of a communications system. Perhaps the most encouraging moment in his journey, therefore, is his discovery that some enslaved communities in Arkansas have received the news of his mission before he arrives in person. Because an underground network allows these people to "get words from each other so far apart," he declares Arkansas "ahead of all the other states" (89). His aim is to extend this regional network to a national or transnational scale, radicalizing it as he goes. When he wants to make his way downriver from Ohio to Kentucky, he catches a ride on a steamer called the "Telegraph No. 2" (122).

Thus Blake becomes a figure for an infrastructure of communication which links together communities of color around the Atlantic. In Delany's time, such a system of circulation was just being built, and Delany himself was one of its messengers. Rollin's biography recalls that, in working with Douglass on the *North Star,* Delany "traveled, holding meetings, and lecturing, so as to obtain subsidies, and endeavored to effect a permanent establishment of a newspaper, as a general organ of the colored people."[77] Emphasizing this phase of Delany's career, Painter notes that his organizing work allowed a black newspaper to reach "a national audience for the first time."[78] In *Blake,* Delany told the story of another traveler whose task was to stitch together a public on a vast, national or "general" scale. *Blake* not only took antislavery protest to a new pitch of intensity; it dramatized the violent activation of a counterpublic sphere. It not only used a literary genre to address, in explicit and militant terms, the historical crisis of its time; it imagined that it could transform the space of its own circulation and reception into a field of fire.

"I have waited long enough on heavenly promises," Blake says as he begins his mission. "I'll wait no longer" (16). With the echoes of Harper's Ferry ringing across the land, the contributors to *The Anglo-African* affirmed the emergence of a militant counterpublic that was national in scope and character. Through the examples of incendiary testimony and revolutionary evangelism—Jacobs's words of fire and Blake's prophecies of vengeance—they imagined that the invocation of justice was now capable of summoning a righteous community to war against the corrupt sovereignty which had assented to the slaveholding legal order. This blazing vision of the curse was a long time coming. Its first sparks, perhaps, had been struck by the enthusiastic self-vindications of offenders in the early republic. It had been kindled into a fire in the class-riven conflicts over blasphemy, the gendered struggle over evil speaking, and the racialized violence of the slavery crisis. In its literary variant, it took an autonomy which had been cast as privacy and returned it to the public sphere, transcending the disciplinary opposition between women's domestic influence and men's authorized speech acts. The networks of transmission and synchronization were in place, and even the disavowal of the curse had contributed to the conception of its inflammatory power. It was time to burn.

Epilogue

The Curse at Sea

By the time *The Anglo-African* published its review of Harriet Jacobs's *Incidents* and the last chapters of Martin Delany's *Blake* in 1861, John Brown's prophecy of a bloody reckoning on a national scale seemed inexorably to be coming true. With the outbreak of the Civil War, Delany turned his efforts from the prospect of a new nation elsewhere to the future of the republic, enlisting in the Union army and recruiting others to the cause. He had circled back, in a sense, from the Caribbean and African scenes of *Blake*'s Part 2 to the U.S. context that dominates Part 1. Like his onetime publishing partner Frederick Douglass, Delany had come to see the United States as the crucial battleground, at least for the moment, and to foresee a racially integrated national community, with equal citizenship rights for all men, as the future most urgently worth fighting for. This forefather of a transnational and cosmopolitan black politics had become a soldier in the service of the nation.

Delany's pivot to the United States was not a renunciation of his radicalism or of his devotion to an African diasporic identity. It was a strategic realignment, responsive to the conditions of conflict that were rapidly changing around him. The lives and political destinies of millions were at stake, and Delany took his side in a war that would determine the geographical borders of the union, redraw the legal boundaries

of citizenship—and, by the time it was over, reconfigure the relation
between the rule of law and the ideal of justice. An earlier period's heterogeneous order, composed of many jurisdictions, would be forged into
a stricter hierarchy. Soon, the promise of inclusion in the national community would appear to foreclose virtually all other spaces and scales of
belonging. Those who cursed the nation or who dreamed of summoning
a counterpublic in opposition to its people would find themselves adrift
in solitude and exile.

Such, at least, was the moral of the most celebrated cursing story
published in the war years, Edward Everett Hale's "The Man without a
Country" (1863). Hale's doomed protagonist is Philip Nolan. As a young
man he is seduced by the "gay deceiver" Aaron Burr, who persuades
him to play a minor part in a treasonous conspiracy. Captured and prosecuted by a military court, Nolan is asked if he can provide any evidence
of his loyalty to the United States. He answers with an obscenity: "D—n
the United States! I wish I may never hear of the United States again."
The Colonel presiding over the court martial, a patriotic veteran of the
Revolution, is so offended by this utterance that he devises an unprecedented penalty: He grants Nolan's wish. The prisoner is condemned to
spend the rest of his life, more than half a century as it turns out, aboard
naval ships, adrift in the seven seas. He never returns to or hears any
news from the United States.[1]

Nolan is treated with courtesy, eventually with affection and indul-
gence, by the officers who oversee his custody. Even so, he comes to
experience his exile as the severest of punishments. Once the child of
a cosmopolitan upbringing in the borderlands of several empires, he
develops a love for a country he can know only in his mind. Scrutiniz-
ing every hint and every silence from his fellow sailors, interpreting the
blank spaces that have been clipped out of his newspapers, he does all
he can to piece together a picture of America. On his deathbed, when he
learns that the republic has extended its reach to Texas in the South and
California in the West, he is moved to tears of joy. (To keep his golden
dream intact, a sympathetic shipmate refrains from telling Nolan about
the recent Southern secession.) The story of the man without a country's redemption teaches its readers that nothing—not liberty, not life

itself—is more precious than their attachment to a chimerical nation, conceived from nostalgia and fantasy.

"The Man without a Country" was loosely based on events from the history of the early republic, but Hale refashioned his material as an allegory of his own legal and political present. He designed the story expressly for the court of public opinion during a wartime crisis of federal authority. President Lincoln had been publicly attacked for suspending the ancient right of *habeas corpus,* imprisoning suspected Confederate sympathizers indefinitely and without trial. Most controversially, Lincoln had permitted the arrest of the Ohio politician Clement Vallandigham for a speech against the abuse of executive power, ordering Vallandigham's banishment from Union territory, into the South. Hale's immediate task in "The Man without a Country" was to defend the legitimacy of the president's decisions. More broadly, as Brook Thomas argues, the story's "major cultural work was to make the country, not the state or the section, the object of affection reserved for one's 'home.'"[2] In this sense it was an allegorical and ideological counterpart to Lincoln's strong assertion of federal sovereignty over the states. The hero's redemption as a patriot serves to justify his extraordinary punishment. For a hundred years, Hale's text was reprinted in popular volumes, a cherished masterpiece of didactic nationalism.

"The Man without a Country" fell out of the canon in the 1960s, During the civil rights and peace movements, critics looked with suspicion on its politics, rejecting Hale's apology for the exceptional expansion of executive power in wartime. More recently, the story has been revisited by scholars interested in its contradictions. The same tale which began as nationalist propaganda can also be turned, by sophisticated readers, to the critique of the nation's history.[3] Yet these contradictions are perhaps less disabling than they seem. For the ideological work of national fantasy, as Lauren Berlant shows, does not depend on the premise that the nation is already perfect. It depends on the promise that it can become so. National fantasy establishes the nation as the final horizon of all reformist struggle and utopian longing, absorbing critiques of the actual nation into the ongoing project of producing the nation as it ought to be.[4] It forecloses other spaces of identification and belonging, in other

words, by plotting every aspiration toward justice along the single tem-
poral arc of the nation's progress toward its destiny.

Whether we approach "The Man without a Country" as patriotic propaganda or as a critique of federal power, then, we can also read it as a
kind of epitaph for the curse. It was not Hale who invented the literature
of national fantasy. (Berlant traces its origins back at least as far as Nathaniel Hawthorne's early tale, "Alice Doane's Appeal.") But the nation under
Lincoln did take hold as never before, establishing its supremacy over
local and sectional attachments. It did so with naked force, through victory in battle and the annihilating strategy of total war. And it did so with
law, through the extraordinary extension of executive authority and the
effective redefinition of sovereignty. The war and its aftermath brought a
paradoxical transformation: just as the federal army revealed its capacity
to put down the largest rebellion in the nation's history, unleashing a terrible violence, the Emancipation Proclamation and the postwar amendments expanded the horizons of citizenship so that the ideal of equal
justice for all men was enshrined as fundamental, positive law.

Equal justice for all men—the phrase suggests an epoch-making
expansion of civil rights but also marks its limits. One of the cruel iro-
nies of the wartime transformation was that the antislavery movement, so
strongly identified with women's influence, ended up reforming the Constitution without extending the franchise to women. In her 1879 autobiography, *A Brand Plucked from the Fire,* the black preacher Julia A. J.
Foote would point out with some bitterness that Chief Justice Taney's
restrictive definition of citizenship rights could still be turned against
her and her sisters, too. "Even the ministers of Christ," she wrote of the
men who excommunicated her from church membership, "did not feel
that women had any rights which they were bound to respect."[5] Like
the women who had preached and exhorted in the decades before the
war, Foote claimed the right to speak in public as a matter of the highest justice. But there was a difference, too. By covertly identifying herself with Dred Scott, Foote adopted the style of rights advocacy that had
become a crucial aspect of U.S. national fantasy only after the war: for
Foote, as for so many others, the ideal of citizenship is derived from the
enfranchisement of black men.[6] The paradigm of this advocacy is the
demand that the federal government recognize and protect the citizen's

rights, unprejudiced by his or her identity. It summons no counterpublic in opposition to the sovereign people; it aspires to full inclusion in the nation's community, to be realized in a time to come. For these reasons, I end my stories of the oracle, the curse, and martyr literature with the conflagration of the Civil War.

Especially after the Fourteenth Amendment to the Constitution (1868), the prevailing mode of justice rhetoric was no longer the appeal to higher law. It was a call for the enforcement of federal law, against the illegal abrogation of civil rights. As Deak Nabers argues, the wartime emancipation of former slaves came to be understood as "a victory of legal process in general and American constitutional law as an expression of that process in particular." Nabers contrasts this emergent project of national inclusion with the higher-law discourse that had characterized the anti-Unionist, Garrisonian abolitionism and sentimental protest literature of the antebellum period. He does not take up Hale's "The Man without a Country," but he does identify the "victory of law" with another writer known for his fictions of judgment and punishment at sea, Herman Melville. More than any other literary text, Nabers argues, it is Melville's volume of war poetry, *Battle-Pieces,* which best "accounts for the ways in which the law can be mobilized to link together the projects of emancipation and Union."[7]

It may come as a surprise to some readers that my own study of the poetics of justice has had so little to say about Melville's work. In my introduction, I mentioned the hero of *Pierre*'s seductive appeal to Isabel, his invitation to ratify an act, backward, with her consent. Pierre's phrases helped me to explain the oracle (and the curse) as a figure calling for a retrospective legitimation, distinct from the authority that is claimed by representative legislatures. But while Melville has been one of the muses of my project from the outset, I have not revisited his well-known allegories of injustice and rebellion, some of which stand at the center of the Law and Literature canon. Melville's writing differs in important ways from the other examples I have taken up, but I would like to conclude by suggesting that it foresees an alternative future for martyr literature.

Bartleby wasting away in the Tombs, Babo dismembered in the public square, Billy dangling from a spar—again and again, Melville dramatizes scenes of martyrdom, where the state, enacting a more or less spectacular legal violence against an offender, also composes on his body the record of its own excesses and injustices. Well acquainted with the law, Melville took up the burning questions that defined antebellum struggles over justice: the tension between the demands of capital and the sentiments of humanity; the contradictions between the slave law's denial of personhood and the practices of resistance and self-preservation among the enslaved; the conflict between formal law and higher law. In almost all of these fictions, though, Melville's figure of the martyr is a cryptic or a silent one. Asked to account for himself, the ghostly Bartleby gives his characteristically evasive reply, "I would prefer not to." Silently submitting to interrogation, to judgment, and to the punishment of death, the rebel slave Babo makes no confession. "Seeing all was over," Melville writes, "he uttered no sound, and could not be forced to. His aspect seemed to say, since I cannot do deeds, I will not speak words." Framed and court-martialed at sea, the handsome sailor Billy Budd is unable to exonerate himself in language. He stammers and strikes his accuser down. Sentenced to hang, he pronounces his blessing on the authority that has condemned him: "God bless Captain Vere!" The lingering presence of these cryptic or silent bodies is unsettling to the men who persecute them, ambiguously prophetic to the public that looks on. Melville's martyrs do not curse. Instead, they seem to haunt.[8]

In his short stories, Melville gestured toward jurisdictions beyond the borders of the nation—a slaver off the coast of Peru, a warship adrift in the Atlantic. And while he set them in the more or less distant past, he also oriented them toward an indefinite future. When, in *Battle-Pieces*, Melville reflected on the legal transformations wrought by the Civil War, he began with the ominous figure of another martyr:

> Hanging from the beam,
> Slowing swaying (such the law),
> Gaunt the shadow on your green,
> Shenandoah!
> The cut is on the crown
> (Lo, John Brown),
> And the stabs shall heal no more.

Hidden in the cap
Is the anguish none can draw;
So your future veils its face,
Shenandoah!
But the streaming beard is shown
(Weird John Brown),
The meteor of the war.[9]

Remarkably, Melville depicts an unspeaking body even when he takes up the case of John Brown, a defendant who became legendary for his old-fashioned, righteous eloquence. Virginia Jackson introduces her reading of "The Portent" by asking who, if anyone, *speaks* its lines. The poem, she concludes, is really about our inability to know the mind of the ambiguous figure whose body sways above the Charles Town green. Indeed, the poem "can't be said to represent anyone's subjective experience."[10] The martyr is an object of legal violence but not a subject of expression—a silent, mysteriously signifying thing.

The curse, as I have described it in this book, also involves an abnegation of the speaking subject. The offender adopts the martyr's posture by disavowing the self, appearing to address the public as the vessel of an impersonal justice. Melville's martyr figures, though, decline even this oddly self-authorizing style of self-evacuation. (The intriguing exception, perhaps, is Billy Budd, whose blessing on his judge is taken up and repeated by the crew, threatening to become the rallying cry of a mutiny. But here Melville is dramatizing the transmission and reception of Billy's words in a way that strongly dissociates them from any sense of justice that the martyr himself would invoke. The handsome sailor is no mutineer.) From the critical perspective that values the self-expressive voice above all else, these silences may seem to communicate an incapacity, a dehumanizing or muzzling of the accused subject. An even more suspicious reading might claim that Melville appropriates political action to the literary field, trading militant intervention for a gothic aesthetics of haunting. From Melville's perspective, though, the martyr's silence may have seemed to be the only way of escaping the bind of subjection—in the context of a jurisprudential compulsion to speak, to give voice to a subjectivity which can be reconstructed as the grounds of criminal intent, the defendant withdraws into cryptic obscurity.

Finally, though, what makes Melville's versions of silent martyrdom so peculiar and so compelling is something other than their ways of evading subjection; it is their weird temporality. Between the Revolution and the Civil War, the development of a large-scale media infrastructure and the prominence of time-sensitive genres like the newspaper had contributed to the fantasy of a synchronized reception that could mediate a national imaginary. Looking into these transformations, Benedict Anderson's *Imagined Communities* famously analyzed the paradoxical mysticism that attended the concept of the national people in a rationalizing, secularizing modernity: "the members of even the smallest nation will never know most of their fellow-members . . . yet in the minds of each lives the image of their communion."[11] For Anderson, cultural nationalism depends on the homogenization of time imposed by print. But the diversification of genres and modes in the mass press actually introduced a multiplicity of temporalities—a variety of ways of being in time, of orienting ourselves toward the past and the future, that characterizes our asynchronous modernity.[12] For most of the era's self-styled martyrs, the prospect of redemption was glimpsed in some more or less distant future. It was only in the decade of crisis before the Civil War, perhaps, that such a future came to seem imminent. Then, for instance, the *Anglo-African* described a vast counterpublic summoned by the lightning wires of the press to witness John Brown's death. And then Delany's Blake announced that the time for patient waiting was over.

Other revisionist critics of early American letters have argued that there was not a single, coherent public sphere but multiple public spheres, in tension with each other. One of my own endeavors in *The Oracle and the Curse* has been to take the work of disaggregation a step further, to suggest that every act of public address spoke the field of its reception into being, summoning its own fantasmatic community. Similarly, where others have charted the emergence of a literary field from an earlier, more unified culture of letters, I have found it more useful to consider the multiple, dissimilar dynamics of estrangement that were laid out in and around particular texts. Still, my stories have followed a certain general trajectory. I have wished to show how the offender's invocation of higher law emerged in the Revolutionary period, with its struggles to define the new foundations of legitimacy; how it was intensified but also regulated and domesticated in the Jacksonian period, with the rise of the mass press; and how radicals in the antebellum period came to affirm the capacity of the curse to summon an insurrection on a national scale. I have told the story of the curse as one in which a provisional withdrawal from the public sphere prepares the way for the return of a counterpublic with a revolutionary design.

Melville's gift, I think, was to see the relation between legal violence and literature less in terms of spatial metaphors, whether of Habermas's spheres or of Bourdieu's fields, and more in terms of time. He recognized that there are multiple temporalities of circulation, and that a martyrdom becomes a "portent" or a prophecy only in retrospect. For others who considered the case in 1859, John Brown's heroic performance had appeared to summon a national community in a synchronic moment. Even Thoreau, who hated newspapers and loved the enduring, time-transcending truths of literary classics, saw a public and a counterpublic conjured by the virtually immediate transmission of Brown's prison writings. For Melville, though, Brown's martyrdom is ambiguously prophetic, seen retrospectively yet oriented toward an indefinite time to come: "so your future veils its face."

Here, perhaps, haunting can be understood as Melville's trope for the martyr's long afterlife in circulation, the figure's becoming-available to receptions not organized by the political coordinates of the present. For if Melville unmoors the power of martyrdom from its anchorage in anyone's subjectivity and sets it afloat in the circuits of transmission and uptake, he also imagines that the time of circulation is unpredictable, unfathomable. In the eighteenth and nineteenth centuries, literature was routinely endowed with the capacity to seduce its readers away from the public obligations that ensured social order and, in the fiery decades just before the Civil War, some dreamed that it could ignite riot and rebellion. Today, from within our highly differentiated and secularized consumer society, it is difficult to see stories and poems as anything more than objects of private use, providing at best a sense of secret knowledge or moral insight that consoles us in our estrangement from power. And yet, as Melville's slowly swaying pendulum indicates, the future's face is veiled. Martyr literature drifts into a mysterious future, awaiting receptions that no prophecy can foresee.

Notes

INTRODUCTION

1. "Address of John Brown to the Virginia Court, Nov. 2, 1859, on Receiving the Sen-
tence of Death, for his Heroic Attempt at Harper's Ferry, to Give Deliverance to the
Captives, and to Let the Oppressed Go Free" (Broadside. Boston: printed by C. C.
Mead, Liberator Office, 1859. Some capitalization omitted). For the legal and politi-
cal dynamics of Brown's case, see Brian McGinty, *John Brown's Trial* (Cambridge,
MA: Harvard University Press, 2009).

2. W. E. B. Du Bois, *John Brown* (New York: Modern Library, 2001), 221, 219.

3. James Redpath, *The Public Life of Captain John Brown* (Boston: Thayer and
Eldridge, 1860). See also Redpath's *Echoes of Harper's Ferry* (Boston: Thayer and
Eldridge, 1860). Many of the letters had been published even before Brown's death,
as antislavery propagandists attempted to use the occasion of his trial to promote
their cause. In *Meteor of War: The John Brown Story* (New York: Brandywine Press,
2004), John Staufffer and Zoe Trodd argue that Brown in prison had deliberately
"mythologized" himself for the purposes of abolitionist propaganda: "He worked
to give the impression that he chose death willingly; his execution could be a martyrdom only if he seemed to die voluntarily as punishment for his beliefs" (133).
See also Paul Filkelman, "Manufacturing Martyrdom," (in Paul Finkelman, ed.,
His Soul Goes Marching On: Responses to John Brown and the Harpers Ferry Raid
[Charlottesville: University of Virginia Press, 1995], 41–66).

4. Frederick Douglass, *John Brown: An Address by Frederick Douglass at the Fourteenth Anniversary of Storer College, Harper's Ferry, West Virginia, May 30, 1881*
(Dover, NH: Morning Star Job Printing House, 1881), 18.

5. William Henry Fish, quoted in Finkelman, "Manufacturing Martyrdom," 43.

6. Du Bois, *John Brown*, 219, 213.

7. See Deak Nabers, *Victory of Law: The Fourteenth Amendment, the Civil War, and American Litearture, 1852–1867* (Baltimore, MD: Johns Hopkins University Press, 2006), especially Chapter 3, "Constitutional Disobedience," 91–131.

8. Henry David Thoreau, "The Last Days of John Brown," *The Liberator* 30 (July 27, 1860), 118. All references are to this first edition, which was printed on a single page.

9. "John Brown as Hero," *The Independent* 11:571 (November 10, 1859), 4.

10. I use the term "historical poetics" to distinguish my endeavor both from an anti-aesthetic ideology critique and from the dehistoricizing practices of rhetorical criticism. I mean to align my project with a developing critical subfield which reconstructs aesthetic theories and practices with reference to specific historical contexts. See, for example, Virginia Jackson, *Dickinson's Misery: A Theory of Lyric Reading* (Princeton, NJ: Princeton University Press, 2005). Just as Jackson and other scholars are reconciling historicism and poetics by recovering the varieties of aesthetic theory and practice that were in play before the imposition of modernist concepts that claimed a transhistorical validity, my historical poetics of justice attends to the ideas about address and reception that informed the public culture of justice before the ideal of "critique" came to dominance with poststructuralism.

11. "John Brown, The Martyr," *Weekly Anglo-African* (December 10, 1859), n.p. "Neither Thoreau nor anyone else," David S. Reynolds notes in a recent biography, "could have had *any* response to John Brown's words if they had not been printed in the press" (*John Brown, Abolitionist: The Man Who Killed Slavery, Sparked the Civil War, and Seeded Civil Rights* [New York: Vintage, 2005], 384). Robert A. Ferguson goes so far as to call Brown's trial "the first modern courtroom event," since it was "the first to claim daily multimedia validation" (*The Trial in American Life* [Chicago: University of Chicago Press, 2007], 118).

12. Jürgen Habermas, *The Structural Transformation of the Public Sphere: An Inquiry into a Category of Bourgeois Society,* trans. Thomas Burger with the assistance of Frederick Lawrence (Cambridge, MA: MIT Press, 1991), 22, 21.

13. Michael Warner, *Publics and Counterpublics* (New York: Zone Books, 2005), 114, 72, 114.

14. Habermas, *Structural Transformation,* 54. See also Warner, *Publics and Counterpublics,* 68.

15. John Adams, *Defence of the Constitutions* (in Charles Francis Adams, ed., *Works of John Adams, Second President of the United States* [Boston: Little, Brown, 1856]), 404.

16. Many others have continued the work of excavation. Of enduring value to literary and cultural studies, for example, is Benedict Anderson, *Imagined Communities: Reflections on the Origin and Spread of Nationalism,* rev. ed. (London: Verso, 2006).

17. Craig Calhoun, Introduction to *Habermas and the Public Sphere* (Cambridge, MA: MIT Press, 1992), 2.

18. Craig Calhoun, "Afterword: Religion's Many Powers (in Eduardo Mendieta and Jonathan VanAntwerpen, eds., *The Power of Religion in the Public Sphere* [New York: Columbia University Press, 2011] 118–134), 119.

19. John L. Brooke, "Consent, Civil Society, and the Public Sphere in the Age of Revolution and the Early American Republic" (in Jeffrey L. Pasley, Andrew W. Robert-
son, and David Waldstreicher, eds., *Beyond the Founders: New Approaches to the
Political History of the Early American Republic* [Chapel Hill: University of North
Carolina Press, 2004] 207–250), 211. I do not adopt Brooke's map of two overlapping
structures because, as I see it, the public sphere has no permanent shape except as
a set of discursive conventions; it is remade anew in every act of public address. For
similar reasons, Warner observes that "there is no necessary conflict between the
public sphere and the idea of multiple publics" (*Publics and Counterpublics* 56).

20. Here I share Steven Wilf's sense that the legal history of the Revolutionary era
should be expanded to include the popular genres and informal practices that made
up a vernacular legal culture. See Wilf, *Law's Imagined Republic: Popular Politics
and Criminal Justice in Revolutionary America* (Cambridge: Cambridge University
Press, 2010). My disagreement with Wilf's account concerns his notion of the "common people," an entity he seems to take for granted as a social group. In my view, the
common people is a construct, the imagined addressee of genres like the execution
sermon and the criminal confession. I return to these questions in Chapter 2.

21. Perry Miller, *The Life of the Mind in America: From the Revolution to the Civil War*
(San Diego: Harcourt Brace Jovanovich, 1965), 118. A strong counterpoint is provided by leftist historians of transatlantic legal culture, including E. P. Thompson,
Douglas Hay, and Peter Linebaugh. Thompson in particular emphasizes the continuity, rather than the contradiction, between a highly ceremonial criminal justice
and the impersonal rule of law. See Thompson's *Whigs and Hunters: The Origin of
the Black Act* (New York: Pantheon, 1975). I return to these debates in Chapter 2.

22. Miller, *The Life of the Mind,* 118.

23. See, for example, Miller, *Life of the Mind,* 122: "The lawyers were gaining control of
the society through their skill in guiding it into their theoretical version of the Common Law." Except in direct quotations, I adopt the convention from Miller's studies of legal literature, where the capitalized "Common Law" refers to the English
customs treated by Blackstone, and "common law" to the American variant, which
emphasized its transnational or universal character.

24. John Adams, *A Dissertation on the Canon and Feudal Law,* in *Works,* 453.

25. William Blackstone, *Commentaries on the Laws of England* (4 vols., 1765–69; fac-
simile edition, Chicago: University of Chicago Press, 1979), I: 69.

26. Jeremy Bentham, *A Fragment on Government* (Oxford: Blackwell, 1948), 22–23.

27. Louis Althusser, "Ideology and Ideological State Apparatuses" (in *Lenin and Philosophy and Other Essays* [New York: Monthly Review Press, 1971]).

28. Pierre Bourdieu, "Authorized Language: The Social Conditions for the Effectiveness of Ritual Discourse" (in *Language and Symbolic Power,* ed. John B. Thompson,
trans. Gino Raymond and Matthew Adamson [Cambridge, MA: Harvard University Press, 1991], 107–126), 113.

29. Jacques Derrida, "Force of Law: The 'Mystical Foundation of Authority'" (in *Acts of
Religion,* ed. Gil Anidjar [New York: Routledge, 2002]), 241.

30. Richard E. Ellis, *The Jeffersonian Crisis: Courts and Politics in the Young Republic*
(1971; New York: Norton, 1974).

31. A Lover of Improvement (Henry Dwight Sedgwick), *The English Practice: A State-ment Showing Some of the Evils and Absurdities of the English Common Law, as Adopted in Several of the United States, and Particularly in the State of New York* (New York: Printed by J. Seymour, 1822), 12.

32. Jesse Root, *The Origins of Government and Laws in Connecticut* (Hartford, CT: Hudson and Goodwin, 1798), x.

33. James Dana, *The Intent of Capital Punishment, a Discourse, Delivered in the City of New-Haven, October 20, 1790, Being the Day of the Execution of Joseph Mountain, for a Rape* (New Haven, CT: T. and S. Green, 1790), 12.

34. Stephen West, *A Sermon Preached in Lenox, in the County of Berkshire, and Common-wealth of Massachusetts; December 6th, 1787: at the Execution of John Bly, and Charles Rose, for Crimes of Burglary* (Pittsfield, MA: Printed by Elijah Russell, 1787), 7.

35. "Sentence of Death," *Salem Mercury,* November 18, 1786, 3.

36. Thomas Jefferson, quoted in Paul Kahn, *Reign of Law: Marbury v. Madison and the Construction of America* (New Haven, CT: Yale University Press, 1997), 15.

37. Kenneth Greenberg, ed., *The Confessions of Nat Turner and Related Documents* (Boston: Bedford, 1996), 56–57.

38. See William Lee Miller, *Arguing about Slavery: The Great Battle in the United States Congress* (New York: Knopf, 1996).

39. *People v. Ruggles*, 8 Johnson 290 (New York 1811). Rpt. in *Reports of Cases Argued and Determined in the Supreme Court of Judicature; and in the Court for the Trial of Impeachments and the Correction of Errors, in the State of New York* (New York: Isaac Riley, 1811).

40. See, for example, David W. Barton, *Original Intent: The Courts, the Constitution, and Religion* (2nd ed.; Aledo, TX: WallBuilder Press, 1997).

41. Jason Frank, *Constituent Moments: Enacting the People in Postrevolutionary Amer-ica* (Durham, NC: Duke University Press, 2010).

42. Louis Hartz, *The Liberal Tradition in America* (1955; New York: Harcourt, 1991), 10.

43. James Wilson, *An Introductory Lecture to a Course of Law Lectures* (Philadelphia: Dobson, 1791), 17–18.

44. Here my argument intersects with recent cultural studies of secularism and secu-larity. Secularization, in the public culture of law as elsewhere, was a paradoxical movement. There was a clear set of institutional transformations—disestablish-ment, expanded freedoms of conscience, a formal respect for religious diversity—and judges, especially in the highest state and federal courts, became more reluctant to cite scripture or to exhort from the bench. Yet secularization meant much more than rationalization. The emergence of a secular society involved transformations much deeper than the proposals of avowed anti-theocrats like Bentham and Jef-ferson; it established new conceptions of religion itself, of the conditions of belief and unbelief, and it produced new styles of enchantment. The secular age was a "haunted" age, as John Lardas Modern says. John Lardas Modern, *Secularism in Antebellum America* (Chicago: University of Chicago Press, 2011), xxix. Modern's account draws from Charles Taylor, *A Secular Age* (Cambridge, MA: Harvard University Press, 2007). On secularism and enchantment, see also Simon During,

Modern Enchantments: The Cultural Power of Secular Magic (Cambridge, MA: Harvard University Press, 2004) and Lee Eric Schmidt, *Hearing Things: Religion, Illusion, and the American Enlightenment* (Cambridge, MA: Harvard University Press, 2002).

45. My treatment of jurisdiction is informed by Bradin Cormack, *A Power to Do Justice: Jurisdiction, English Literature, and the Rise of Common Law, 1509-1625* (Chicago: University of Chicago Press, 2007). To claim jurisdiction, Cormack argues, is to assert normative authority over a single territory within a larger order of multiple, hetero-geneous territories. It is thus to wield power while acknowledging the simultaneous existence of diverse normative frameworks. In setting aside the question of sovereignty for that of jurisdiction, Cormack's study (like other recent revisions of early modern legal history) decenters the nation and attends to the practice of law in local and trans-national contexts. Cormack also shows how the vexed coexistence of multiple jurisdic-tions was understood in English legal and literary culture. Along these lines, literature's assertion of moral autonomy can be seen as continuous with a legalistic worldview, as yet another normative partitioning: the invention of a new jurisdiction.

46. Death sentence in John Brown's case, reproduced in McGinty, *John Brown's Trial*, 232-233. All quotations are from these two pages.

47. The role of law in keeping the peace was crucial to the ideology of the Southern judiciary and a key point of negotiation between local and state jurisdictions. See Laura F. Edwards, *The People and Their Peace: Legal Culture and the Transforma-tion of Inequality in the Post-Revolutionary South* (Chapel Hill: University of North Carolina Press, 2009).

48. Robert Cover, *Justice Accused: Antislavery and the Judicial Process* (New Haven, CT: Yale University Press, 1975), 15.

49. David Walker, *Walker's Appeal, in Four Articles* (3rd ed.; Boston: David Walker, 1830), 4.

50. James Morgan, quoted in Karen Halttunen, *Murder Most Foul: The Killer and the American Gothic Imagination* (Cambridge, MA: Harvard University Press, 1998), 20.

51. Michel Foucault, *The History of Sexuality, Volume I: An Introduction,* trans. Robert Hurley (New York: Vintage, 1990), 61–62. Foucault was neither the first nor the last to describe the confession as a ritual of submission, retrospectively conjuring a specter of subjectivity. Friedrich Nietzsche, in *The Genealogy of Morals* (trans. Walter Kaufmann [New York: Vintage, 1989]) took this damaged, ghostly figment as a general model for the modern self. He traced the origins of a reflexive, inward-looking subjectivity—the "bad conscience," as he called it—to the development of a "sphere of legal obliga-tions" where personal responsibility is enforced with violence (65). In Judith But-ler's reading of Nietzsche's text, "there can be no subject without a blameworthy act, and there can be no 'act' apart from a discourse of accountability and, accord-ing to Nietzsche, without an institution of punishment" ("Burning Acts—Injurious Speech" [in Andrew Parker and Eve Kosofsky Sedgwick, eds., *Performativity and Performance* (New York: Routledge, 1995)], 200). Applications of these theoreti-cal insights to legal, literary and cultural criticism include Peter Brooks, *Troubling Confessions: Speaking Guilt in Law and Literature* (Chicago: University of Chicago

Press, 2000) and Susan David Bernstein, *Confessional Subjects: Revelations of Gender and Power in Victorian Literature and Culture* (Chapel Hill: University of North Carolina Press, 1997).

52. Shakespeare, *The Tempest,* I. ii. 365–66. On performative language and power in the play, see Stephen Greenblatt, "Learning to Curse," in *Learning to Curse* (New York: Routledge, 1990) 16–39.

53. Geoff Eley, "Nations, Publics, and Political Cultures: Placing Habermas in the Nineteenth Century," in Craig Calhoun, ed., *Habermas and the Public Sphere* (Cambridge, MA: MIT Press, 1992, 289–339), 307. Calhoun goes so far as to claim that the bourgeois public sphere was created "precisely by exclusion" (*The Roots of Radicalism: Tradition, The Public Sphere, and Early Nineteenth-Century Social Movements* [Chicago: University of Chicago Press, 2012]), 124.

54. Jacques Rancière, *Dis-Agreement: Politics and Philosophy,* trans. Julie Rose (Minneapolis: University of Minnesota Press, 1999), 29.

55. Daniel A. Cohen, *Pillars of Salt, Monuments of Grace: New England Crime Literature and the Origins of American Popular Culture, 1674–1860* (Amherst: University of Massachusetts Press, 1993, 2006), 79. Along similar lines, Jeannine DeLombard argues in *In the Shadow of the Gallows: Race, Crime, and American Civic Identity* (Philadelphia: University of Pennsylvania Press, 2012) that the gallows literature attributed to black offenders in the eighteenth century prepared the way for the self-asserting black personhood that flourished in the slave narratives of the antebellum period. See especially Chapter 2, "Black Catalogues: Crime, Print, and the Rise of the Black Self," 87–116. DeLombard does not associate minority self-assertion with a preliterate orality but locates it within print culture, and she fully recognizes that the attribution of agency in the context of criminal trials served to affix blame and to justify punishment.

56. See, for example, William Lee Miller, *Arguing about Slavery* and Michael T. Gilmore, *The War on Words: Slavery, Race, and Free Speech in American Literature* (Chicago: University of Chicago Press, 2010).

57. Calhoun, "Afterword: Religion's Many Powers," 120.

58. Abraham Lincoln, "Address at Cooper Institute," (in *Selected Speeches and Writings,* ed. Don E. Fehrenbacher [New York: Library of America, 1992], 240–252), 246.

59. Abner Kneeland, *Review of the Trial, Conviction, and Final Imprisonment in the Common Jail of the County of Suffolk, of Abner Kneeland, for the Alleged Crime of Blasphemy, Written by Himself* (Boston: George A. Chapman, 1838), 36.

60. William Ellery Channing, *Memoir of William Ellery Channing* (2 vols.; London: Routledge, 1850), II: 245–246.

61. Elleanor Knight, *A Narrative of the Christian Experience, Life and Adventures, Trials and Labors of Elleanor Knight, Written by Herself* (Providence, RI, 1839), 18, 52.

62. Israel Chamberlayne, *Evil Speaking, or, A Bridle for the Unbridled Tongue* (Rochester, NY: Jerome and Brother, 1849).

63. Nabers, *Victory of Law,* 47.

64. Cover, *Justice Accused,* 210.

65. Lemuel Shaw, quoted in Cover, *Justice Accused,* 169.

66. Theodore Parker, *The Trial of Theodore Parker, for the 'Misdemeanor' of a Speech in Faneuil Hall Against Kidnapping* (Boston: Published for the Author, 1855), 69.

67. Jeannine Marie DeLombard, *Slavery on Trial: Law, Abolitionism, and Print Culture* (Chapel Hill: University of North Carolina Press, 2007), 1.

68. George Thompson, *Prison Life and Reflections* (2nd ed.; Hartford: A. Work, 1851), 29, 86. This George Thompson was not the more famous English abolitionist, who also played a major role in the development of abolition's public sphere. A brief biographical sketch of the author of *Prison Life and Reflections* can be found in Clyde S. Kilby, "Three Antislavery Prisoners" (*Journal of the Illinois State Historical Society* 52:3 [Autumn 1959], 419–30), 425–426.

69. Greenberg, ed., *Confessions of Nat Turner,* 48.

70. The vast, contradictory literature on higher law and slavery is surveyed in George Edward Carter, "The Use of the Doctrine of Higher Law in the American Anti-Slavery Crusade, 1830–1860" (PhD. Thesis, University of Oregon, 1970). See also Nabers, *Victory of Law* and DeLombard, *Slavery on Trial.*

71. Samuel T. Spear, "The Law-Abiding Conscience and the Higher Law Conscience; with Remarks on the Fugitive Slave Question: A Sermon, Preached in the South Presbyterian Church, Brooklyn, Dec. 12, 1850" (New York: Lambert and Lane, 1850), 5, 6, 7, 16, 19.

72. Spear, "Law-Abiding Conscience," 6.

73. Nancy Fraser, "Abnormal Justice" (*Critical Inquiry* 34 [Spring 2008] 393–422), 396, 393, 395. Fraser's concepts of "normal" and "abnormal" discourse are drawn from Richard Rorty, especially *Philosophy and the Mirror of Nature* (Princeton, NJ: Princeton University Press, 1979). Fraser expands on some of these concepts in her own *Scales of Justice: Reimagining Political Space in a Globalizing World* (New York: Columbia University Press, 2009).

74. George B. Cheever, *The Curse of God Against Political Atheism: With Some of the Lessons of the Tragedy at Harper's Ferry* (Boston: Walker, Wise, and Co., 1859).

75. Habermas, *Structural Transformation,* 142.

76. The standard account is Robert Ferguson, *Law and Letters in American Culture* (Cambridge, MA: Harvard University Press, 1987). Similar analyses of the emergent literary field have been offered by several other critics. William Charvat argues that the literary press before 1835 was an arena dominated by "lawyers and ministers," the Whiggish "privileged classes" whose moral and political conservatism produced a "homogeneity" of critical standards (Charvat, *The Origins of American Critical Thought, 1810–1835* [1936. New York: A.S. Barnes, 1961] 5). The century leading up to the Civil War, Lawrence Buell observes, was thus a period of "literary emergence. . . , in which belles letters were moving toward, yet still far from attaining, their present degree of autonomy" (Buell, *New England Literary Culture: From Revolution through Renaissance* [Cambridge: Cambridge University Press, 1986], 13). According to Richard Brodhead, it was precisely "the fracturing of the cultural field that brought a distinctly high-literary culture into existence" (Brodhead,

Cultures of Letters: Scenes of Reading and Writing in Nineteenth-Century America [Chicago: University of Chicago Press, 1993], 9).

77. Brook Thomas, *Cross-Examinations of Law and Literature: Cooper, Hawthorne, Stowe, and Melville* (Cambridge: Cambridge University Press, 1987), 2.

78. Wai Chee Dimock, *Residues of Justice: Literature, Law, Philosophy* (Berkeley: University of California Press, 1996), 8, 10.

79. F. O. Matthiessen explicitly opposes the "masterworks" of Emerson, Hawthorne, and company to the "best sellers" of popular female writers (*American Renaissance: Art and Expression in the Age of Emerson and Whitman* [London: Oxford University Press, 1941], x–xi). See also Nina Baym, *The Shape of Hawthorne's Career* (Ithaca, NY: Cornell University Press, 1976); Ann Douglas, *The Feminization of American Culture* (1977; New York: Noonday/Farrar, Strauss and Giroux, 1998); and Henry Nash Smith, *Democracy and the Novel: Popular Resistance to Classic American Writers* (New York: Oxford University Press, 1978). Against this received wisdom, David S. Reynolds argues in *Beneath the American Renaissance: The Subversive Imagination in the Age of Emerson and Melville* (New York: Knopf, 1988) that American literature achieved its distinctive character through its openness to the rhetorical variety and intensity of antebellum popular culture.

80. Thus Jean Fagan Yellin, in "Hawthorne and the American National Sin," (in H. Daniel Peck, ed., *The Green American Tradition: Essays and Poems for Sherman Paul* [Baton Rouge: Louisiana State University Press, 1989]), indicts Hawthorne by charging that "the studied ambiguity of [his] works, usually understood as the result of deliberate artistic decisions, must also be considered as a strategy of avoidance and denial" (97). Fagan's argument is taken up by Jennifer Fleischner, "Hawthorne and the Politics of Slavery," (*Studies in the Novel* 23:1 [Spring 1991] 96–106) and Teresa A. Goddu, "Letters Turned to Gold: Hawthorne, Authorship, and Slavery" (*Studies in Short Fiction* 29:1 [Spring 2001] 49–76).

81. Lauren Berlant, "Poor Eliza," (*American Literature* 70:3 [1998] 635–668), 641.

82. See Milette Shamir, *Inexpressible Privacy: The Interior Life of Antebellum American Literature* (Philadelphia: University of Pennsylvania Press, 2006), 147–174.

83. Jon Mee, *Romanticism, Enthusiasm, and Regulation: Poetics and the Policing of Culture in the Romantic Period* (Oxford: Oxford University Press, 2003), 5.

84. Guyora Binder and Robert Weisberg make the point forcefully: "A precondition of the application of literary theory to legal interpretation is their initial separation. Yet before the nineteenth century, literature was less the discrete enterprise it is today" (*Literary Criticisms of Law* [Princeton, NJ: Princeton University Press, 2000], 7).

85. John Guillory, *Cultural Capital: The Problem of Literary Canon Formation* (Chicago: University of Chicago Press, 1995), 36. Even F. O. Matthiessen's *American Renaissance,* which was steeped in modernist aesthetics, recognized the "desire" in all of its authors "that there should be no split between art and the other functions of the community" (Matthiessen, *American Renaissance,* xi, xiv–xv).

86. "Linda" (*Weekly Anglo-African,* April 13, 1861 [Rpt. in Jean Fagan Yellin, ed., *Harriet Jacobs Family Papers* [2 vols. Chapel Hill: University of North Carolina Press, 2008] 1:349–350), 349.

1. ORACLES OF LAW

1. Nathaniel Hawthorne, *The House of the Seven Gables,* ed. Robert S. Levine (New York: Norton, 2006). Unless otherwise noted, subsequent references are to this edition and cited parenthetically in the text.

2. Hawthorne took the line from published accounts of the 1692 trial and punishment of the condemned witch Sarah Good.

3. See Brook Thomas, *Cross-examinations of Law and Literature: Cooper, Hawthorne, Stowe, and Melville* (Cambridge: Cambridge University Press, 1987), Walter Benn Michaels, "Romance and Real Estate" (in Walter Benn Michaels and Donald Pease, eds., *The American Renaissance Reconsidered* [Baltimore, MD: Johns Hopkins University Press, 1985] 156–82; rpt. in Hawthorne, *The House of the Seven Gables,* 364–385), and Gillian Brown, "Hawthorne, Inheritance, and Women's Property" (*Studies in the Novel* 23 [1991] 107–118). Milette Shamir argues that the key legal concept in *The House of the Seven Gables* is privacy, not property. See Shamir, *Inexpressible Privacy: The Interior Life of Antebellum American Literature* (Philadelphia: University of Pennsylvania Press, 2006), 147–174.

4. Thomas, *Cross-examinations,* 47, 54.

5. Pierre Bourdieu, "Authorized Language: The Social Conditions for the Effectiveness of Ritual Discourse" (in *Language and Symbolic Power,* ed. John B. Thompson, trans. Gino Raymond and Matthew Adamson [Cambridge, MA: Harvard University Press, 1991], 107–126), 107, 109, 113.

6. William Blackstone, *Commentaries on the Laws of England* (4 volumes, 1765–1769; Chicago: University of Chicago Press, 1979). Unless otherwise indicated, all references are to this edition, and cited parenthetically in the text.

7. In 1804, when the poet Edward Leicomb published a "versification" of the *Commentaries,* an American reviewer noticed that the passage on natural law "varies little from Blackstone's original." "Commentaries on the Laws of England, Versified by Edward Leicomb, from the Text of Sir William Blackstone," anonymous review, *The Companion and Weekly Miscellany* 1:2 (November 10, 1804), 14.

8. Douglas Hay, "Property, Authority and the Criminal Law" (in Douglas Hay, et al., *Albion's Fatal Tree: Crime and Society in Eighteenth-Century England* [New York: Pantheon, 1975], 17–63), 23.

9. J. G. A. Pocock, *The Ancient Constitution and the Feudal Law: English Historical Thought in the Seventeenth Century* (1957; New York: Norton, 1967), 30.

10. Guyora Binder and Robert Weisberg, *Literary Criticisms of Law* (Princeton, NJ: Princeton University Press, 2000), 32. On the transition from local customary regimes to an international order organized around sovereign nation-states, see Lauren Benton, *Law and Colonial Cultures: Legal Regimes in World History, 1400–1900* (Cambridge: Cambridge University Press, 2002).

11. On juridical nationalism, see Donald Kelley, *The Human Measure: Social Thought in the Western Legal Tradition* (Cambridge, MA: Harvard University Press, 1990), 175–177.

12. David Lieberman, *The Province of Legislation Determined: Legal Theory in Eighteenth-Century Britain* (Cambridge: Cambridge University Press, 1989), 37.

13. Lieberman, *Province,* 13–16. See also Kelley, *The Human Measure,* on the shift "from jurisprudence to legislation" (222).

14. When the "critical public" in Britain became the "new forum" before which state authorities sought to "legitimate [their] demands," Habermas argues, "the assembly of estates became transformed into a modern parliament" (*The Structural Transformation of the Public Sphere: An Inquiry into a Category of Bourgeois Society* [trans. Thomas Burger with the assistance of Frederick Lawrence [Cambridge, MA: MIT Press, 1991], 57).

15. Blackstone disavowed any claim that, in any circumstances, would place "the judicial power above that of the legislature"; such a reversal in the distribution of authority, he wrote, "would be subversive of all government" (I: 91).

16. Lieberman, *Province,* 64.

17. Blackstone quoted the maxim that English "laws . . . are mixed as our language: and as our language is so much the richer, the laws are the more complete" (I: 64).

18. Daniel R. Coquillette, *The Anglo-American Legal Heritage* (Durham, NC: Carolina Academic Press, 1999), 437.

19. St. George Tucker, *Blackstone's* Commentaries: *With notes of reference to the Constitution and laws of the federal government of the United States and of the commonwealth of Virginia* (Philadelphia: W. Y. Birch and A. Small, 1803), vi.

20. Jeremy Bentham, *A Fragment on Government* and *An Introduction to the Principles of Morals and Legislation,* ed. Wilfrid Harrison (Oxford: Basil Blackwell, 1948), 4. Unless otherwise noted, further references to Bentham's *Fragment* and *Introduction* are to this edition and cited parenthetically in the text.

21. Kelley, *Human Measure,* 183, 224.

22. In 1932, C. K. Ogden attempted to make a place for Bentham in the history of linguistic philosophy in *Bentham's Theory of Fictions* (London: Kegan Paul, Trench, Trubner, and Company, 1932). The project is taken up in Lieberman, *Province of Legislation,* and Angela Esterhammer, *The Romantic Performative: Language and Action in British and German Romanticism* (Stanford, CA: Stanford University Press, 2000). See also Sue Chaplin, "Law and Literature in the Romantic Era: The Law's Fictions" (*Literature Compass* 3–4 [2006] 804–817) and Kathleen Blake, *The Pleasures of Benthamism* (Oxford: Oxford University Press, 2009).

23. Esterhammer discovers in Bentham's writings a richly developed theory of language as social action that anticipates the late modern ideas of speech act theorists including J. L. Austin and Jacques Derrida. Bentham's writings on law, she argues, "articulated a range of speech-act principles, exploring issues of authority, uptake, felicity and infelicity in sociopolitical discourse" (*Romantic Performative,* 42–43).

24. See Bentham, *Fragment and Introduction,* 432 n. 1: "the constitutional branch [of law] is chiefly employed in conferring, on particular persons, *powers,* to be exercised for the good of the whole society, or of considerable parts of it, and prescribing *duties* to the persons invested with those powers."

25. See also Esterhammer's discussion of Bentham's pedagogic mission (*Romantic Performative,* 50).

26. Quoted in Esterhammer, *Romantic Performative,* 45. Esterhammer observes that, in Bentham's own analysis, "the success of the law-as-command depends on the authority of the law-giver, but the authority of the law-giver depends equally on the pragmatic success of the law-as-command" (44).

27. Quoted in Lieberman, *Province,* 230.

28. Quoted in Lieberman, *Province,* 232.

29. Arendt suggests that the Declaration creates a political community, the revolutionary nation, by articulating a common faith, the people's collective recognition of a transcendent law. The document is a deed performed in language, "the perfect way for an action to appear in words" (Arendt, *On Revolution* [New York: Viking, 1965], 192–93). Jay Fliegelman takes up the rhetoric of the document and the rituals of its performance in *Declaring Independence: Jefferson, Natural Language, and the Culture of Performance* (Stanford, CA: Stanford University Press, 1993). Derrida, much more suspicious of the performative language that establishes a new legal order, seeks to deconstruct "the mystical foundation of authority" as laid in such proclamations. Since authority is founded on a performative that creates the world it seems to refer to, Derrida argues, the origin of the law recedes beyond any standard of judgment. Jacques Derrida, "Force of Law: The 'Mystical Foundation of Authority'" (in *Acts of Religion,* ed. and trans. Gil Anidjar [New York: Routledge, 2002], 228–298). Along the same lines, Benjamin Lee argues that the Declaration "follows a speech act model of performativity that it secures within a constative order established by God" (*Talking Heads: Language, Metalanguage, and the Semiotics of Subjectivity* [Durham: Duke University Press, 1997], 334). A poetics of justice might extend this tradition by observing that the God of the Declaration is neither the Puritan God of vengeful revelation nor the detached, deistic composer of natural law but the imagined space of national belonging itself.

30. Lawrence M. Friedman, *A History of American Law* (New York: Simon and Schuster, 1973), 88.

31. Robert Bell, "To the American World," rpt. in Coquillette, *Legal Heritage,* 421.

32. Friedman, *History of American Law,* 89.

33. Morton J. Horwitz, *The Transformation of American Law, 1780–1860* (Cambridge, MA: Harvard University Press, 1977), 4.

34. The distinction between natural law and national custom was not clearly drawn by the lawyers of the Revolutionary period. See James Q. Whitman, "Why Did the Revolutionary Lawyers Confuse Custom and Reason?" (*University of Chicago Law Review* 58:4 [Autumn 1991] 1321–1368).

35. Maxwell Bloomfield, *American Lawyers in a Changing Society* (Cambridge, MA: Harvard University Press, 1976), 32, 40.

36. Horwitz, *Transformation of American Law,* 19. Similarly, William E. Nelson observes that "the attempts of the revolutionary generation to explain and justify the war and its political results set loose new intellectual and social currents which ultimately transformed the legal and social structure" of the United States (*The Americanization of the Common Law: The Impact of Legal Change on Massachusetts Society, 1760–1830* [Cambridge, MA: Harvard University Press, 1975], 5).

37. See Perry Miller, *The Legal Mind in America: From Independence to the Civil War* (Ithaca, NY: Cornell University Press, 1962), 121: "the cry for codification would be identified with a nationalistic spirit."

38. Thomas Paine, quoted in Friedman, *History of American Law,* 96. Discussing the reception of English Common Law in New York State, Friedman goes on to write that "an undefinable, unknowable group of old laws somehow maintained a ghostly presence" in the postrevolutionary period (97).

39. Peter Van Schaak, quoted in Bloomfield, *American Lawyers,* 24.

40. Jesse Root, *The Origin of Government and Laws in Connecticut* (Hartford, CT: Hudson and Goodwin, 1798), iv, xiii.

41. Whitman, "Custom and Reason."

42. Nathaniel Chipman, *Sketches of the Principles of Government* (1793; rpt. in Miller, *Legal Mind,* 19–30), 26–27.

43. Miller, *Legal Mind,* 21.

44. Root, *Origin,* ix.

45. "Obituary" (*The Evangelist,* August 1824, 313–319), 314, 317. The author suggested that the death of Root's brother in the French and Indian War had left the family in need of money, forcing him to pursue his fortune in the law: "Mr. Root did not leave the desk for the bar from any degree of coldness towards the cause of Christ, nor a disaffection to the Christian ministry" (315).

46. Root, *Origin,* ix–x.

47. Root, *Origin,* xiii, xii.

48. Robert Rantoul, Jr., "An Oration Delivered before the Democrats and Antimasons, of the County of Plymouth, at Scituate, on the Fourth of July, 1836" (Boston: Beals and Greene, 1836) 40–41. The phrase "Jacksonian Benthamite" is from Robert Cover, *Justice Accused: Antislavery and the Judicial Process* (New Haven, CT: Yale University Press, 1975), 176.

49. Rantoul, "Oration," 38.

50. A Lover of Improvement (Henry Dwight Sedgwick), *The English Practice: A Statement Showing Some of the Evils and Absurdities of the English Common Law, as Adopted in Several of the United States, and Particularly in the State of New York* (New York: Printed by J. Seymour, 1822), preface (n.p.), 7.

51. "The English Practice," (anonymous review, *The Literary and Scientific Repository, and Critical Review,* May 1, 1822, 286–311), 289–290.

52. "More than any of his contemporaries," Bloomfield suggests, "Sampson dramatized the issues of legal dissent for a lay audience, initiating a continuing dialogue on the uses of juridical power whose end is not yet in sight." Bloomfield, *American Lawyers,* 60.

53. *The Trial of Amos Broad and His Wife, on Three Several Indictments for Assaulting and Beating Betty, a Slave, and her Little Female Child Sarah, Aged Three Years* (New York: Printed by Henry C. Southwick, 1809). For some background on the Broad trial and a reprint of the pamphlet, see Daniel E. Williams, ed., *Liberty's Captives: Narratives of Confinement in the Print Culture of the Early Republic* (Athens: University of Georgia Press, 2006), 131–154. My quotation is from this reprinted edition, 149–150. On Amos Broad, see also Paul A. Gilje, *The Road to Mobocracy:*

Popular Disorder in New York City, 1763–1834 (Chapel Hill: University of North Carolina Press for the Institute for Early American History and Culture, 1987).

54. "The Common Law" (*The Atlantic Magazine,* May–October 1824, 23–31), 24.

55. William Hamersley, "Connecticut: The Origin of Her Courts and Laws" (in William T. Davis, ed. *The New England States: Their Constitutional, Judicial, Educational, Commercial, Professional and Industrial History* [Boston: D. H. Hurd and Co., 1897], 472–498), 491. Dwight Loomis and Joseph Calhoun, eds. *The Judicial and Civil History of Connecticut* (Boston: Boston History Company, 1895), 144.

56. James Wilson, *An Introductory Lecture to a Course of Law Lectures* (Philadelphia: Dobson, 1791), 41–42.

57. Wilson, *Introductory Lecture,* 36.

58. Wilson, *Introductory Lecture,* 31–32.

59. Wislon, *Introductory Lecture,* 31–32. Some capitalization omitted.

60. Wilson, *Introductory Lecture,* 8–9.

61. Wilson, *Introductory Lecture,* 15. Some capitalization omitted.

62. James Kent, *Commentaries on American Law* (New York: O. Halsted, 1826), I: 439.

63. Roger B. Taney, "Supplement to Dred Scott Opinion" (September, 1858. Cited as rpt. in Samuel Tyler, *Memoir of Robert Brooke Taney, LL.D.* [Baltimore, MD: John Murphy and Co., 1872] 578–608), 600.

64. Some background on the case, including some details based on unpublished sources, is provided in Alan Rogers, *Murder and the Death Penalty in Massachusetts* (Amherst: University of Massachusetts Press, 2008), 46–47.

65. [Untitled article], *Massachusetts Gazette,* December 26, 1786, 3. Rpt. in *Charleston* [South Carolina] *Morning Post and Daily Advertiser,* March 14, 1787, 2.

66. "A Sketch of the Life and Confession of Isaac Coombs," *Continental Journal,* December 28, 1786, 4.

67. "A Sketch of the Life and Confession of Isaac Coombs." Coombs's mystical vision was also discussed by the court, as evidence that the defendant recognized his own guilt, in the unsigned "Sentence of Death."

68. Joshua Spalding, *The Prayer of a True Penitent for Mercy; or, the Publican's Prayer, Illustrated. A Sermon Delivered at Salem, Dec. 21, 1786, Previous to the Execution of Isaac Coombs, an Indian, Whose Crime was the Murder of His Wife* (Salem, MA: Dabney and Cushing, 1787), 22.

69. Spalding, *Prayer of a True Penitent,* 22; Rogers, *Murder and the Death Penalty,* 47.

70. Blackstone, *Commentaries,* IV: 369. This justification for the legitimacy of punishment was by no means unique to the postrevolutionary United States. Blackstone, in discussing the grounds of the government's authority to punish crimes, or "public wrongs," wrote that its power came "by the consent of individuals; who, in forming societies, did either tacitly or expressly invest the sovereign power with a right of making laws, and of enforcing obedience to them when made, by exercising, upon their non-observance, severities adequate to the evil" (*Commentaries,* IV: 8).

71. The article, under the title "Sentence of Death," was reprinted in the following papers: *Essex Journal,* November 22, 1786, 3; *The American Recorder and the Charlestown Advertiser,* November 24, 1786, 2; *The Massachusetts Gazette,*

November 24, 1786, 4; *The American Herald,* November 27, 1786, 4; *Loudon's New-York Packet,* November 28, 1786; *The Connecticut Journal,* November 29, 1786, 3; *Pennsylvania Packet, and Daily Advertiser,* December 1, 1786, 2; *The Independent Gazetteer,* December 8, 1786, 2.

72. "Sentence of Death" (*Salem Mercury,* November 18, 1786, 3). Subsequent citations are to the same text and page.

2. ORACLES OF GOD

1. Douglas Hay, "Property, Authority and the Criminal Law" (in Douglas Hay et al., *Albion's Fatal Tree: Crime and Society in Eighteenth-Century England* [New York: Pantheon, 1975], 16–64), 22. For a useful reconsideration of Hay's influential study, see Peter King, "Decision-Makers and Decision-Making in the English Criminal Law, 1750–1800" (*Historical Journal* 27 [March 1984] 25–58).

2. Hay, "Property, Authority and the Criminal Law," 27. Since the 1970s, scholarship on public executions in the critical humanities has drawn from the vocabulary of the theater and performance. For an overview of this scholarship, with special reference to the hangings performed in colonial New England, see Dwight Conquergood, "Lethal Theatre: Performance, Punishment, and the Death Penalty" (*Theatre Journal* 54:3 [October 2002] 339–367).

3. David Brion Davis, *Homicide in American Fiction, 1798–1860: A Study in Social Values* (Ithaca, NY: Cornell University Press, 1957, 1968), viii. Over the past several decades, cultural histories of criminal justice have shared Davis's guiding principle. Louis P. Masur, for example, opens his *Rites of Execution: Capital Punishment and the Transformation of American Culture, 1776–1865* (New York: Oxford University Press, 1989), by suggesting that changing paradigms of punishment "embodied the triumphs of new sensibilities and the reconstitution of cultural values throughout the Western world" (3). My point is not to discredit the premises of cultural historiography; I share some of them. But I argue that the rhetorical function of American crime genres was not limited to the "expression" of widely shared norms. These documents did not only articulate the beliefs and values that held societies together; they produced a sense of social belonging by reinventing such norms.

4. I refer to a body of critical studies informed especially by Michel Foucault, *Discipline and Punish,* trans. Alan Sheridan (New York: Vintage, 1977). See, for example, my first book, *The Prison and the American Imagination* (New Haven, CT: Yale University Press, 2009). But even Foucault's famous study of the drawing and quartering of Damiens, the paradigm of the ancien regime's "spectacle of the scaffold," was based on works of popular crime literature.

5. Some recent scholarship in early U.S. legal and political history has emphasized the political aspects of legal rituals. See, for example, Larry Kramer, *The People Themselves: Popular Constitutionalism and Judicial Review* (New York: Oxford University Press, 2004) and Jason Frank, *Constituent Moments: Enacting the People in*

Postrevolutionary America (Durham, NC: Duke University Press, 2010). In *Law's Imagined Republic: Popular Politics and Criminal Justice in Revolutionary America* (Cambridge: Cambridge University Press, 2010), Steven Wilf places the ceremonies of criminal justice at the center of an argument about the mutually constitutive fields of law and politics in the Revolutionary period. The vernacular, intertextual conversation about justice that was carried on in newspapers, pamphlets, sermons and confessions helped to shape both the statues and the jurisprudence of the early Republic.

6. V. A. C. Gatrell, *The Hanging Tree: Execution and the English People, 1770–1868* (Oxford: Oxford University Press, 1994), vii–viii.

7. Peter Linebaugh, "The Tyburn Riot Against the Surgeons," (in Hay et al., *Albion's Fatal Tree*, 65–117), 66. On the execution as a carnival, see T. W. Laqueur, "Crowds, Carnival, and the State in English Executions, 1604–1868," (in A. L. Beier et al., eds., *The First Modern Society: Essays in Honor of Lawrence Stone* [Cambridge: Cambridge University Press, 1989], 305–399). Laqueur's thesis is taken up and revised in Gatrell, *The Hanging Tree,* especially 90–105.

8. Edgar J. McManus, *Law and Liberty in Early New England: Criminal Justice and Due Process, 1620–1692* (Amherst: University of Massachusetts Press, 1993).

9. Nathaniel Hawthorne, *The Scarlet Letter* (1850; New York: Penguin, 1986), 47, 53.

10. Daniel A. Cohen, *Pillars of Salt, Monuments of Grace: New England Crime Literature and the Origins of American Popular Culture, 1674–1860* (Amherst: University of Massachusetts Press, 1993; 2006), vii. Along the same lines, Scott D. Seay writes that "until the American Revolution, virtually [the clergy] alone were authorized to make meaning of the activities of hanging day" (*Hanging Between Heaven and Earth: Capital Crime, Execution Preaching, and Theology in Early New England* [DeKalb: Northern Illinois University Press, 2009], 17).

11. Cohen, *Pillars of Salt, Monuments of Grace*, 5. Comparing New England crime literature to the popular genres of seventeenth- and eighteenth-century London, Cohen argues that the execution sermon, as an "autonomous literary genre," was a new world "innovation" devised by the Puritans (3).

12. Seay, *Hanging Between Heaven and Earth,* 24.

13. My study of early American execution literature draws especially from the following: Masur, *Rites of Execution*; Daniel E. Williams, *Pillars of Salt: An Anthology of Early American Criminal Narratives* (Madison, WI: Madison House, 1992); Karen Halttunen, *Murder Most Foul: The Killer and the American Gothic Imagination* (Cambridge, MA: Harvard University Press, 1998); Stuart Banner, *The Death Penalty: An American History* (Cambridge, MA: Harvard University Press, 2002); Cohen, *Pillars of Salt, Monuments of Grace;* Seay, *Hanging Between Heaven and Earth;* and Wilf, *Law's Imagined Republic.*

14. On gallows literature and the racialization of New England's Indian populations, see Katerine Grandjean, "'Our *Fellow-Creatures* & Our *Fellow-Christians*': Race and Religion in Eighteenth-Century Narratives of Indian Crime" (*American Quarterly* 62:4 [December 2010] 925–950).

15. Samson Occom, "A Sermon Preached by Samson Occom" (1772; rpt. in Myra Jehlen and Michael Warner, eds. *The English Literatures of America, 1500–1800.* [New York: Routledge, 1997] 643–659), 648.

16. Occom, "Sermon," 656.

17. See McManus, *Law and Liberty,* which describes how "Scripture became a force for progress and legal reform" in the colonies (36). By comparison to English law, the seventeenth-century colonies had far fewer capital statutes, since they enforced the death penalty only when an explicit scriptural sanction could be found.

18. Charles Chauncy, *The Horrid Nature and Enormous Guilt of Murder* (Boston: Printed by Thomas Fleet, 1754), 22.

19. Seay, *Hanging Between Heaven and Earth,* 35.

20. Halttunen, *Murder Most Foul,* 37.

21. Peres Fobes, *The Paradise of God Opened to a Penitent Thief* (Providence, RI: Bennett Wheeler, 1784), 26–27.

22. Fobes, *Paradise,* 4, 29, 35, 26.

23. Cohen, *Pillars of Salt, Monuments of Grace,* 107–109.

24. Fobes, *Paradise,* 31.

25. Cohen, *Pillars of Salt, Monuments of Grace,* 107.

26. Halttunen, *Murder Most Foul,* 25. Even in the seventeenth century, Edgar J. McManus observes, "there was constant harping on the theme that the churches had had their best day and that neither in faith nor behavior did the colonists equal their fathers" (*Law and Liberty,* 180).

27. Fobes, *Paradise,* 46.

28. Fobes, *Paradise,* 35.

29. Stephen West, *A Sermon Preached in Lenox, in the County of Berkshire, and Commonwealth of Massachusetts; December 6th, 1787: at the Execution of John Bly, and Charles Rose, for Crimes of Burglary* (Pittsfield, MA: Printed by Elijah Russell, 1787).

30. Lawrence M. Friedman, *A History of American Law* (New York: Simon and Schuster, 1973), 94. See also Maxwell Bloomfield, *American Lawyers in a Changing Society, 1776–1876* (Cambridge, MA: Harvard University Press, 1976) 26–27. On the rebellion more generally, see David P. Szatmary, *Shays' Rebellion: The Making of an Agrarian Insurrection* (Amherst: University of Massachusetts, 1980); and Leonard L. Richards, *Shays's Rebellion: The American Revolution's Last Battle* (Philadelphia: University of Pennsylvania Press, 2003).

31. Richards, *Shays's Rebellion,* 40, 41.

32. Masur, *Rites of Execution,* 31.

33. "Extracts from the Last Words and Dying Speeches of John Bly and Charles Rose, Who Were Executed at Lenox, in the Commonwealth of Massachusetts, on Thursday the Sixth Day of December, 1787, for Burglary" (*Worcester Magazine* 4:15 [January 1788] 186–187), 187.

34. West, *A Sermon,* 3, 9, 10, 6.

35. West, *A Sermon,* 3.

36. West, *A Sermon,* 10.

37. West, *A Sermon,* 3, 7.

38. Fobes, *Paradise of God,* 11.

39. Lawrence M. Friedman, *Crime and Punishment in American History* (New York: Basic, 1993), 43. On the two-witness rule, see also McManus, *Law and Liberty,* 35–36.

40. Cohen, *Pillars of Salt, Monuments of Grace,* 10.

41. Patience Boston, "A Faithful Narrative of the Wicked Life and Wicked Conversion of Patience Boston" (rpt. in Williams, *Pillars of Salt,* 11–141), 123. On the composition and ceremonial function of the narrative, and on the discursive construction of Boston's identity, see Tamara Harvey, "'Taken from Her Mouth': Narrative Authority and the Conversion of Patience Boston" (*Narrative* 16:3 [October 1998] 256–270).

42. *A Narrative of the Life, Together with the Last Speech, Confession, and Solemn Declaration, of John Lewis* (New Haven, CT: James Parker, 1762. Quoted in Stuart Banner, *The Death Penalty: An American History,* 40).

43. Halttunen, *Murder Most Foul,* 18–19; Seay, *Hanging Between Heaven and Earth,* 33–34.

44. Halttunen, *Murder Most Foul,* 16.

45. Williams, *Pillars of Salt,* 283.

46. Fobes, *Paradise,* 46, 47.

47. Daniel E. Williams, "In Defense of Self: Author and Authority in the 'Memoirs of Stephen Burroughs'" (*Early American Literature* 25:2 [1990] 96–122), 98. On the relations between Burroughs's narrative and other popular genres, see also Christopher W. Jones, "Praying upon Truth: The Memoirs of Stephen Burroughs and the Picaresque" (*Early American Literature* 30:1 [1995] 32–50). In "Personating Stephen Burroughs: The Apparitions of a Public Specter" (*Early American Literature* 44:3 [2009] 569–603), Peter Jaros shows how Burroughs disrupted the early republic's vocabulary of identity, appearing not as himself but as a "singularly plural . . . public specter" (572).

48. Whiting Sweeting, *Narrative of Whiting Sweeting* (Concord, NH: Russell, 1793), 31.

49. Cohen, *Pillars of Salt, Monuments of Grace,* 147–149, 161–162.

50. Halttunen, *Murder Most Foul,* 90, 87.

51. Joseph Mountain, *Sketches of the Life of Joseph Mountain, A Negro* (New Haven: T. and S. Green, 1790).

52. Wilf, *Law's Imagined Republic,* 111, 113, 112. Mountain's execution is also discussed in Masur, *Rites of Execution,* 25–26.

53. Mountain, *Sketches,* 17, 16.

54. Mountain, *Sketches,* 10.

55. Williams, *Pillars of Salt,* 53.

56. "Address to the Prisoner," (*Connecticut Courant,* August 23, 1790, 2). On the death sentence, see also Wilf, *Law's Imagined Republic,* 118–119.

57. James Dana, *The Intent of Capital Punishment, a Discourse, Delivered in the City of New-Haven, October 20, 1790, Being the Day of the Execution of Joseph Mountain, for a Rape* (New Haven, CT: T. and S. Green, 1790), 5. Subsequent references cited parenthetically in the text.

58. See Wilf, *Law's Imagined Republic,* 119–124.

59. Jeannine Marie DeLombard, *In the Shadow of the Gallows: Race, Crime, and American Civic Identity* (Philadelphia: University of Pennsylvania Press, 2012), 103.

60. James Dana, *The African Slave Trade: A Discourse Delivered in the City of New-Haven, September 9, 1790, before the Connecticut Society for the Promotion of Freedom* (New Haven, CT: Thomas and Samuel Green, 1790), 24.

61. John Marsh, *The Great Sin of Striving with God* (Hartford, CT: Hudson and Goodwin, 1783), 21.

62. Beadle, quoted in Marsh, *Great Sin,* 21.

63. "Poem, Occasioned by the Most Shocking and Cruel Murder" (Broadside, Boston, 1782).

64. On the strange career of Beadle's corpse, see Wilf, *Law's Imagined Republic,* 135–137.

65. Marsh, *Great Sin,* 19.

66. James Dana, *Man's Sins not Chargeable on God, but on Themselves* (New Haven, CT: T. and S. Green, 1782), 21, 6, 25.

67. [Stephen Mix Mitchell], *A Narrative of the Life of William Beadle* (Hartford, CT: Bavil Webster, 1783), 16.

68. See Marsh, *Great Sin,* 19: "Had he left no written account of his intentions and views respecting the destruction of himself and his family, we should have been ready to consider it as the effect of a sudden and most vehement frenzy. But by his writings he appears to have had it in contemplation for three years."

69. Mitchell, *Life of William Beadle,* 16.

70. "An Account of a Murder Committed by Mr. J—— Y——, upon His Family, in December, A.D. 1781" (*New York Weekly Magazine* 2:55 [July 20, 1796], 20. Cited as rpt. in Charles Brockden Brown, *Wieland; or, The Transformation: An American Tale* (New York: Modern Library, 2002), 361–365. All references to "Account of a Murder" and to *Wieland* are to this edition and cited parenthetically in the text.

71. On Brown, Bleecker, and the Yates case, see James C. Hendrickson, *A Note on Wieland* (*American Literature* 8:3 [November 1936] 305–306). On the connections to the Beadle case, see Shirley Samuels, "*Wieland:* Alien and Infidel" (*Early American Literature* 25:1 [1990] 46–66); and Daniel E. Williams, "Writing under the Influence: An Examination of *Wieland*'s 'Well-Authenticated Facts' and the Depiction of Murderous Fathers in Post-Revolutionary Print Culture" (*Eighteenth-Century Fiction* 15:3 [2003] 643–668).

72. Davis refers to *Wieland* as a "drama of historical allegory" (*Homicide in American Fiction,* 89). The allegory, according to Christopher Looby, "operates in terms of a deep correspondence between the conceptual grammar of the gothic plot and the predominant representations of history and politics given in the culture of postrevolutionary America" (*Voicing America: Language, Literary Form, and the Origins of the United States* [Chicago: University of Chicago Press, 1996], 146).

73. Jane Tompkins, *Sensational Designs: The Cultural Work of American Fiction, 1790–1860* (New York: Oxford University Press, 1985), 49. Many other critics have explored *Wieland*'s critique of radical democracy. Samuels, in "*Wieland:* Alien and

Infidel," shows how Brown engages the conservative, moralizing discourse which, in the era of the Alien and Sedition Acts, associated the security of the nation with the inviolate purity of the nuclear family. Jason Frank reads *Wieland* as a patently "antidemocratic novel" (*Constituent Moments,* 157).

74. See, for example, Nicholas Rombes, Jr., "'All Was Lonely, Darkson, and Waste'": *Wieland* and the Construction of the New Republic" (*Studies in American Fiction* 22:1 [Spring 1994] 37–46). With its "multivocalic" formal ambiguities, Rombes argues, "*Wieland* implicitly calls into question the true nature of Federalist authority" (38, 37).

75. In the antebellum period, the popular Whig historian William H. Prescott hailed Brown's works as the nation's "first decidedly successful attempts in the walk of romantic fiction." Prescott noted that Brown's literary ambitions had led him to "retreat" from a legal career, and the episode has remained central to the legend of Brown as a literary founder. William H. Prescott, "Charles Brockden Brown, The American Novelist," (in *Biographical and Critical Miscellanies* [New York: Harper and Brothers, 1845], 1–56), 27.

76. Robert Ferguson, *Law and Letters in American Culture* (Cambridge, MA: Harvard University Press, 1987), 142.

77. Laura H. Korobkin, "Murder by Madman: Criminal Responsibility, Law, and Judgment in *Wieland*" (*American Literature* 72:4 [December 2000] 721–750), 723. Korobkin goes so far as to read *Wieland* as a defense of customary jurisprudence, including the standards of judgment and punishment laid out in Blackstone's *Commentaries.* The many ambiguities of motive and method in the plot, she argues, do not disable the kind of analysis that characterized eighteenth-century criminal law; "they demand it" (723). I would qualify this strong claim by suggesting that, while *Wieland* does concede to the law's authority in judging cases of public wrong, it is also concerned to open a private space for literary, philosophical, and moral judgments, beyond the reach of law.

78. The question of enthusiasm in *Wieland* has been addressed in several critical studies. See especially Nancy Ruttenberg, *Democratic Personality: Popular Voice and the Trial of American Authorship* (Stanford, CA: Stanford University Press, 1998), 210–258; and Lee Eric Schmidt, *Hearing Things: Religion, Illusion, and the American Enlightenment* (Cambridge, MA: Harvard University Press, 2000), which argues that *Wieland* develops a secular-rationalist critique of "the clamoring voices of religious inspiration" (150). On the connection between Brown's antienthusiasm and his political conservatism, see Samuels, "*Wieland:* Alien and Infidel" and Frank, *Constituent Moments,* 156–181.

3. BLASPHEMY "AT THE COURT OF HELL"

1. "Essay on Profanity" (*The Lay-Man's Magazine* 1:2 [November 23, 1815], 9–20], 11.

2. Samuel Gridley Howe, "Atheism in New England" (*New-England Magazine* 7 [December 1834] 500–509; 8 [January 1835] 53–62), 501, 500.

3. Leonard W. Levy, *Blasphemy: Verbal Offense against the Sacred, from Moses to Salman Rushdie* (New York: Alfred A. Knopf, 1993), 400. See also Leonard W. Levy, ed., *Blasphemy in Massachusetts: Freedom of Conscience and the Abner Kneeland Case* (New York: Da Capo, 1973). Roderick Stuart French, in "Liberation from Man and God in Boston: Abner Kneeland's Free-Thought Campaign, 1830–1839" (*American Quarterly* 32:2 [1980] 202–221), argues that "Kneeland was just slightly ahead of a segment of the American people who were relinquishing religious ideas" (203). In *Word Crimes: Blasphemy, Culture, and Literature in Nineteenth-Century England* (Chicago: University of Chicago Press, 1998), Joss Marsh similarly links the crime to "the struggle for freedom of the press and of publication" (10). These cultural histories of blasphemy trials share a liberal conception of the free press that links publication to the diffusion of knowledge, power, and political freedom. For a critique of these premises, see Talal Asad, et al., *Is Critique Secular?: Blasphemy, Injury, and Free Speech* (Berkeley: University of California Press, 2009).

4. Aristides, "Blaspehmy" (*The Correspondent* 3:25 [July 12, 1828] 385–386), 386.

5. Robert C. Post, "Cultural Heterogeneity and Law: Pornography, Blasphemy, and the First Amendment" (*California Law Review* 76:2 [March 1988] 297–335), 308.

6. Sarah Barringer Gordon, "Blasphemy and the Law of Religious Liberty in Nineteenth-Century America" (*American Quarterly* 52:4 [December 2000] 682–719), 683.

7. *Commonwealth v. Kneeland*. 37 Mass. 206 (1838). Cited as rpt. in Levy, ed., *Blasphemy in Massachusetts* (419–460), 434.

8. Lyman Beecher, *Works, Volume I: Lectures on Political Atheism and Kindred Subjects* (Boston: John P. Jewett and Company, 1852), 94.

9. Abner Kneeland, *Review of the Trial, Conviction, and Final Imprisonment in the Common Jail of the County of Suffolk, of Abner Kneeland, for the Alleged Crime of Blasphemy, Written by Himself* (Boston: George A. Chapman, 1838), 41.

10. My treatment of the legal details of the Ruggles case follows Levy, *Blasphemy*, 400–404, and Gordon, "Blasphemy and Liberty."

11. *People v. Ruggles*, 8 Johnson 290 (New York 1811). Rpt. in *Reports of Cases Argued and Determined in the Supreme Court of Judicature; and in the Court for the Trial of Impeachments and the Correction of Errors, in the State of New York* (New York: Isaac Riley, 1811).

12. Perry Miller, *The Legal Mind in America: From Independence to the Civil War* (Ithaca, NY: Cornell University Press, 1969), 92–93.

13. Scott Douglas Gerber, *Seriatim: The Supreme Court before John Marshall* (New York: New York University Press, 1998).

14. James Wilson, *An Introductory Lecture to a Course of Law Lectures* (Philadelphia: Dobson, 1791), 53. Some capitalization and italics omitted.

15. Thomas Jefferson, quoted in Paul Kahn, *Reign of Law: Marbury v. Madison and the Construction of America* (New Haven, CT: Yale University Press, 1997), 113.

16. Kahn, *Reign of Law*, 115.

17. Kahn, *Reign of Law*, 218.

18. Gordon, "Blasphemy and Liberty," 686.

19. Gordon, "Blasphemy and Liberty," 693.

20. "Blasphemy &c. Punishable at the Common Law," (*Weekly Recorder* 2:11 [September 20, 1815] 85–86), 85.

21. *Updegrath v. Commonwealth*, 11 Sergeant and Rawle 394 (Pennsylvania 1824).

22. Henry Steele Comager, "The Blasphemy of Abner Kneeland" (*New England Quarterly* 8:1 [March 1935] 29–41), 30.

23. Beecher, *Political Atheism*, 94.

24. On Kneeland's life and the scandal of his trial, see Levy, *Blasphemy in Massachusetts;* Comager, "The Blasphemy of Abner Kneeland," and French, "Liberation from Man and God."

25. Howe, "Atheism in New England," 502.

26. *Commonwealth v. Kneeland*, 421.

27. French, "Liberation from Man and God," 213.

28. Kneeland, *Review of the Trial*, 39.

29. Democratus, "Blasphemy" (*Universalist Watchman, Repository, and Chronicle* 10:4 [July 21, 1838] 28–29), 28.

30. Quoted in Democratus, "Blasphemy," 29.

31. Comager, "Blasphemy of Abner Kneeland," 30.

32. *Commonwealth v. Kneeland*, 425. Kneeland publicly speculated that Chief Justice Shaw himself had hesitated to uphold the conviction (*Review of the Trial*, 33).

33. *Commonwealth v. Kneeland*, 434.

34. *Commonwealth v. Kneeland*, 427.

35. *Commonwealth v. Kneeland*, 435.

36. Edgar Allan Poe, "The Pit and the Pendulum" (in *Complete Tales and Poems* [New York: Vintage, 1975], 246–257), 250.

37. Kneeland, *Review of the Trial*, 37, 41, 38–41, 37, 57.

38. Karen Halttunen, *Murder Most Foul: The Killer and the American Gothic Imagination* (Cambridge, MA: Harvard University Press, 1998), 36.

39. Daniel A. Cohen, *Pillars of Salt, Monuments of Grace: New England Crime Literature and the Origins of American Popular Culture, 1674–1860* (Amherst: University of Massachusetts Press, 1993, 2006), 28.

40. Kneeland, *Review of the Trial*, 3.

41. Kneeland, *Review of the Trial*, 48, 43.

42. Kneeland, *Review of the Trial*, 66.

43. Democratus, "Blasphemy," 28.

44. *Commonwealth v. Kneeland*, 452, 456.

45. S. D. Parker, quoted in Comager, "The Blasphemy of Abner Kneeland," 32–33.

46. Peter Thatcher, quoted in Comager, "The Blasphemy of Abner Kneeland," 35.

47. *State v. Chandler*, 2 Harrington 553 (Delaware 1837).

48. French, "Liberation from Man and God," 215, 216.

49. This interpretation of Kneeland's populist politics would be consistent with the account of multiple public spheres developed by Craig Calhoun in *The Roots of Radicalism: Tradition, The Public Sphere, and Early Nineteenth-Century Social Movements* (Chicago: University of Chicago Press, 2012).

50. Marsh, *Word Crimes*, 123.

51. William Ellery Channing, *Memoir of William Ellery Channing* (2 vols.; London: Routledge, 1850), II: 245–246.

52. A. B. G., "Abner Kneeland" (*Evangelical Magazine and Gospel Advocate* 9:29 [July 20, 1838] 231).

53. Kneeland, *Review of the Trial*, 53, 44.

54. Robert E. Burkholder, "Emerson, Kneeland, and the Divinity School Address" (*American Literature* 58:1 [March 1986] 1–14), 7.

55. Nathaniel Hawthorne, "Alice Doane's Appeal" (in *Selected Tales and Sketches*, ed. Michael J. Colacurcio [New York: Penguin, 1987], 110–123. Subsequent references are to this edition and cited parenthetically in the text. Even in the late nineteenth and early twentieth centuries, after Hawthorne's canonization, the tale was usually overlooked or unappreciated by his critics. Seymour L. Gross summarizes the critical consensus of the mid-twentieth century when he describes "Alice Doane's Appeal" as "the most poorly structured and chaotically organized of all of Hawthorne's stories" ("Hawthorne's 'Alice Doane's Appeal'" [*Nineteenth-Century Fiction* 10:3 (December 1955) 232–236], 232). Neal Frank Doubleday, in *Hawthorne's Early Tales: A Critical Study* (Durham, NC: Duke University Press, 1972), dismisses "Alice Doane's Appeal" as "at best apprentice work" (58) and notes that "Hawthorne never collected or acknowledged the tale" (27). Nancy Bunge, in *Nathaniel Hawthorne: A Study of the Short Fiction* (New York: Twayne, 1993), makes no mention of the tale at all. On the development of Hawthorne's place in the canon of American literature, see Bertha Faust, *Hawthorne's Contemporaneous Reputation: A Study of Literary Opinion in America and England, 1828–1864* (New York: Octagon Books, 1968), Nina Baym, *The Shape of Hawthorne's Career* (Ithaca, NY: Cornell University Press, 1976), Jane Tompkins, *Sensational Designs: The Cultural Work of American Fiction, 1790–1860* (New York: Oxford University Press, 1985), especially Chapter 1, "Masterpiece Theater: The Politics of Hawthorne's Literary Reputation" (3–39), and John L. Idol, Jr., and Buford Jones, eds., *Nathaniel Hawthorne: The Contemporary Reviews* (Cambridge: Cambridge University Press, 1994).

56. Michael J. Colacurcio, *The Province of Piety: Moral History in Hawthorne's Early Tales* (Cambridge, MA: Harvard University Press, 1984), 78–93. The phrase "specter evidence" appears on p. 83 and elsewhere.

57. Charles Wentworth Upham, *Lectures on Witchcraft: Comprising a History of the Delusion in Salem, in 1692* (Boston: Carter, Hendee and Babcock, 1831).

58. Lauren Berlant, *The Anatomy of National Fantasy: Hawthorne, Utopia, and Everyday Life* (Chicago: University of Chicago Press, 1991), 43. Berlant suggests that "love, in the central tale of 'Alice Doane's Appeal,' is not romantic, or even sexual, but a love of law" (43).

59. Taking their cues from the narrator, several critics have argued that Hawthorne's project is to develop a genre of literary fiction that will restore a proper respect for the national past. See Colacurcio, *Province*, 92, and Berlant, *Anatomy*, 37. On moral historiography in Hawthorne's tales, see also Baym, *Shape* 54–55.

60. Meredith L. McGill, "The Problem of Hawthorne's Popularity" (in Steven Fink and Susan S. Williams, eds., *Reciprocal Influences: Literary Production, Distribution,*

and Consumption in America [Columbus: Ohio State University Press, 1999], 36–54). McGill further develops the argument in *American Literature and the Culture of Reprinting, 1834–1853* (Philadelphia: University of Pennsylvania Press, 2003), especially Chapter 6, "Suspended Animation: Hawthorne and the Relocation of Narrative Authority" (218–269).

61. This defense of Hawthorne's aesthetic project is argued, for example, by Henry Nash Smith, who locates its subversive power in its "subordination of the outer world of institutions and observed behavior to the inner universe of private experience" (*Democracy and the Novel: Popular Resistance to Classic American Writers* [New York: Oxford University Press, 1978]), 18.

62. Nathaniel Hawthorne, *The House of the Seven Gables,* ed. Robert S. Levine (New York: Norton, 2006), 151. Further citations are to this edition and cited parenthetically in the text.

63. McGill, *Culture of Reprinting,* 220.

64. McGill, *Culture of Reprinting,* 269.

4. EVIL SPEAKING, "A BRIDLE FOR THE UNBRIDLED TONGUE"

1. These attacks are quoted and discussed, with reference to women's preaching, in Catherine A. Brekus, *Strangers and Pilgrims: Female Preaching in America, 1740–1845* (Chapel Hill: University of North Carolina Press, 1998), 279.

2. Elijah Hedding, *The Substance of an Address Delivered to the Oneida Annual Conference of Ministers of the Methodist Episcopal Church, August 31; and to the Genesee Conference, September 21, 1837* (Auburn, NY: Printed at the Office of the Auburn Banner, 1837), 22.

3. Elijah Hedding, "Self-Government" (in *The Methodist Preacher: Containing Twenty-Eight Sermons, on Doctrinal and Practical Subjects* [Auburn, NY: Derby and Miller, 1853], 202–218), 204.

4. Sally Thompson, *The Trial and Defence of Mrs. Sally Thompson* (Lowell, MA: A. B. F. Hildreth, 1839), 2.

5. Harriet Beecher Stowe, *Dred: A Tale of the Great Dismal Swamp* (2 vols.; Boston: Phillips, Sampson, and Company, 1856), I: 305.

6. John Lardas Modern, *Secularism in Antebellum America* (Chicago: University of Chicago Press, 2011), 21.

7. Lyman Beecher, "Dr. Beecher's Letter to Mr. Beman," December 15, 1827 (cited as rpt. in *The Religious Intelligencer,* January 12, 1828, 513–518), 513. The letter also appeared in the *New-York Observer,* the *Christian Observer,* and other periodicals.

8. Daniel Walker Howe, *The Political Culture of the American Whigs* (Chicago: University of Chicago Press, 1979), 150. A few years later, in the 1830s, Beecher would embrace a more enthusiastic revivalism, going so far as to entertain some doctrines which sounded suspiciously like the anti-Calvinist creed that went by such names as "holiness" or "perfectionism." Associated with the radical faction in the antislavery movement, this brand of faith was preached by William Lloyd Garrison in

Boston and propagated by a faction of immediate abolitionists at the newly founded Lane Seminary, in Cincinnati, where Beecher had been appointed President in 1833. Although he tried to manage the controversy, a perfectionist-abolitionist camp meeting threw the school into crisis in 1834. The following year, Beecher was forced to defend himself, in a Presbyterian church trial, against charges of heresy, slander, and hypocrisy. In one of the Second Great Awakening's many ironic reversals, a minister known for his moderation was denounced for "the propagation of dangerous doctrines." The *New York Observer* sent a correspondent to produce a trial report for general circulation. See Arthur Joseph Stansbury, *Trial and Acquittal of Lyman Beecher, D. D., before the Presbytery of Cincinnati* (Cincinnati, OH: Published by Eli Taylor, 1835). My account of the Lane controversy draws from Miller, *Arguing about Slavery,* 79–93.

9. Beecher, "Letter to Mr. Beman," 513.
10. Benjamin Franklin, *The Autobiography of Benjamin Franklin,* ed. Kenneth Silverman (New York: Penguin, 1986), 116–117.
11. The movement known as the Great Awakening is still a matter of controversy. Some historians suggest that the evangelicals prepared the way for a political revolution and a new national culture. Perry Miller describes the Awakening as a decisive phase in the development of American religious and philosophical traditions, inaugurating the line of new-world thought that would lead from Jonathan Edwards to Ralph Waldo Emerson. See Miller, *Errand into the Wilderness* (Cambridge, MA: Harvard University Press, 1956) and Alan Heimert and Perry Miller, eds., *The Great Awakening: Documents Illustrating the Crisis and its Consequences* (Indianapolis, IN: Bobbs-Merrill, 1967). Harry S. Stout argues that the Awakening created a style of oratory that appealed to a popular audience, bound the several colonies more closely together, and prepared the way for a national imaginary. See Stout, "Religion, Communications, and the Ideological Origins of the American Revolution" (*William and Mary Quarterly* 34 [October 1977], 519–541) and *The New England Soul: Preaching and Religious Culture in Colonial New England* (New York: Oxford University Press, 1986). The connection between evangelicalism and revolution is made even more forcefully by Nathan O. Hatch in *The Democratization of American Christianity* (New Haven, CT: Yale University Press, 1989). On the class dynamics of the evangelical uprisings, see Gary B. Nash, *The Urban Crucible: Social Change, Political Consciousness, and the Origins of the American Revolution* (Cambridge, MA: Harvard University Press, 1979) and Rhys Isaac, *The Transformation of Virginia, 1740–1790* (Chapel Hill: University of North Carolina Press, 1982). Susan Juster sees in the Awakening a "feminization" of evangelical congregations in New England that gave a new authority to women's speech (*Disorderly Women: Sexual Politics and Evangelicalism in Revolutionary New England* [Ithaca, NY: Cornell University Press, 1994], 44). Another line of historians, however, questions the coherence and the consequences of the various local events that were later described as one Awakening. See Jon Butler, "Enthusiasm Described and Decried: The Great Awakening as Interpretive Fiction," (*Journal of American History* 69:2 [September 1982] 305–325). As a possible origin of this fiction, Butler cites the antebellum historian

Joseph Tracy, *The Great Awakening: A History of the Revival of Religion in the Time of Edwards and Whitefield* (Boston: Tappan and Dennet, 1842). In the "Letter to Mr. Beman" and elsewhere, Lyman Beecher contributed to the nineteenth century's retrospective creation of a "first" Great Awakening as a kind of origin myth. Synthesizing these two opposing views, to a degree, Frank Lambert traces the concept of the Great Awakening back to the 1730s and 1740s, when evangelicals themselves first "reported local awakenings in scores of congregations" and "interpreted them as a single intercolonial occurrence" (*Inventing the "Great Awakening"* [Princeton, NJ: Princeton University Press, 1999], 11).

12. Charles Chauncy, *Enthusiasm Described and Caution'd Against* (Boston: J. Draper for S. Eliot and J. Blanchard, 1742), 3. By the early 1740s, the problem of enthusiasm had the full attention of the clergy in the American colonies. The South Carolina minister Alexander Garden, in a 1740 sermon against Whitefield, described how an itinerant preacher's voice, like *"a very lovely song,"* seduced the public. The effect was "the Charming of the Ear," a kind of verbal mystification that worked "to rivet fast the *Chains* of Error and Delusion" (*Take heed how ye hear* [Charles-Town: Printed by Peter Timothy, 1741], 21–23). In Massachusetts, Benjamin Doolittle acknowledged that enthusiasm had become a common subject of concern among people of letters: "Many wise and learned Men have written of ENTHUSIASM, and discoursed well concerning it" (*An Enquiry into Enthusiasm* [Boston: Rogers and Fowle, 1743], 7–8). Charles Chauncy joined his voice to this chorus.

13. See Juster, *Disorderly Women,* on "the inversion of sexual mores which seemed to follow close on the heels of the Holy Spirit as it blazed a path across New England" (35).

14. Chauncy, "Enthusiasm Described," 5. The radical, utopian tendencies of the revivals, Butler suggests, found their most elaborate expression in the "nightmares of the antirevivalist Chauncy" ("Enthusiasm Described and Decried," 317).

15. Chauncy, *Seasonable Thoughts on the State of Religion in New England* (Boston: Rogers and Fowle, 1743. Rpt. Hicksville, New York: Regina Press, 1975), 103.

16. See Ann Taves, *Fits, Trances, and Visions: Experiencing Religion and Explaining Experience from Wesley to James* (Princeton, NJ: Princeton University Press, 1999), especially 20–33. Quotation p. 25. According to Taves, the critique of enthusiasm, as developed in this curious collaboration between conservative religious authorities and rationalist skeptics, continues to inform the modern, secularized study of religion in the academy.

17. Chauncy, "Enthusiasm Described," 6.

18. Chauncy, *Seasonable Thoughts,* 95.

19. Chauncy, "Enthusiasm Described," 15. The lines are discussed in Nancy Ruttenberg, *Democratic Personality: Popular Voice and the Trial of American Authorship* (Stanford, CA: Stanford University Press, 1998), 126. Drawing from Chauncy's sermons, Ruttenberg describes the enthusiast as a figure who "transcended the limitations of a merely private existence and acceded to the public sphere by means of a voice inexorably rising, as if summoned by an external power" (116).

20. Benjamin Doolittle, "An Enquiry into Enthusiasm" (Boston: Rogers and Fowle, 1743), 14, 29.

21. Doolittle, "Enquiry into Enthusiasm," 33, 5.

22. James Davenport, *The Reverend Mister Davenport's Confession and Retractions* (Boston: S. Kneeland and T. Green, 1744), 4–6.

23. Beecher, "Letter to Mr. Beman," 514.

24. Beecher, "Letter to Mr. Beman," 514-515.

25. Beecher, "Letter to Mr. Beman," 516, 517.

26. "A Presbyterian," "Female Exhorters" (*The Religious Intelligencer* 17:40 [March 2, 1833], 629–630), 630.

27. Brekus, *Strangers and Pilgrims*, 271.

28. Brekus, *Strangers and Pilgrims*, 282.

29. Elleanor Knight, *A Narrative of the Christian Experience, Life and Adventures, Trials and Labors of Elleanor Knight, Written by Herself* (Providence, RI, 1839), 125.

30. Knight, *Narrative*, 8.

31. Knight, *Narrative*, 111.

32. Knight, *Narrative*, 99–100.

33. Knight, *Narrative*, 125.

34. Thompson, *Trial and Defence*, 3.

35. Thompson, *Trial and Defence*, 5.

36. John Wesley, *The Cure of Evil Speaking* (London: G. Paramore, 1795), 2. The Tract Society of the Methodist Episcopal Church of New York brought out at least two editions of this sermon in the early nineteenth century, in 1827 and 1837.

37. Wesley, *Cure of Evil Speaking*, 2.

38. Horatio Wood, *Evil Speaking: A Sermon Preached to the Congregational Church in Tyngsborough, February 4, 1844* (Boston: James Monroe and Company, 1844), 9.

39. Israel Chamberlayne, *Evil Speaking, or, A Bridle for the Unbridled Tongue* (Rochester, NY: Jerome and Brother, 1849), 23.

40. Chamberlayne, *Evil Speaking*, 3, 4, For Chamberlayne's position on conversion and church membership, see his *Saving Faith* (New York: Carlton and Lanahan, 1871). Chamberlayne was also known to some antebellum readers as the author of a sensational captivity narrative. See William Jackman (Israel Chamberlayne), *The Australian Captive* (Auburn, NY: Derby and Miller, 1853).

41. Chamberlayne, *Evil Speaking*, 3, 4, 20.

42. Thompson, *Trial and Defence*, 8.

43. Thompson, *Trial and Defence*, 3.

44. Catherine Reed Williams, *Fall River: An Authentic Narrative* (Providence, RI: Marshall, Brown, and Company, 1834), quoted in Brekus, *Strangers and Pilgrims*, 268.

45. Matteson Baker, *A Brief Statement of the Administration of Westford Circuit, in Relation to Mrs. Sally Thompson: Arraigned, Tried and Expelled from the Methodist Episcopal Church* (Lowell, MA: A. B. F. Hildreth, 1839), 3, 2, 16n.

46. Brekus, *Strangers and Pilgrims*, 270, 271.

47. Mary P. Ryan, "Gender and Public Access: Women's Politics in Nineteenth-Century America" (in Craig Calhoun, ed., *Habermas and the Public Sphere* [Cambridge, MA: MIT Press, 1992], 259–288), 266.

48. Chauncy, *Seasonable Thoughts,* 77.

49. Baker, *Brief Statement,* 24.

50. "A Presbyterian," "Female Exhorters," 630. On the evangelical movement and its contribution to the creation of the mass press and large-scale social movements, see David Paul Nord, *Faith in Reading: Religious Publishing and the Birth of Mass Media in America* (Oxford: Oxford University Press, 2004) and Michael P. Young, *Bearing Witness against Sin: The Evangelical Birth of the American Social Movement* (Chicago: University of Chicago Press, 2006).

51. Elizabeth Dillon, *The Gender of Freedom: Fictions of Liberalism and the Literary Public Sphere* (Stanford, CA: Stanford University Press, 2004), 25. See also Stacey Margolis, *The Public Life of Privacy in Nineteenth-Century American Literature* (Durham, NC: Duke University Press, 2005).

52. R. Babcock, "Christian Females Exhorted to Use Their Utmost Influence in Favor of Christianity" (*Christian Secretary* 8:48–49 [1829] 191–195), 191. A more famous version of the same polemic was Jonathan F. Stearns, *Female Influence: and the True and Christian Mode of Its Exercise* (Newburyport, MA: John G. Tilton, 1837). See Barbara Welter's classic feminist critique, "The Cult of True Womanhood" (*American Quarterly* 18:2 [Summer 1966] 151–174).

53. Ann Douglas, *The Feminization of American Culture* (1977; New York: Noonday/Farrar, Straus and Giroux, 1998), 46, 58.

54. Gregg D. Crane, "Dangerous Sentiments: Sympathy, Rights, and Revolution in Stowe's Antislavery Novels" (*Nineteenth-Century Literature* 51:2 [September 1996] 176–204), 188.

55. Harriet Beecher Stowe, *Uncle Tom's Cabin,* ed. Elizabeth Ammons (New York: Norton 1994), 70. Subsequent references cited parenthetically in the text. On the relationship between public authority and private sentiments in this scene, see also Dillon, *The Gender of Freedom,* 228–229.

56. Brook Thomas, *Cross-Examinations of Law and Literature: Cooper, Hawthorne, Stowe, and Melville* (Cambridge: Cambridge University Press, 1987), 122.

57. Zilpha Elaw, *Memoirs of the Life, Religious Experience, Ministerial Travels, and Labours of Mrs. Zilpha Elaw, an American Female of Colour* [(London: "Published by the Authoress," 1846). Cited as rpt. in William L. Andrews, *Sisters of the Spirit: Three Black Women's Autobiographies of the Nineteenth Century* (Bloomington: Indiana University Press, 1986), 49–160], 77-78, 104. See also Yolanda Pierce's account of Elaw in "African American Women's Spiritual Narratives" (in Dale M. Bauer and Philip Gould, eds., *The Cambridge Companion to Nineteenth-Century American Women's Writing* [Cambridge: Cambridge University Press, 2001], 244–261).

58. Elaw, *Memoirs,* 52.

59. Dawn Coleman, "The Unsentimental Woman Preacher of *Uncle Tom's Cabin*" (*American Literature* 80:2 [June 2008] 265–292), 283.

60. Stowe, afterword to *Uncle Tom's Cabin,* cited as rept. in Coleman, "Unsentimental Woman Preacher," 278–279.

61. Coleman, "Unsentimental Woman Preacher," 278–279.

62. Knight, *Narrative,* 41.

5. THE CURSE OF SLAVERY

1. Nathaniel Hawthorne, *The House of the Seven Gables*, ed. Robert S. Levine (New York: Norton, 2006). Unless otherwise noted, subsequent references are to this edition and cited parenthetically in the text.
2. Harriet Beecher Stowe, *Dred: A Tale of the Great Dismal Swamp* (2 vols.; Boston: Phillips, Sampson, and Company, 1856), 1: 256, 320.
3. Stowe, *Dred,* 1: iv. On the abolition movement's conception of the revolutionary heritage and the archaism of the public sphere, see Robert Fanuzzi, *Abolition's Public Sphere* (Minneapolis: University of Minnesota Press, 2003).
4. Stowe, *Dred,* 1: iv.
5. Larua H. Korobkin, "Appropriating Law in Harriet Beecher Stowe's *Dred*" (*Nineteenth-Century Literature* 62:3 [December 2007] 380–406), 388.
6. Stowe, *Dred,* 2:103.
7. Robert Cover, *Justice Accused: Antislavery and the Judicial Process* (New Haven, CT: Yale University Press, 1975), 77.
8. Stowe, *Dred,* 2:105, 99, 105.
9. Stowe, *Dred,* 1: 256, 2:105.
10. Gregg D. Crane, "Dangerous Sentiments: Sympathy, Rights, and Revolution in Stowe's Antislavery Novels" (*Nineteenth-Century Literature* 51:2 [September 1996] 176–204), 180, 181, 178.
11. Stephen Howard Browne, "'This Unparalleled and Inhuman Massacre': The Gothic, the Sacred, and the Meaning of Nat Turner" (*Rhetoric and Public Affairs* 3:3 [2000] 309–331), 309.
12. Henry Irving Tragle, *The Southampton Slave Revolt of 1831: A Compilation of Source Material* (Amherst: University of Massachusetts Press, 1971), 430.
13. The lines are from an apocryphal account by William Wells Brown, from *The Negro in the American Rebellion: His Heroism and His Fidelity* (Boston: Lee and Shepherd, 1867), 19–25. Tragle reprints Brown's section on Turner's insurrection but suggests that such details "are products of the author's imagination, not historical detail" (349). See also Herbert Aptheker, *Nat Turner's Slave Rebellion* (New York: Grove, 1966), 45–46.
14. On the complex legacies of the Southampton rebellion, see Mary Kempt Davis, *Nat Turner before the Bar of Justice: Fictional Treatments of the Southampton Slave Insurrection* (Baton Rouge: Louisiana State University Press, 1999); Scot French, *The Rebellious Slave: Nat Turner in American Memory* (Boston: Houghton Mifflin, 2004); and Kenneth S. Greenberg, *Nat Turner: A Slave Rebellion in History and Memory* (New York: Oxford University Press, 2002). On literary treatments, see also Adélékè Adéèkó, *The Slave's Rebellion: Literature, History, Orature* (Bloomington: Indiana University Press, 2005), 22–49.
15. *The Confessions of Nat Turner* (Baltimore: Thomas R. Gray, 1831). Rpt. in Kenneth S. Greenberg, ed., *The Confessions of Nat Turner and Related Documents* (New York: Bedford, 1996). Subsequent references cited parenthetically in the text.
16. French, *The Rebellious Slave,* 51. Aptheker's classic study reclaimed the Southampton struggle for a tradition of black resistance, using the *Confessions* to refute the

claims of William S. Drewry, a racist and Southern apologist who had portrayed Turner as a deluded fanatic. See Drewry, *The Southampton Insurrection* (1900; Murfreesboro, NC: Johnson Publishing, 1968). Protesting Styron's depiction of the rebellion, a number of critics discovered in the *Confessions* not the troubled character of postmodern fiction but a hero of African American militancy. See John Henrik Clarke, ed., *William Styron's Nat Turner: Ten Black Writers Respond* (Boston: Beacon, 1968).

17. Literary critics have called attention, especially, to the editorial role of Gray, who may have emphasized Turner's religious fanaticism in order to quell the widespread fear of an organized conspiracy. Thus Seymour Gross and Eileen Bender argue that the *Confessions* is little more than "an exercise in reassurance" for the benefit of a traumatized white public ("History, Politics, Literature: The Myth of Nat Turner" [*American Quarterly* 23:4 (October 1971) 487–518], 497). Similarly, Mary Kempt Davis suggests that "a primary purpose of Gray's *Confessions* is to sedate the (white) public mind" (*Nat Turner before the Bar of* Justice, 64).

18. Eric J. Sundquist, *To Wake the Nations: Race in the Making of American Literature* (Cambridge, MA: Harvard University Press/Belknap Press, 1993), 37.

19. Sundquist's reading is not always attentive to the peculiar ways in which texts operate within history to produce and deploy voice, with its aura of authenticity. As Dwight A. McBride argues in *Impossible Witness: Truth, Abolition, and Slave Testimony* (New York: New York University Press, 2001), the testifying subject is in important respects an effect, rather than an origin, of the speech act that asserts his or her subjectivity.

20. Davis, *Nat Turner before the Bar of Judgment,* 68. More recently, Jeannine Marie DeLombard's *In the Shadow of the Gallows: Race, Crime, and American Civic Identity* (Philadelphia: University of Pennsylvania Press, 2012), restores the *Confessions* to the tradition of gallows literature. See especially pp. 171–183.

21. Sundquist, *Wake the Nations,* 39.

22. See also Davis, *Nat Turner before the Bar of Judgment,* 16, and Tragle, *Southampton Slave Revolt,* 38.

23. Quoted in Thomas C. Parramore, *Southampton County, Virginia* (Charlottesville: University of Virginia Press, 1978), 100.

24. Richard Eppes, quoted in Aptheker, *Nat Turner's Slave Rebellion,* 61.

25. Stephen B. Oates, *The Fires of Jubilee: Nat Turner's Fierce Rebellion* (New York: Harper and Row, 1975), 102.

26. Tragle, *Southampton Slave Revolt,* 174. Floyd insisted: "It is important that the evidence be taken verbatim as given in Court and that it be so certified" (174).

27. Tragle, *Southampton Slave Revolt,* 221.

28. The official record is reprinted in Tragle, *Southampton Slave Revolt,* 221–223. As James M. Campbell shows in his history of criminal slave trials in Richmond, the Virginia courts of oyer and terminer that decided such cases generally disregarded common-law conventions of due process. Convictions, Campbell observes, were "often based on the uncorroborated testimony of whites or on evidence from slaves and free African Americans. Indeed, the summary nature of oyer and terminer

proceedings meant that even in some capital cases slave defendants might be convicted upon depositions that did little more than raise the suspicion of guilt" (*Slavery on Trial: Race, Class, and Criminal Justice in Antebellum Richmond, Virginia* [Gainesville: University Press of Florida, 2007], 88).

29. Tragle, *Southampton Slave Revolt,* 222.

30. Tragle, *Southampton Slave Revolt,* 405. See also 244.

31. Tragle, *Southampton Slave Revolt,* 223.

32. Peter H. Wood, "Nat Turner: The Unknown Slave as Visionary Leader" (in Leon Litwack and August Meier, eds., *Black Leaders of the Nineteenth Century* [Urbana: University of Illinois Press, 1988], 21–42), 37, 38.

33. Parramore, *Southampton,* 105–107.

34. My account of Thomas Ruffin Gray and the making of the *Confessions* follows Parramore, *Southampton,* and his "Covenant in Jerusalem" (in Greenberg, ed., *Nat Turner,* 58–77), as well as David F. Allmendinger, Jr., "The Construction of *The Confessions of Nat Turner*" (in Greenberg, *Nat Turner,* 24–42).

35. Parrmore, *Southampton,* 113.

36. On the *Confessions* and the conventions of gothic literature, see Browne, "Unparalleled and Inhuman Massacre."

37. "The Confessions of Nat Turner," *Richmond Enquirer,* December 2, 1831. Rpt. in Tragle, *Southampton Slave Revolt,* 141–143. The review was reprinted in the [Amherst, MA] *Farmer's Cabinet;* the *Eastern Argus* [ME] *Semi-Weekly;* the *Essex* [MA] *Gazette;* the *Ithaca* [NY] *Journal and General* Advertiser; the *Macon* [GA] *Telegraph;* the *New York Mercury;* the *New Hampshire Gazette;* the *Norwich* [CT] *Courrier;* the *Rhode Island American and Gazette;* and elsewhere. Unless otherwise noted, all references are to Tragle's reprint.

38. "The Confessions of Nat Turner," *Carolina Observer,* November 16, 1831, n.p.

39. "The Confessions of Nat Turner," *Connecticut Mirror,* December 17, 1831.

40. Tragle, *Southampton,* 141–143.

41. See Allmendinger, "Construction," 37.

42. Campbell notes that "the only instances in which the thoughts of the accused were heard by the magistrates occurred when witnesses testified that the defendant had confessed to the alleged crime" (*Slavery on Trial,* 88). A key text on the status of slave testimony is the state's standard handbook of legal procedure in the antebellum period, William Waller Hening's *The Virginia Justice: Comprising the Office and Authority of a Justice of the Peace, in the Commonwealth of Virginia* (4th ed.; Richmond, VA: Shepherd and Pollard, 1825). According to Hening, the testimony of slaves was generally considered an inferior kind of evidence at trial, and in some cases a slave's testimony was not admissible at all. In other cases, the court would admonish slaves in the harshest of terms against perjury. However, when the court sought the conviction of a slave in a criminal trial, the standards of evidence were significantly less severe (649–650). On the status of confessions by enslaved persons, see Hening's rules of evidence: "a confession . . . which is obtained from a defendant, either by the flattery of hope, or by the impression of fear . . . is not admissible evidence" (200).

43. Saidiya Hartman, *Scenes of Subjection: Terror, Slavery, and Self-Making in Nineteenth-Century America* (New York: Oxford University Press, 1997), 80. For an opposing view, emphasizing the contradictory effects of this attribution of criminal responsibility, see DeLombard, *In the Shadow of the Gallows.*

44. On the status of slave confessions, see McBride, *Impossible Witness.* On the abolitionist effort to open a space in the press for African American civil subjectivity, see Jeannine Marie DeLombard, *Slavery on Trial: Law, Abolitionism, and Print Culture* (Chapel Hill: University of North Carolina Press, 2007), 71–100.

45. Histories of the rebellion disagree about whether to call Turner a preacher. Aptheker prefers the term "exhorter," which emphasizes Turner's informal religious authority and his power to move his listeners to action (*Nat Turner's Slave Rebellion,* 36–37).

46. For Sundquist, Turner's "messianic" voice arises from its "syncretic blend of Christian and African" practices; his story is "infused with African belief and communal leadership" (*Wake the Nations,* 61).

47. Randolph Ferguson Scully, "'I Come Here Before You Did and I Shall Not Go Away': Race, Gender, and Evangelical Community on the Eve of the Nat Turner Rebellion" (*Journal of the Early Republic* 27 [Winter 2007], 661–684), 665.

48. Tragle, *Southampton,* 432.

49. Quoted in Aptheker, *Nat Turner's Slave Rebellion,* 81.

50. DeLombard, *Slavery on Trial,* 6–7.

51. William Lloyd Garrison, *A Brief Sketch of the Trial of William Lloyd Garrison for an Alleged Libel on Francis Todd of Newburyport, Mass.* (Boston: Garrison and Knapp, 1834), iii.

52. See George Edward Carter, "The Use of the Doctrine of Higher Law in the American Anti-Slavery Crusade, 1830–1860" (PhD. Diss., University of Oregon, 1970), 96.

53. Lydia Maria Child, *An Appeal in Favor of That Class of Americans, Called Africans* (Boston: Allen and Ticknor, 1833).

54. Paul Simon, *Freedom's Champion—Elijah Lovejoy* (Carbondale: Southern Illinois University Press, 1994). On the riots and the murder, a key text from the period is Edward Beecher, *Narrative of the Riots at Alton* (Alton, IL: G. Holton, 1838). In *Voicing Abjection: Evangelical Publicity, Race, and Suffering in Early American Literature* (Philadelphia: University of Pennsylvania Press, forthcoming), Mark J. Miller argues compellingly that Beecher's account of the Lovejoy murder inaugurated a new age of abolitionist "martyrology."

55. Harriet Martineau, *The Martyr Age of the United States* (Boston: Weeks, Jordan, 1839).

56. Tragle, *Southampton,* 141.

57. Garrison, *Brief Sketch of the Trial,* iii.

58. There is a vast scholarly literature on religion and the abolition movement. On the role of evangelical conversion in the campaign, see, for example, John Stauffer, *The Black Hearts of Men: Radical Abolitionists and the Transformation of Race* (Cambridge, MA: Harvard University Press, 2001) and Michael Young, *Bearing Witness Against Sin: The Evangelical Birth of the American Social Movement* (Chicago: University of Chicago Press, 2007).

59. Garrison, *Trial,* iii.

60. [William Lloyd Garrison], "Slavery Record: Confessions of Nat Turner" (*Liberator,* December 17, 1831, 2–3). All citations are to this original edition.

61. "Incendiary Publications" (*Liberator,* October 8, 1831, 1).

62. Elizabeth Barrett Browning, "The Runaway Slave at Pilgrim's Point," *The Liberty Bell,* January 1, 1848, 29–35. Further citations are to this first printing and cited parenthetically in the text.

63. Isobel Armstrong, *Victorian Poetry: Poetry, Poetics, and Politics* (London: Routledge, 1993), 360.

64. Tricia Lootens, "States of Exile" (in Meredith L. McGill, ed., *The Traffic in Poems: Nineteenth-Century Poetry and Transatlantic Exchange* [Piscataway, NJ: Rutgers University Press, 2008], 15–36), 29. Lootens emphasizes that "the speaker abandons her intention to curse in the name of the Pilgrim Fathers," deciding "to entrust vengeance to a higher authority" (30, 31).

65. Marjorie Stone, "Elizabeth Barrett Browning and the Garrisonians: 'The Runaway Slave at Pilgrim's Point,' the Boston Female Anti-Slavery Society, and Abolitionist Discourse in the *Liberty Bell*" (in Alison Chapman, ed., *Victorian Women Poets* [Cambridge: D. S. Brewer, 2003], 33–55), 39, 46, 54.

66. Stone, "Browning and the Garrisonians," 48.

67. Stone, "Browning and the Garrisonians," 34.

68. See Sarah Brophy, "Elizabeth Barrett Browning's 'The Runaway Slave at Pilgrim's Point' and the Politics of Interpretation" (*Victorian Poetry* 36:3 [Fall 1998] 273–288): "the moral and political role of women (the poem's female speaker but also Barrett Browning as author) is to exercise an emotional influence over men" (277). This critique is consistent with the argument developed in Mark Reinhardt's work on the literary legacies of the historical Margaret Garner, with whom Browning's speaker is often compared. See Reinhardt, "Who Speaks for Margaret Garner?: Slavery, Silence, and the Politics of Ventriloquism" (*Critical Inquiry* 29:1 [Autumn 2002] 81–119). Such a reading would also conform to the account of antislavery literature's preoccupation with death and martyrdom in Russ Castronovo, *Necro Citizenship: Death, Eroticism, and the Public Sphere in the Nineteenth-Century United States* (Durham, NC: Duke University Press, 2001).

6. WORDS OF FIRE

1. "The Nat Turner Insurrection" (*Anglo-African Magazine,* December 1859, n.p.).

2. George B. Cheever, *The Curse of God Against Political Atheism: With Some of the Lessons of the Tragedy at Harper's Ferry* (Boston: Walker, Wise, and Co., 1859), 6.

3. Cheever, *Curse of God,* 24.

4. George Thompson, *Prison Life and Reflections* (2nd ed.; Hartford, CT: A. Work, 1851), 29.

5. Theodore Parker, *The Trial of Theodore Parker, for the 'Misdemeanor' of a Speech in Faneuil Hall Against Kidnapping* (Boston: Published for the Author, 1855), 69.

6. J. G. Forman, *The Christian Martyrs: Or, The Conditions of Obedience to the Civil Government* (Boston: Wm. Crosby and H. P. Nichols, 1851), 30.

7. Anonymous, *The Higher Law Tried by Reason and Authority: An Argument Pro and Con* (Cincinnati, OH: Truman and Spofford, 1851), 6.

8. J. M. Peck, *The Duties of American Citizens: A Discourse, Preached in the State-House, Springfield, Illinois, January 26, 1851* (St. Louis, MO: Published by Request, Printed by T. W. Ustick, 1851), 20.

9. John C. Lord, *"The Higher Law" and Its Application to the Fugitive Slave Bill* (New York: Published by Order of the "Union Safety Committee," 1851), 16, 15.

10. *Higher Law Tried by Reason,* 42.

11. Richard S. Storrs, Jr., *The Obligation of Man to Obey the Civil Law: Its Ground and its Extent* (New York: Mark H. Newman and Co., 1850), 6. Some capitalization omitted.

12. Henry David Thoreau, "Civil Disobedience" (in Carl Bode, ed., *The Portable Thoreau* [New York: Viking, 1966], 109–137), 111.

13. Thoreau, "Civil Disobedience," 111.

14. As Michael P. Young shows in *Bearing Witness against Sin: The Evangelical Birth of the American Social Movement* (Chicago: University of Chicago Press, 2006), the evangelical movements of the nineteenth century acquired their compelling force by reconfiguring the relation between "the intimate and the far-flung," the integrity of conscience and the large-scale entanglements of economic and political systems (3). Thus they created a politics of self-purification, animated by anxieties about complicity, which endures in the social movements of the present.

15. Here I distinguish my approach from one of the most sustained and original discussions of higher law in recent criticism, Deak Nabers's *Victory of Law: The Fourteenth Amendment, the Civil War, and American Literature, 1852–1867* (Baltimore, MD: Johns Hopkins University Press, 2006). Nabers observes that "it is often difficult to determine whether Garrison was more committed to the constative matter of the arguments he prosecuted or the performative matter of the social and political effects those arguments might have had in the immediate contexts in which he delivered them" (49). Whereas Nabers focuses on arguments that can be extrapolated from their immediate contexts, my interest is precisely in performative utterances and their reception in a specific historical period. Along the same lines, I suggest that the abolition movement made free use of exhortation, seduction, and other non-rational modes of persuasion, in addition to the deliberative rationalism emphasized by Robert Fanuzzi in *Abolition's Public Sphere* (Minneapolis: University of Minnesota Press, 2003).

16. Henry Ward Beecher, "A Sermon by Henry Ward Beecher, Preached at Plymouth Church, Brooklyn, on Sunday Evening, October 30, 1860" (in James Redpath, ed., *Echoes of Harper's Ferry* [Boston: Thayer and Eldridge, 1860], 257–279), 263, 266, 264.

17. Beecher, "A Sermon," 263, 265.

18. Albert J. Von Frank, "John Brown, James Redpath, and the Idea of Revolution" (*Civil War History* 52:2 [June 2006] 142–160), 148. John Brown's own thinking

about insurrection, according to Von Frank, was significantly informed by his "contact" with "refugees from the English and Continental revolutions of 1848" (143).

19. Redpath, *Echoes of Harper's Ferry*, 7, 5.

20. Beecher, "A Sermon," 267.

21. Beecher, "A Sermon," 267.

22. Beecher, "A Sermon," 277-278.

23. Jean Fagan Yellin, *Harriet Jacobs: A Life* (New York: Basic Civitas Books, 2004), 140. Throughout, my account of Jacobs's life and times is informed by Yellin's biography and by her collection of documentary sources, *The Harriet Jacobs Family Papers* (2 vols.; Chapel Hill: University of North Carolina Press, 2008).

24. On the founding of Thayer and Eldridge, see Ted Genoways, *Walt Whitman and the Civil War: America's Poet during the Lost Years of 1860–1862* (Berkeley: University of California Press, 2009), 14–15.

25. Harriet Jacobs, *Incidents in the Life of a Slave Girl* (1861; New York: Oxford University Press, 1988), title page. Subsequent references are to this edition and cited parenthetically in the text.

26. Yellin, *Harriet Jacobs*, 140.

27. Lydia Maria Child, letter to Harriet Jacobs, August 13, 1860 (in Yellin, ed., *Harriet Jacobs Family Papers*, 1:277–280), 279. See also Yellin, *Harriet Jacobs*, 141.

28. My study of the episode builds on Bruce Mills, "Lydia Maria Child and the Ending to Harriet Jacobs's *Incidents in the Life of a Slave Girl*" (*American Literature* 64:2 [June 1992], 255–272) and Albert H. Tricomi, "Harriet Jacobs's Autobiography and the Voice of Lydia Maria Child" (*ESQ: A Journal of the American Renaissance* 53:3 [2007] 216–252).

29. Lydia Maria Child, *Correspondence between Lydia Maria Child and Gov. Henry Wise and Mrs. Mason, of Virginia* (Boston: American Anti-Slavery Society, 1860), 14.

30. Child, *Correspondence*, 13.

31. Tricomi, "Jacobs's Autobiography," 244. The sales figure for Child's pamphlet is given in David S. Reynolds, *John Brown, Abolitionist: The Man Who Killed Slavery, Sparked the Civil War, and Seeded Civil Rights* (New York: Vintage, 2005), 462.

32. Child, *Correspondence*, 14.

33. Tricomi, "Jacobs's Autobiography," 219.

34. Tricomi, "Jacobs's Autobiography," 219.

35. [Amelia Chesson], "Domestic Slave-Life in the Southern States" (*Morning Star and Dial,* March 10, 1862. Rpt. in Yellin, ed. *Harriet Jacobs Family Papers*, 366–373), 366.

36. Yellin, *Harriet Jacobs* and *Harriet Jacobs Family Papers*. On the tradition of writing by enslaved and free black women in the eighteenth and nineteenth century, see also Frances Smith Foster, *Written by Herself: Literary Production of African American Women, 1746–1892* (Bloomington: Indiana University Press, 1993).

37. See William L. Andrews, *To Tell a Free Story: The First Century of Afro-American Autobiography* (Urbana: University of Illinois Press, 1986), especially 240–241, and Jacqueline Goldsby, "'I Disguised My Hand': Writing Versions of the Truth in Harriet Jacobs's *Incidents in the Life of a Slave Girl* and John Jacobs's "A True Tale of Slavery'" (in Deborah M. Garfield and Rafia Zafar, eds., *Harriet Jacobs and*

Incidents in the Life of a Slave Girl: *New Critical Essays* [New York: Cambridge
University Press, 1996], 11–43).

38. Hazel Carby describes Jacobs's book as "the most sophisticated, sustained narrative
dissection of the conventions of true womanhood by a black woman author before
emancipation" (*Reconstructing Womanhood: The Emergence of the Afro-American
Woman Novelist* [Oxford: Oxford University Press, 1987], 47). In similar terms,
Mark Rifkin calls it "an incredibly sophisticated analysis of the relation between
law, white privilege, and ideologies of private space" ("'A Home Made Sacred by
Protecting Laws': Black Activist Homemaking and Geographies of Citizenship in
Incidents in the Life of a Slave Girl" [*Differences* 18:2 (2007) 72–102], 75). Placing
Jacobs's work in the context of antebellum criminal trials, Saidiya Hartman argues
that *Incidents* "reveal[s] the role of law in sustaining and defining virtue" (*Scenes of
Subjection: Terror, Slavery, and Self-Making in Nineteenth-Century America* [New
York: Oxford University Press, 1997], 104).

39. Charles H. Nichols, "Who Read the Slave Narratives" (*Phylon Quarterly* 20:2
[1959] 149–162),151, 152.

40. Some of the conventions of testimony, as a genre of antislavery literature, are discussed
in Dwight A. McBride, *Impossible Witnesses: Truth, Abolition, and Slave Testimony*
(New York: New York University Press, 2001). On Jacobs's narrative as testimony, see
Deborah M. Garfield, "Earwitness: Female Abolitionism, Sexuality, and *Incidents in
the Life of a Slave Girl*" (in Garfield and Zafar, *Harriet Jacobs*, 76–99).

41. Jacobs's story, as Hartman observes, is recounted "from the perspective of the dispossessed and non-contractual subject" (*Scenes of Subjection*, 103).

42. See Rifkin, "A Home Made Sacred," 75: "One of the most notable . . . aspects of
Jacobs's critique of white power," Rifkin notes, "is the extent to which it references
national law and symbols."

43. On the Dred Scott case, see Jacobs, letter to Amy Kirby Post, March 1857 (in Yellin,
ed., *Harriet Jacobs Family Papers*, 231–233) and Rifkin, "A Home Made Sacred."

44. Hartman, *Scenes of Subjection*, 104, 106. Hartman is building from Hazel Carby's
argument that *Incidents* "demystified a convention that appeared as the obvious,
common sense rules of behavior and revealed the concept of true womanhood to be
an ideology, not a lived set of social relations" (*Reconstructing Womanhood*, 49).

45. "At the time Child was revising Jacobs's manuscript," as Tricomi acknowledges,
"John Brown had become a polarizing figure not only for the North and South but
among abolitionists as well" ("Jacobs's Autobiography," 244).

46. Mills, "Child and the Ending," 257.

47. Jacobs, letter to Amy Kirby Post, November 8, 1860 (Rpt. in Yellin, *Harriet Jacobs
Family Papers*, 1:284–285), 284.

48. "Our Boston Correspondence," (*National Anti-Slavery Standard*, February 16,
1861. Rpt. in Yellin, ed. *Harriet Jacobs Family Papers*, 1:328–329), 328.

49. "New Publications," (*National Anti-Slavery Standard*, February 23, 1861. Rpt. in
Yellin, ed. *Harriet Jacobs Family Papers*, 1:329–334). 333.

50. "Linda" (*Weekly Anglo-African*, April 13, 1861. Rpt. in Yellin, ed. *Harriet Jacobs
Family Papers*, 1:349–350), 349.

51. "The Nat Turner Insurrection" (*Anglo-African Magazine*, December, 1859, n.p.).

52. "John Brown, The Martyr" (*Weekly Anglo-African*, December 10, 1859, n.p.). On cross-racial alliances among the militants, see John Mead, "Declarations of Liberty: Representations of Black/White Alliance Against Slavery by John Brown, James Redpath, and Thomas Wentworth Higginson" (*Journal for the Study of Radicalism* 3:1 [2009] 111–143).

53. On Redpath, see John R. McKivigan, *Forgotten Firebrand; James Redpath and the Making of Nineteenth-Century America* (Ithaca, NY: Cornell University Press, 2008). On the Haytian Emigration Bureau, see also Willis D. Boyd, "James Redpath and Negro Colonization in Haiti, 1860–1862" (*The Americas* 12:2 [October 1955] 169–182).

54. See "Resignation" (*Weekly Anglo-African*, April 6, 1861, n.p.).

55. "A Carbonari Wanted" (*Weekly Anglo-African*, April 13, 1861, n.p.).

56. Redpath, *Echoes of Harper's Ferry*, 5.

57. Martin R. Delany, *Blake, or The Huts of America*, ed. Floyd J. Miller (1859 and 1861–1862; Boston: Beacon, 1970). Subsequent references cited parenthetically.

58. Nell Irvin Painter, "Martin R. Delany: Elitism and Black Nationalism" (in Leon Litwack and August Meier, eds., *Black Leaders of the Nineteenth Century* [Urbana: University of Illinois Press, 1988], 149–171), 149. On Delany's reclamation, see also Robert S. Levine, *Martin Delany: A Documentary Reader* (Chapel Hill: University of North Carolina Press, 2003), 4–5.

59. John Zeugner, "A Note on Martin Delany's *Blake,* and Black Militancy" (*Phylon* 32:1 [1971] 98–105), 98.

60. Eric Sundquist, *To Wake the Nations: Race in the Making of American Literature* (Cambridge, MA: Harvard University Press/Belknap Press, 1993), especially 135–221.

61. Paul Gilroy, *The Black Atlantic: Modernity and Double Consciousness* (Cambridge, MA: Harvard University Press, 1993), especially 19–29.

62. Gilroy, *Black Atlantic,* 26,

63. Sundquist, *Wake the Nations,* 194.

64. More recently, a few scholars have reopened the question of Delany's gender politics. See, for example, Jordan Alexander Stein, "'A Christian Nation Calls for Its Wandering Children': Life, Liberty, Liberia" (*American Literary History* 19:4 [Winter 2007] 849–873), which describes surprising affinities between the Christian nationalisms of Delany and Sarah J. Hale.

65. Frank [Frances] A. Rollin, *Life and Public Services of Martin R. Delany* (Boston: Lee and Shepard, 1883), 33–39.

66. See Jeffory A. Clymer, "Martin Delany's *Blake* and the Transnational Politics of Property" (*American Literary History* 15:4 [Winter 2003] 709–731).

67. *Scott v. Sanford.* 60 U.S. 393, 404, 405.

68. *Scott v. Sanford,* 404.

69. *Scott v. Sanford* 426.

70. *Scott v. Sanford,* 404.

71. Gregg D. Crane, "The Lexicon of Rights, Power, and Community in *Blake:* Martin R. Delany's Dissent from *Dred Scott*" (*American Literature* 68:3 [September 1996] 527–553).

72. Roger B. Taney, "Supplement to Dred Scott Opinion" (September 1858. Cited as rpt. in Samuel Tyler, *Memoir of Roger Brooke Taney, LL.D.* [Baltimore, MD: John Murphy and Company, 1872], 578–608), 607. The Supplement is discussed at some length in Crane, "Lexicon of Rights."
73. Crane, "Lexicon of Rights," 538.
74. Gilroy, *Black Atlantic,* 28.
75. Stein, "Christian Nation," 867.
76. On Delany and the historical Plácido, see Ifeoma Kiddoe Nwankwo, *Black Cosmopolitanism: Racial Consciousness and Transnational Identity in the Nineteenth-Century Americas* (Philadelphia: University of Pennsylvania Press, 2005), especially Chapter 2, "The View from Next Door: Plácido through the Eyes of U.S. Black Abolitionists" (48–80). On Manzano, see Miller's note in Delany, *Blake,* 319 n. 27. On Delany and Whitfield, see Sundquist, *Wake the Nations,* especially pp. 203–204.
77. Rollin, *Life,* 55.
78. Painter, "Martin Delany," 151.

EPILOGUE

1. Edward Everett Hale, "The Man without a Country," *Atlantic Monthly,* December 1863. Cited as rpt. in Hsuan Hsu and Susan Kalter, eds., *Two Texts by Edward Everett Hale: "The Man without a Country" and* Philip Nolan's Friends (Lantham, MD: Lexington Books, 2010, 19–37), 20, 21.
2. Brook Thomas, *Civic Myths: A Law-and-Literature Approach to Citizenship* (Chapel Hill: University of North Carolina Press, 2007), 58.
3. Hsuan Hsu, for example, shows that this patriotic story is also a dream of empire: "it is as much a tale of the state's own investments in extraterritorial and extralegal force as it is a parable of treason and redemption" ("Contexts for Reading 'The Man without a Country'" [in Hsu and Kalter, eds., *Two Texts,* 1–16], 6). Carrie Hyde places Hale's text in the tradition of didactic literature on crime and punishment to show how these genres of "negative instruction" threaten to undermine their own design ("Outcast Patriotism: The Dilemma of Negative Instruction in 'The Man without a Country'" [*ELH* 77:4 (December 2010) 915–939]).
4. Lauren Berlant, *The Anatomy of National Fantasy: Hawthorne, Utopia, and Everyday Life* (Chicago: University of Chicago Press, 1991).
5. Julia A. J. Foote, *A Brand Plucked from the Fire* (Cleveland, OH: W. F. Schneider, 1879. Cited as rpt. in William L. Andrews, *Sisters of the Spirit: Three Black Women's Autobiographies of the Nineteenth Century* [Bloomington: Indiana University Press, 1986], 161–234), 207.
6. See Berlant, *National Fantasy,* 13.
7. Deak Nabers, *Victory of Law: The Fourteenth Amendment, the Civil War, and American Literature, 1852–1867* (Baltimore, MD: Johns Hopkins University Press, 2006), viii, 21.

8. Herman Melville, *Billy Budd, Sailor, and Other Stories* (New York: Penguin, 1986), 13, 25, 258.

9. Herman Melville, "The Portent," in *Battle-Pieces and Aspects of the War* (1866; New York: Da Capo, 1995), n.p.

10. Virginia Jackson, "Who Reads Poetry?" (*PMLA* 123:1 [January 2008] 181–187).

11. Benedict Anderson, *Imagined Communities: Reflections on the Origin and Spread of Nationalism* (rev. ed.; London: Verso, 2006).

12. See Lloyd Pratt, *Archives of American Time: Literature and Modernity in the Nineteenth Century* (Philadelphia: University of Pennsylvania Press, 2010).

Acknowledgments

S peaking of John Brown, Ralph Waldo Emerson came around to "love, whose other name is justice." One thing I've been trying to say in *The Oracle and the Curse* is this: even when we read in private, we don't read alone. Working on the book, I spent many days in solitude, with no better companion than a handful of weird, obscure old documents. What kept my heart in it, some of those lonely times, was the wish to understand the kinds of power and pleasure we encounter when a work of the imagination calls us together. When we feel like we've been summoned to one side, against another, in a divided world. I'm grateful to feel that I belong among many generous souls.

Michael Warner provoked me to think about how public speech creates the space of its own circulation as a gathering place for publics and counterpublics. Virginia Jackson and Lawrence Buell read an early draft and helped me to redesign the project at an important stage. Conversations with Meredith McGill taught me about Nathaniel Hawthorne and the dynamics of literary renunciation. Along the way, I learned from Lauren Berlant, Pete Coviello, Colin Dayan, Jeannine DeLombard, Elizabeth Dillon, Wai Chee Dimock, Jacqueline Goldsby, Kathryn Lofton, Jessica Pressman, and Aaron Ritzenberg. Following my inexpert guidance, Ryan Carr, Thomas Koenigs, Stephen Krewson, and Cooper Wilhelm went uncomplaining into the archives, searching out forgotten cases and eccentric offenders. The people who work at the Beinecke, the Huntington, Brown University's Special Collections, and the New York Historical Society are a bunch of angels. Some sections of Chapter 6 appeared, in an earlier version, as "Harriet Jacobs among the Militants," in *American Literature*, vol. 84, issue 4, pp. 743–767, © 2012 Duke University Press, and are reprinted with permission.

And two more things: I made the last of my revisions in the middle of a hurricane, and Jenny Mellon kept me company that day; having her around reminds me that justice can also be a name we give to love. And *The Oracle and the Curse* is dedicated to my father down in Arkansas, Stephen Austin Smith, one of the all-time great raisers of hell.

Index

abnormal justice, 27–28, 223n73
abolitionists, 1, 2, 6, 15, 25–26, 28, 32, 35, 36, 104, 106, 151–55, 166, 168–184, 186, 187, 190–194, 211, 240n8, 249n15
Adams, John, 7, 11; *Dissertation on the Canon and Feudal Law*, 11
allegory, 32, 35, 38, 90, 91, 173, 197, 209, 211, 234n72
Althusser, Louis, 12
amendments to the Constitution, 210–211
American Anti-Slavery Society, 168
American Colonization Society, 168, 170, 195
American Revolution, 4, 11, 12, 17, 19, 25, 29, 33, 49–52, 55, 58–59, 65, 69–73 passim, 79, 87, 98, 101, 153, 174, 208, 214
Anderson, Benedict, 214, 218n16
Anglo-African, The, 6, 176–178, 193–195, 197, 205, 207, 214
Aptheker, Herbert, 244n16, 247n45
Arendt, Hannah, 50, 227n29
Armstrong, Isobel, 171
atheists, 15, 28, 96–97, 105, 108
Atlantic Magazine, The, 57
Austin, James T., 106, 112
autonomy. *See* literary autonomy

Baker, Matteson, 142, 143
Baptists, 80, 104, 138
Beadle, William, 23, 87–89, 90, 92, 161
Beecher, Henry Ward, 181–184, 185, 191, 193
Beecher, Lyman, 99, 132–133, 136–137, 143, 145, 169, 181, 239n8, 241n11
Bell, Robert, 50
Beman, Nathaniel, 132
Bender, Eileen, 245n17
Bentham, Jeremy, 11–12, 13, 45–50, 54, 56, 57, 220n44; *A Fragment on Government*, 46; *Introduction to the Principles of Morals and Legislation*, 49
Berlant, Lauren, 30, 117, 209, 210, 238n58
Binder, Guyora, 43, 224n84
Blackstone, William, 11–13, 16, 19, 41, 51, 53, 56, 57–58, 61, 63, 64, 101, 154, 177; *Commentaries on the Laws of England*, 11–13, 41–49, 50, 54, 55, 57, 64, 83, 198, 229n70, 235n77
blasphemy, xi–xii, 9, 15, 23, 26, 33, 35, 79, 87, 96–116, 117, 118, 122, 123, 126, 128–130, 134, 169, 206, 236n3
Bleecker, Ann Eliza, 89
Bloomfield, Maxwell, 50
Bly, John, 74–77

Boston, Patience, 78, 79

Boston Investigator, 23, 104–105, 109, 112–113, 115, 129

Bourdieu, Pierre, 12, 39, 47, 215

Brantley, Etheldred T., 165–166

Brekus, Catherine A., 138, 142–143

Broad, Amos, 55–56, 228n53

Brooke, John L., 8, 219n19

Brophy, Sarah, 174

Brown, Charles Brockden 30, 31, 90–91; *Wieland*, 23, 30, 31, 90–95, 116, 118, 120

Brown, John, x, 1–5, 6, 18, 23, 28–29, 32, 35–36, 171, 176–178, 181–186, 191–195 passim, 197, 207, 212–215, 217n3, 249n18, 255; "Address to the Virginia Court," 1, 3, 192

Brown, William Wells, 156

Browning, Elizabeth Barrett: "The Runaway Slave at Pilgrim's Point," 35, 171–175, 204

Buell, Lawrence, 223n76

Burkholder, Robert E., 115

Burr, Aaron, 208

Burroughs, Stephen: *Memoirs of the Notorious Stephen Burroughs*, 80

Butler, Jon, 240n11, 241n14

Butler, Judith, 221n51

Cain, 14

Calhoun, Craig, 8, 22, 222n53, 237n49

Campbell, James M., 245n28, 246n42

Carolina Observer, 163

Chamberlayne, Israel, 24, 140–141, 242n40

Channing, William Ellery, 114, 115, 169

Chartists, 182

Charvat, William, 223n76

Chauncy, Charles, 71, 79, 133–135, 143, 241n12

Cheever, George B.: *The Curse of God Against Political Atheism*, 28, 177–178

Child, Lydia Maria, 24, 28, 168, 181, 184–186, 187, 190–192

Chipman, Nathaniel, 103; *Sketches of the Principles of Government*, 52

circulation, ix, x, xii, 2–8 passim, 14, 23, 26, 29, 35, 45, 55, 56, 70, 75, 77, 93, 103, 105, 112–114, 115, 118, 126, 138, 142, 144, 147, 149, 166, 175, 186, 192, 199, 203–206, 214–216

civil death, 70

civil disobedience, x, 3, 25, 26, 28, 30, 111, 179–181, 183, 188–193 passim

Civil War, 4, 11, 17, 19, 25, 30, 33, 153, 178, 190, 195, 207–211, 212, 214, 215

Cobb, Jeremiah, 15, 160–162, 163, 166, 170, 176

codification, 10, 13, 48, 54–55, 56, 228n37

Cohen, Daniel, 21, 68, 73, 78, 80, 109, 231n11

Colacurcio, Michael, 116

Coleman, Dawn, 149

common law, 5, 7, 11, 12–13, 15–19 passim, 23, 30, 40–59, 74, 97, 100–104, 105, 107, 108, 153, 219n23

common people, 4, 13, 16, 21, 23, 60, 63–66, 68, 70–73, 76, 77, 79, 86, 96, 134, 136, 219n20

confessions, ix, x, 18, 19–20, 21, 65–67, 77–81, 82, 89–90, 91–94 passim, 117, 136, 159, 162, 164, 172–174, 188–189, 191, 212, 213–214, 219n20, 221n51, 231n5, 246n42

Confessions of Nat Turner, The, 15, 26, 31, 156–171, 172, 176, 201, 245n17

Congregationalists, 13, 24, 53, 70, 71, 80, 132–136

conjure, 165, 200–201, 202

Connecticut Courant, 82, 86

Connecticut Mirror, 160, 163

Connecticut Society for the Promotion of Freedom, 84

conscience, xii–xiii, 2, 14, 26, 27, 30–32, 34, 36, 38, 77, 86, 89, 91, 95, 97–100, 106, 107–108, 110–111, 115, 144, 150, 153, 154, 169, 171, 178, 179–181, 183, 203, 220n44

Coombs, Isaac, 14, 60–63

Cormack, Bradin, 221n45

counterpublics, 4, 9, 35, 36, 82, 113, 116, 118, 147, 165–167, 171, 174, 175, 203–206, 208, 211, 214, 215

court of public opinion, 3, 25–26, 93, 98, 110, 129, 131, 141, 155, 185, 168, 188, 192, 199, 209

Cover, Robert, 19, 25, 153, 154

Crane, Gregg D., 145, 155, 199, 201

critique, xi, 11, 12, 16–17, 19, 29–30, 32, 35, 39, 46, 47, 50, 56, 57, 66, 91, 120, 121, 125,

127, 147, 149–150, 154, 178, 187–188, 190, 199, 209–210, 218n10

culture of letters, 29, 57, 69, 99, 114–115, 118, 214

Cushing, William, 61–62

Daggett, David, 81, 82

Dana, James, 83–88, 161

Davenport, James, 23, 69, 133–137; "Confession and Retraction," 136

Davis, David Brion, 65–66

Declaration of Independence, 49–50, 227n29. *See also* American Revolution

death sentences. *See* sentences

deists, 23, 51, 87–89, 90

Delany, Martin, 36, 197, 205, 207–208; *Blake*, 36, 178, 195–206, 207, 214

deliberation, xi, 8–9, 12, 16, 21, 24, 35, 47, 48, 99, 102, 107–108, 110, 113, 126, 129, 143, 146–147

DeLombard, Jeannine, 25–26, 84, 168, 222n55, 245n20, 247n43

Derrida, Jacques, 12, 50, 227n29

Dillon, Elizabeth, 144

Dimock, Wai Chee, 29

disestablishment, 10, 16, 97, 100, 105, 132, 136, 220n44

Dixson, John, 72–73, 77, 79, 80

Doolittle, Benjamin, 135–136, 241n12

Douglas, Ann, 144–145

Douglass, Frederick, 2, 152, 196, 201, 205, 207

Drewry, William S., 245n16

Du Bois, W. E. B., 2

Dyer, Eliphat, 82–83

Eastern Argus Semi-Weekly, 162

Edwards, Jonathan, 133, 136, 240n11

Elaw, Zilpha, 147–148, 149

Eley, Geoff, 21

Ellis, Richard E., 12

emancipation (in law), 182, 210–211

Emerson, Ralph Waldo, 115–116, 224n79, 240n11

enthusiasm, xi, 9, 10, 22–23, 24, 26, 28, 31, 33, 86, 90, 92–93, 95, 111, 129–131,
133–137, 138, 139, 140, 143, 145, 148, 149, 151, 155, 160, 161, 169, 171, 176, 180, 182, 193, 206, 235n78, 241n12, 241n16

Eppes, Richard, 158

Esterhammer, Angela, 226n23, 227n26, *Evangelical Magazine*, 114

evangelicals, 10, 15, 23–24, 26, 28, 30, 35, 69, 71, 78, 80, 93, 103, 129–150, 154, 168, 179, 180, 187, 240n11, 249n14

evil speaking, xi–xii, 23–24, 35, 128–131, 133, 136, 137, 139–144, 182, 206

exclusion (from the public sphere), xiii, 8, 21–22, 23, 24, 118, 130, 132, 138, 143–145, 147–148, 150, 222n53

execution sermons, ix, 13–16, 60–61, 65, 67–79, 81, 82, 83–86, 89, 163, 219n20

exhortation, xii, 9, 24, 31, 35, 61, 69, 74, 76, 83, 88, 92, 120, 129–131, 136–150 passim, 151–153, 156, 160, 165–169 passim, 175, 177, 179, 180, 182, 184, 197, 210, 247n45

Fanuzzi, Robert, 244n3, 249n15

Ferguson, Robert A., 91, 223n76

Finney, Charles Grandison, 132

First Society of Free Enquirers, 105

Fletcher, Mary Bosanquet, 140

Fliegelman, Jay, 227n29

Floyd, John, 156, 158, 167

Fobes, Peres, 72–74, 76, 77, 79, 86

Foote, Julia A. J.: *A Brand Plucked from the Fire*, 210

Forman, J. G., 179

Foucault, Michel, 19–20, 221n51, 230n4

Frank, Jason, 16, 235n73

Franklin, Benjamin, 133

Fraser, Nancy, 27–28

freethinkers, 23, 98, 105, 114, 128–130

French, Roderick Stuart, 105, 113, 236n3

Friedman, Lawrence, 50, 74

fugitive slave laws, 145, 177, 178, 179, 181, 183, 189, 191, 192, 197

Gabriel, 200

Gallows Hill, 119–120

Garden, Alexander, 241n12

Garner, Margaret, 248n68
Garnet, Henry Highland, 194
Garrison, William Lloyd, 26, 28, 35, 152,
    154, 166, 168, 170–171, 175, 178, 181, 185,
    195, 239n8, 249n15. *See also* abolition-
    ists, *Liberator*
Gatrell, V. A. C., 67
Geffrard, Fabre, 194
Gibbon, Edward, 112
Gilroy, Paul, 196, 201–202
Godey's Lady's Book, 124
Gordon, Sarah Barringer, 98, 103
Graham's Magazine, 124
Gray, Thomas (father of Thomas Ruffin
    Gray), 160
Gray, Thomas Ruffin, 156, 157, 159–160,
    163, 164, 170, 176, 245n17. See also *Con-
    fessions of Nat Turner*
Great Awakening, 71, 133–136, 143, 240n11.
    See also Second Great Awakening
Gross, Seymour, 238n55, 245n17
Guillory, John, 34

habeas corpus, 179, 209
Habermas, Jürgen, 6–9, 12, 29, 215
Hale, Edward Everett: "The Man without
    a Country," 208–211
Halttunen, Karen, 78–79, 80–81, 109
Hamilton, Thomas, 6, 193
Harper's Ferry, 1, 23, 177, 182–185, 191
Hartman, Saidiya, 164, 189–190, 251n38
Hartz, Louis, 16
Harvard Divinity School, 115
Hatch, Nathan O., 240n11
Hawthorne, Nathaniel, xii, 30, 31, 60,
    116–127; "Alice Doane's Appeal," 31,
    116–121, 122, 124, 126, 128, 172, 210,
    238n55; *The House of the Seven Gables*,
    31, 37–40, 68, 121–127, 128, 199–200; *The
    Scarlet Letter*, 68
Hay, Douglas, 64–65
Haytian Emigration Bureau, 194, 195
Hedding, Elijah, 129
Hening, William Waller: *The Virginia
    Justice*, 246n42
higher law, ix, xiii, 1–4, 5, 19, 25–28, 30, 54,
    59, 63, 67, 68, 76, 92, 95, 99, 103, 109–111,
    116, 144, 145, 150–155 passim, 165–167,

168, 169, 171, 175, 177–184, 190, 201, 211,
    212, 215, 223n70
Horwitz, Morton J., 50
Howe, Daniel Walker, 132
Howe, Samuel Gridley, 96–98, 114
Hsu, Hsuan L., 253n3
Hume, David, 112, 134
Hyde, Carrie, 253n3

Independent, The, 3
influence (in evangelical reform discourse),
    xii, 24, 31, 131, 137, 144–152, 155, 169, 171,
    172, 174, 183–184, 185, 191, 193, 194, 196,
    206, 210, 248n68
insanity, 87, 90, 170
Irving, Washington, 28–29

Jacobs, Harriet, 184: *Incidents in the Life
    of a Slave Girl*, 36, 178, 184–194, 195, 197,
    205, 207
Jackson, Andrew, 96
Jackson, Virginia, 213, 218n10
Jaros, Peter, 233n47
Jefferson, Thomas, 10, 14, 54, 102, 220n44
jeremiads, 73, 86, 148
juridical nationalism, 43. *See also* national
    fantasy
jurisdiction, 17–18, 69, 70–71, 158, 208, 212,
    221n45
Juster, Susan, 240n11

Kahn, Paul, 102–103
Kelley, Abby, 128
Kelley, Donald, 45
Kent, James, 10, 15, 23, 97, 101–104, 107; *Com-
    mentaries on American Law*, 58–59, 101
Kneeland, Abner, 23, 98–99, 104–116, 120,
    128–130, 237n32
Knight, Elleanor, 24, 138–139, 149
Knight, Jr., Harding (husband of Elleanor
    Knight), 138
Korobkin, Laura H., 91, 152, 235n77

Lambert, Frank, 241n11
Lane Seminary, 168, 240n8

lawcraft, xi, 14, 16, 18, 22, 40, 50, 56–63 passim, 65, 71, 77, 83, 98, 101, 104, 109, 120, 121, 154–155
Lee, Benjamin, 227n29
Lee, Robert E., 1
legal treatises, ix, 12, 13, 16, 40, 43, 45, 46, 51–52, 58, 60, 64–65, 101
legislation, xi, 7–9, 11, 12, 25, 44–46, 49, 58, 59, 68, 70–71, 73, 76, 179
Levy, Leonard, 98, 236n3
Lewis, John, 78
Liberator, The, 2, 168–170, 176
Liberty Bell, The, 171
Lieberman, David, 44
Lincoln, Abraham, 23, 209, 210
Lincoln's Inn, 55
Linebaugh, Peter, 67, 219n21
Literary and Scientific Repository, 55
literary autonomy, xii, xiii, 29–36 passim, 38, 86, 91, 95, 125–127, 197, 203, 206, 214–216, 221n45, 223n76
literary regulation, xii, xiii, 22, 31, 36, 99–100, 118–121, 124–127, 130–131, 144, 149, 155, 175, 192, 215
Locke, John, 50, 134
Lockwood, Samuel, 52
Looby, Christopher, 234n72
Lootens, Tricia, 171, 248n64
Lord, John C., 180
Lovejoy, Elijah, 106, 112, 168, 247n54
Lowther, George W., 192
Ludlow, Henry, 128

Manzano, Juan Francisco, 203
Marbury v. Madison, 102
Marsh, John, 87–88
Marsh, Joss, 114, 236n3
Marshall, John, 10, 102–103
Martineau, Harriet, 168
martyr literature, xii, 20, 26, 27, 28–36, 37, 155, 172, 174, 211–216
Masur, Louis P., 75, 230n3
Mather, Cotton, 69, 120
McBride, Dwight A., 245n19
McGill, Meredith L., 125–126
McManus, Edgar J., 68, 232n17, 232n26
Mee, Jon, 31

Melville, Herman, xii, 15, 30, 211–216; "Bartleby," 211–212; *Battle-Pieces*, 211–213; "Benito Cereno," 211–212; *Billy Budd*, 211–212, 213; *Pierre*, 15–16, 211
Methodists, 24, 129, 138, 139–144, 158
militancy, ix, x, xi, 19, 27–28, 32, 33, 36, 151, 155, 166, 169, 171, 174–178, 180, 182, 185–186, 192–194, 195–206, 213
Miller, Mark J., 247n54
Miller, Perry, 10, 40, 52, 101, 219n21, 240n11
Mills, Bruce, 186
Mitchell, Stephen Mix, 87–88, 90
Modern, John Lardas, 131–132, 220n44
Montaigne, Michel de, 87
Montesquieu, Baron de, 50
Moore, Henry, 140
Morgan, James, 19
Morton, Marcus, 111
Mountain, Joseph, 81–86, 161

Nabers, Deak, 24, 211, 249n15
National Anti-Slavery Standard, 192
National Era, 148–149
national fantasy, 209–211
National Gazette and Literary Register, 160
New York Mercury, 162
New York Observer, 240n8
New-York Weekly Magazine, 89
Newgate Prison (London), 81
Nichols, Charles H., 187
Nietzsche, Friedrich, 221n51
North Star, The, 205

Occom, Samson, 69–70, 77, 133
opinion of the court, 15, 16, 59, 97–98, 99, 100, 101–104, 107, 111–113, 197–199
Owen, Robert, 105

Paine, Thomas, 50, 55, 104; *The Age of Reason*, 90
Painter, Nell Irvin, 195, 205
pantheists, 104, 115
Parker, James W., 159
Parker, Richard, 18–19
Parker, S. D., 112

Parker, Theodore, 25, 179
Parramore, Thomas C., 160
Paul, Moses, 69
Peck, J. M., 180
People v. Ruggles, 15, 23, 100–104, 107
Philadelphia Minerva, 89
Phillips, Wendell, 154
Phylon, 196
Pierce, Franklin, 195
Plácido (Gabriel de la Concepción Valdés), 203
Pocock, J. G. A., 43
Poe, Edgar Allan: "The Pit and the Pendulum," 108
poetics of justice, ix, x, xiii, 4, 9–17 passim, 33–36, 40, 42, 52, 60, 65–67, 78, 101, 114, 126, 130–131, 157, 178, 186, 194, 196, 203, 211, 218n10, 227n29
Post, Amy, 192
Presbyterians, 27, 137, 240n8
Prescott, William H., 235n75
private sphere, xii, 30–32, 35, 91, 95, 120–121, 126–127, 131, 144–150 passim, 191, 203
public opinion, 7, 8, 21, 41, 46, 47, 114, 182, 183, 190, 193, 198. *See also* court of public opinion
public sphere, ix–xiii passim, 4, 5–9, 12, 21, 24, 26–27, 30–31, 34–36 passim, 40–47 passim, 52, 56, 57, 66–67, 71, 74, 81, 86, 89, 91, 97–99, 102, 103, 108, 111, 113, 114, 121, 129, 130, 131, 144, 146–147, 149–150, 152, 154, 155, 166–172 passim, 176–178, 186, 187, 190, 196–197, 206, 214, 219n19
Pynchon, William, 60

Rancière, Jacques, 21
Rantoul, Robert, 13, 25, 54–55, 59, 153–154
Redpath, James, 2, 182–184, 194, 195; *Echoes of Harper's Ferry*, 182, 184, 194; *The Public Life of Captain John Brown*, 2, 184
reform, x–xiii passim, 5, 7, 11, 12, 15, 21–28 passim, 30, 32, 35, 36, 47, 51, 56, 84, 103, 104–105, 114–115, 118, 144, 155, 169–171, 182, 186
revivals, 9, 10, 15, 78, 93, 129, 130, 132–133, 135, 136, 165

Revolution. *See* American Revolution
Richards, Leonard L., 75
Richmond Enquirer, 162, 169
Richmond Whig, 158
Rogers, Alan, 61
Rollin, Frances, 197, 205
Rombes, Jr., Nicholas, 235n74
Root, Jesse, 13, 51, 52–54, 57, 63, 103, 153, 154, 177, 179, 228n45; *Origin of Government and Laws in Connecticut*, 52–54, 64
Rose, Charles, 74–77
Ruffin, Thomas, 25, 152–154
Ruggles. See *People v. Ruggles*
Ruttenberg, Nancy, 241n19

Sage (wife of Isaac Coombs), 14, 60
Salem Mercury, 62
Salem witch trials, 37, 116, 119, 120
Sampson, William, 13, 25, 55–57, 59, 153–154, 228n52; *Anniversary Discourse*, 56–57
Samuels, Shirley, 234n73
Scott, Dred. See *Scott v. Sanford*
Scott v. Sanford, 59, 177, 178, 188, 189, 195, 197–199, 201, 210. *See also* Taney, Roger B.
Scully, Randolph, 167
Seay, Scott D., 69, 231n10
secession, 208
Second Great Awakening, 23, 132, 136, 169, 240n8
secularization, ix–xi, 5, 8, 10, 11, 12, 15, 16, 19, 22, 26, 61–63, 65–66, 68, 71, 73, 75–76, 79–81, 98, 101, 105, 109–110, 116, 119–120, 130, 154, 179, 214–215, 220n44. *See also* disestablishment
Sedgwick, Henry Dwight, 12–13, 55; *The English Practice*, 55
sentences (in criminal cases), 1–6 passim, 14, 16, 18–19, 23, 56, 61–63, 70, 74, 76, 81, 82–83, 84, 86, 87, 100, 109, 114, 158, 159, 160–166, 170
sentimentalism, xi, 9, 10, 24, 30, 34, 36, 66–67, 80, 85–86, 131, 144–150, 155, 162, 171, 173, 185–186, 196, 211
seriatim opinions, 102

sermons, xiii, 27, 87–88, 106, 134, 140, 177–178, 180, 181–184, 191, 193, 231n5; *see also* execution sermons
Seward, William H., 179
Shakespeare, William, 87; *The Tempest*, 20
Shaw, Lemuel, 23, 25, 97, 98–99, 107–108, 109, 111, 113, 114, 154, 179, 237n32
Shays, Daniel (and Shays's Rebellion), 74–77
Sims, Thomas, 178–179
slavery, xiii, 1–2, 18, 19, 22, 24–28, 30, 35, 55, 59, 82, 84–85, 123, 132, 139, 145–146, 150, 151–155, 159, 162, 164, 166–206 passim, 212; *see also* abolitionists; emancipation; fugitive slave laws
Smith, Henry Nash, 239n61
social contract, 16, 42, 47, 68, 76
Spalding, Joshua, 60–61
Spear, Samuel T., 27
specter evidence, 116, 117
stare decisis, 42
State v. Mann, 25, 152–153
statutes. *See* legislation
Stearns, Jonathan F.: *Female Influence*, 243n52
Stein, Jordan, 203
Stone, Marjorie, 171–172, 174
Storrs, Richard S., 180
Story, Joseph, 10, 25
Stout, Harry S., 240n11
Stowe, Harriet Beecher, xii, 30, 31, 34, 35, 130–131, 145, 181, 184, 201; *Dred*, 31, 131, 151–156, 174; *Key to Uncle Tom's Cabin*, 184; *Uncle Tom's Cabin*, 24, 30, 31, 145–150, 151–152, 174, 183, 189, 196, 199–200
Styron, William, 156, 245n16
Sundquist, Eric, 157, 196, 245n19, 247n47
Sweeting, Whiting: *Narrative of Whiting Sweeting*, 80

Taney, Roger B., 59, 197–199, 201, 210. See also *Scott v. Sanford*
Taves, Ann, 134, 241n16
testimony, 20, 26, 36, 91–95, 117, 158–159, 164, 173, 184, 186–192, 205, 246n42
Thatcher, Peter, 112

Thayer and Eldridge, 184
Thomas, Brook, 29, 38, 146, 209
Thompson, E. P., 219n21
Thompson, George, 26, 178, 223n68
Thompson, Sally, 24, 129–130, 138–144
Thoreau, Henry, 2–6, 8, 30, 32, 34, 35, 180, 181, 182, 215; "A Plea for Captain John Brown," 2; "The Last Days of John Brown," 2, 28–29
Thornton, Sarah, 138
Token, The, 116
Tompkins, Jane, 90
Tracy, Joseph, 241n11
Tragle, Henry Irving, 158, 159
Trezevant (or Trezvant), Samuel, 159, 164
Tricomi, Albert H., 185–186
trial reports, ix, 20, 23, 25, 55, 62, 65, 67, 68, 71, 87, 97, 100, 108–111, 118, 129, 140, 141, 155, 157, 160, 240n8
true religion, 131–132, 139
Trumpet, The, 105
Tucker, St. George, 45, 64, 101
Turner, Nat, x, xiii, 14–15, 26, 156–171, 176–177, 191, 195, 196, 200, 201, 247n45. See also *Confessions of Nat Turner*
Tyburn, 67

Union Safety Committee, 180
Unitarians, 114, 136
Universalist Watchman, 111
Universalists, 104–106, 108, 111, 115, 136
Updegraph, Abner, 104
Upham, Charles W.: *Lectures on Witchcraft*, 116, 118, 120

Vallandigham, Clement, 209
Van Schaak, Peter, 51
Vesey, Denmark, 200
Volney, Constantin-François Chassebœuf, comte de, 112
Voltaire, 104
Von Frank, Albert J., 182

Walker, David, 19, 22, 26, 152, 166, 169; *Walker's Appeal*, 19, 168, 170

Wall, Rachel, 79
Waller, Levi, 158–159, 164
Warner, Michael, 6, 219n19
Weber, Max 12
Weekly Recorder, 103–104
Weisberg, Robert, 43, 224n84
Welter, Barbara, 243n52
Wendell, John L., 100
Wesley, John, 140
West, Stephen, 74-77, 86
Whitefield, George, 133
Whitfield, James M., 203
Whitman, James Q., 52

Whittemore, Thomas, 105, 111
Wilf, Steven, 81, 219n20, 230n5
Williams, Catherine, 142, 144
Williams, Daniel, 80, 82
Wilson, James, 17, 57–58, 64, 102
Wise, Henry, 185
Wood, Horatio, 140
Wright, Frances ("Fanny"), 105, 128, 130

Yates, James, 23, 89–90, 92, 161
Yellin, Jean Fagan, 184, 187, 224n80
Young, Michael P., 249n14